MW
TP100 13110
KSSPSSR

Beveridge and voluntary action in Britain and the wider British world

MANCHESTER
1824

Manchester University Press

Beveridge and voluntary action in Britain and the wider British world

Edited by Melanie Oppenheimer and Nicholas Deakin

Manchester University Press

Manchester and New York

distributed in the United States exclusively

by Palgrave Macmillan

Published by Manchester University Press
Oxford Road, Manchester M13 9NR, UK
and Room 400, 175 Fifth Avenue, New York, NY 10010, USA
www.manchesteruniversitypress.co.uk

Distributed in the United States exclusively by
Palgrave Macmillan, 175 Fifth Avenue, New York,
NY 10010, USA

Distributed in Canada exclusively by
UBC Press, University of British Columbia, 2029 West Mall,
Vancouver, BC, Canada V6T 1Z2

British Library Cataloguing-in-Publication Data
A catalogue record for this book is available from the British Library

Library of Congress Cataloging-in-Publication Data applied for

ISBN   978 07190 8381 5   hardback

First published 2011

The publisher has no responsibility for the persistence or accuracy of URLs for any external or third-party internet websites referred to in this book, and does not guarantee that any content on such websites is, or will remain, accurate or appropriate.

Typeset in 10.5/12.5pt Arno Pro
by Graphicraft Limited, Hong Kong
Printed in Great Britain
by TJ International Ltd, Padstow

Contents

Figures

Acknowledgements

There are a number of people that we would like to thank specifically because without them the original symposium 'William Beveridge's *Voluntary Action* 60 Years On' held in November 2008 in London and the subsequent book would not have happened. In terms of the symposium, we would like to thank our financial sponsors, Amanda Andrews from Andrews Communications Systems, Sydney, Australia, and the Faculty of Arts at Monash University, Australia. Pat Starkey and Georgina Brewis from the Voluntary Action History Society and Frank Bongiorno and Kirsten McIntyre from the Menzies Centre for Australian Studies at King's College, London, University of London, provided invaluable support in co-convening the symposium and assisting with the venue, the splendid Downer Room at the Australian High Commission in The Strand. We would also like to thank Baroness Julia Neuberger DBE for addressing the symposium. Others including Justin Davis Smith, Colin Rochester, Angela Ellis Paine, Jenny Harrow, Karl Wilding, Ann Blackmore and Cynthia Messeleka-Boyer, as well as the contributors to this book, all helped in their various ways to make the symposium a great success. We would also like to thank Manchester University Press, especially Emma Brennan, Reena Jugnarain, Lianne Slavin and copy-editor Fiona Little. It has been a pleasure to work with them all.

Melanie Oppenheimer
Nicholas Deakin
September 2010

1

Beveridge and voluntary action

Melanie Oppenheimer and Nicholas Deakin

William Beveridge's report *Voluntary action: a report on methods of social advance* was published in October 1948. When his earlier and more well-known report *Social insurance and allied services* appeared in December 1942, the winter cold failed to put off long queues of purchasers. A second report on tackling unemployment had a similarly warm reception. Beveridge became a household name across the world as the 'father of the welfare state'. Yet in sharp contrast *Voluntary action*, his third report, provoked very little interest and rapidly disappeared from view.

Beveridge himself continued to attract considerable attention for his contribution to the creation of the British social security system and the impact across the world of his ideas on a social service state.[1] Yet even his biographer, Jose Harris, who contributes a chapter to this book, barely mentioned *Voluntary action* in the first edition of her book. However, the profound shift in attitudes in Britain and elsewhere during the last two decades about the respective roles of governments and the voluntary sector and their relationship was reflected in Harris's second edition, which now included a full critical account of *Voluntary action*.[2] For the promotion of voluntary action has become a very popular concept across and beyond politics, and voluntary organisations are now significant players in public policy, across the political spectrum and in many different countries. As a result, many people are now looking at Beveridge's *Voluntary action* in a new light while exploring possible answers to many twenty-first-century dilemmas. In order to reflect upon the significance of *Voluntary action* and explore its contemporary relevance, a group of historians from Britain, Australia, Canada and New Zealand gathered together in November 2008 at a symposium to mark the sixtieth anniversary of its publication. Convened by the United Kingdom Voluntary Action History Society and hosted by the Menzies Centre for Australian Studies in London, the symposium sought to explain and evaluate the legacy of Beveridge's *Voluntary action* in Britain and the 'wider British world'.

In assessing the impact of Beveridge's *Voluntary action* over the last sixty years, this book also provides a reminder that the terms 'voluntary action' and 'voluntary sector' are both fluid and contestable. In this book we use Beveridge's own definition of voluntary action as outlined in his 1948 report, as encompassing mutual aid, self-help and philanthropy. The term 'voluntary sector' is especially debatable: it is difficult to quantify, and definitions vary enormously across the literature.[3] Kendall and Knapp took a phrase from Henry James, describing it as a 'loose and baggy monster'. Here, we take Kendall's view that the sector covers organisations 'which are formal, non profit distributing, constitutionally independent of the state, self-governing and benefiting from voluntarism'.[4]

Other labels are also often employed, such as 'third sector', 'not-for-profit sector', 'non-profit sector' and 'charitable sector'. Under whatever title, there has been considerable academic interest in this area since the 1990s, reflecting the increasing importance of the voluntary sector in delivering an expanding range of services, separately or in partnership with government. The Johns Hopkins Comparative Nonprofit Sector Project, begun in 1990 and now covering more than forty countries, provides a valuable comparative resource for understanding the relationship between the state and the voluntary sector. This pattern of increasing government reliance in recent years on the voluntary sector has been repeated in all the countries under consideration in this book – Britain, Canada, Australia and New Zealand. Academics such as Mark Lyons in Australia, Margaret Tennant in New Zealand and Kathy L. Block in Canada have joined others in Britain like Diana Leat, Marilyn Taylor and Jeremy Kendall who are concerned with analysing recent developments in voluntary action.[5] The connections between the 'mother country' and the British dominions in the period from the end of the Second World War in terms of different approaches to voluntary action provides us with a new lens with which to examine the relationship.

The historical relationship between the state and the voluntary sector and its development over time are therefore a major theme of the book. As the individual chapters demonstrate, the ideas that William Beveridge developed in his *Voluntary action* in the late 1940s have regained currency in recent times. What he had to say then has proved to be still relevant to us today, in an era which has seen increased co-operation and formal partnerships, or 'compacts', but also widely expressed concerns about the basis of relations between third-sector organisations and the state.

Beveridge's 'third report'

Voluntary action, a lengthy report of over 200,000 words, was commissioned by one of Britain's largest mutual aid and insurance associations, the National Deposit Friendly Society, which was concerned for its future and that of its 1,600,000 members after the passage of the National Insurance Act of 1946. Beveridge himself was very unhappy with the Attlee Labour government's treatment of the friendly societies, whose legislation effectively killed them off. Beveridge had specifically recommended in his 1942 report that as well as providing their own benefits, the friendly societies should be allowed to continue administering the state benefits of insurance against sickness as they had done since Lloyd George's legislation of 1911.[6]

Until 1946, the National Deposit Friendly Society had administered its own voluntary benefits to members through the National Insurance Act of 1911, under which approved societies were allowed to administer both state and voluntary society benefits.[7] At the time of the report in 1948, friendly societies in Britain had about 8,000,000 members.[8]

Beveridge agreed to write the report, for a fee of £10,000, on condition that he could write about friendly societies in general and other topics as well to ensure engaging 'a much wider audience' that would make the final report more relevant.[9] For in Beveridge's view voluntary action was much broader than just friendly societies. Voluntary action was:

> everything that citizens do outside their duties to the State, to improve the conditions of life for themselves and their fellows . . . to improve conditions for himself and his fellows. That really falls into two main sections, which I distinguish as mutual aid and philanthropy. These lead people to band themselves together to improve social conditions by their direct action and not by getting the State to do something.[10]

Friendly societies, trade unions, co-operatives, building societies, housing societies, social clubs, trustee savings banks and hospital contributory schemes all fell under the rubric of what Beveridge called 'mutual aid', which he described as a 'consciousness of a common need' that 'leads to combined action to meet that need, to helping oneself and one's fellows together'.[11] The second feature of voluntary action, according to Beveridge, was philanthropy, people with a social conscience seeking to make life better for the less fortunate in society. Beveridge identified up to seventeen areas where philanthropic organisations were continuing to evolve as social needs changed. These areas included work with the disabled, prisoners, unmarried mothers and the infirm as well as organisations that assisted the arts and national heritage, and protected animals and the environment.[12]

Voluntary action received reasonably positive press coverage on its release but nowhere near the volume and range of commentary on Beveridge's earlier reports. *The Times* devoted a generally favourable editorial as well as a general news item to the report, and Beveridge himself wrote a 'turnover' article entitled 'Voluntary action above a national minimum'.[13] Other reviews were mixed. G. D. H. Cole, writing in the *Economic Journal*, said he did not mind Beveridge's thesis on voluntary action as such but criticised the over-emphasis on friendly societies, which was to the detriment of other forms of mutual aid such as consumers' co-operative societies and women's co-operative guilds, organisations that, Cole believed, did so much for working-class women and active citizenship. Cole also found the report poorly constructed, and 'interesting, but scrappy'. It was, he noted, as if Beveridge had 'got tired of his task before he had achieved a satisfactory arrangement of his material'.[14]

Some subsequent evaluations have also been quite harsh. The British historian of voluntarism Geoffrey Finlayson has argued that the report was largely 'an exercise in special pleading for the voluntary sector friendly societies' but also stated that its importance was that it revealed the strength of voluntary action, its size and its cumbersome nature.[15] His third report may seem unfocussed simply because of the scale of voluntarism unearthed: Beveridge and his committee may have been simply overwhelmed by their material and what they uncovered.[16] Jose Harris, when she eventually came to discuss *Voluntary action* and its research papers, dismissed it as displaying none of the 'inventiveness and intellectual coherence' of his earlier two reports.[17]

Why, then, has *Voluntary action* now belatedly become such an influential text, widely quoted by policy analysts and politicians? Partly because voluntary organisations never faded away, as Beveridge and other commentators had feared they might. Although voluntary action was initially overshadowed by the development of the welfare state after 1945, the need and scope for such action, as defined by Beveridge in his report, continued. And although, through the early growth of welfare states, governments took on a much larger role in overall service delivery, voluntary action continued to be a crucial component. The boundary between voluntary and state action shifted through time – the 'moving frontier' identified originally by Beveridge himself and later taken up by Margaret Brasnett in her 1969 history of the National Council of Social Service and by Geoffrey Finlayson in his 1994 book *Citizen, state and social welfare in Britain*.[18] Eventually, the balance began to tip the other way, with widespread scepticism about the effectiveness of statutory agencies in delivering services and an increasingly assertive attitude among campaigning voluntary organisations. By the end of the century, voluntary action was firmly back in the centre of the picture as both partner and critic of government. So, as the contributors to this book demonstrate, the influences of Beveridge and voluntary action now extend not only beyond the period of the original publication of his report but also outside Britain to the wider 'British world'.

The first six chapters of this book place Beveridge in the world in which he wrote *Voluntary action* as well as exploring the ideas, philosophies and experiences that influenced his intellectual development up to, and during, the 1940s. Beveridge's background and motivations behind the themes contained in *Voluntary action* are explored in various contexts. In Chapter 2, Jose Harris provides us with an overview and discusses some of the issues surrounding Beveridge's three reports, situating *Voluntary action* within the context of Beveridge's earlier reports of 1942 and 1944. As Harris suggests, many today see *Voluntary action* as a blueprint for what has happened since 1948 with the development of the partnerships between government and the voluntary sector in the twenty-first century. Yet in the late 1940s what Beveridge was proposing was perceived as old-fashioned and not part of the new world order of post-war politics. She wonders how representative Beveridge's views on voluntarism were, and how realistic was his vision in *Voluntary action*. Her analysis helps to explain why there was a shift in Beveridge's ideas, providing us with a key to the tensions between statism and voluntarism, and between public and private freedom.

In the following chapter, Nicholas Deakin draws on Beveridge's experiences of the 1930s with special reference to his role in assisting academics to escape from Nazi Germany as one possible explanation for the development of Beveridge's attitudes towards the role of voluntary action. On *Voluntary action* itself, Deakin describes the report as inherently confusing, providing no clear plan or programme – unlike his earlier reports. One reason why the report is more popular today, he suggests, is that it contains 'something for everyone'.

Two of the main areas of voluntary action – philanthropy and mutual aid – are the subjects of the next two chapters. In Chapter 4, Frank Prochaska asserts that 'Beveridge . . . has never been enough for Beveridge' and argues that, perhaps as a result of the visible damage inflicted by enemy action on charitable services during the Second World War, Beveridge began to have second thoughts about his earlier reports. Prochaska suggests that the adverse affects of the war on the charitable sector and the perceived failure of many voluntary health and social service provisions also provided the post-war Labour government with a rationale to nationalise services. These developments impacted on Beveridge's ideas of the importance of voluntary action, and in that sense *Voluntary action* can be seen as a form of *mea culpa*.

In the next chapter, Daniel Weinbren takes a look at the role of friendly societies, a key feature of *Voluntary action*. He suggests that Beveridge's view reflects an idealised image of friendly societies, representative of his own youthful experience rather than Britain in the late 1940s. Beveridge was describing a 'lost world', a disappearing way of life that harked back to the nineteenth century. While *Voluntary action* was in press, Beveridge and his wife, Janet, accepted an invitation from New Zealand to present the De Carle lectures. In Chapter 6, Melanie Oppenheimer sketches out the little-known six-month Antipodean tour from February to July 1948. Scrambling to complete his report, Beveridge submitted his manuscript to the publishers only days before setting sail. The chapter introduces the influences of Beveridge in these British dominions and reflects on Beveridge and voluntary action in the immediate post-war period.

The next three chapters focus on specific areas of voluntary action with special relevance today. James McKay argues in Chapter 7 that the voluntary sector remains a key player in British politics. Using two major reports, Beveridge's 1948 *Voluntary action* and a 1996 report by one of the present contributors (Nicholas Deakin) for the National Council for Voluntary Organisations, *Meeting the challenge of change*, as his book-ends, McKay contends that any analysis of British politics overlooks the voluntary sector at its peril. The voluntary sector, McKay argues, has a varied but important political role which includes the ability to pioneer new causes, develop social capital and citizen participation and direct political engagement. One way to appreciate the wider spectrum of the voluntary sector's political involvement is to broaden how we define politics itself, moving outside the traditional Westminster–Whitehall axis.

In Chapter 8, Georgina Brewis argues that one of the areas that has changed significantly since Beveridge's time is that of organised volunteer programmes for young people, especially overseas volunteer programmes. Brewis charts the rise of what is called the youth 'volunteer boom' from the late 1950s to 1970. Another area of social need has been the plight of the rural poor. In Chapter 9, Jill Roe looks at the principles of voluntary action favoured by Beveridge and uses her Australian experiences to consider rural poverty, arguing that there has been a distortion of Beveridge's idealistic views of voluntary action in recent years. But she also suggests that voluntary action may be vital to the survival of rural communities in Australia and beyond, especially Indigenous Australians, who are the poorest of the poor.

The final four chapters are surveys of different national situations, focussing on the influence of voluntary action in Britain, New Zealand, Australia and Canada in the aftermath of the publication of Beveridge's report. As one would expect, there are both interesting commonalities and differences in the themes exposed in these national studies. In Chapter 10, Pat Thane examines voluntary action in Britain in the post-war period, from the introduction of the welfare state, through the 1960s and 1970s and the emergence of a highly professionalised voluntary sector, to the rise of neo-liberalism, New Labour and the third way. She discusses how changeable the term 'voluntary action' is and how difficult it is to quantify over time owing to the lack of data, and argues that one of the ongoing difficulties when discussing voluntary action and the voluntary sector is not just its sheer size but also the complexity of its form.

In Chapter 11, Margaret Tennant considers to what degree New Zealanders regarded themselves as being in advance of Beveridge and what they learnt from his report. She argues that *Voluntary action* was only one influence on debates concerning the relationship between voluntarism and the state, and that voluntary action in New Zealand was influenced by a number of historical forces, including the role its Indigenous peoples have played, especially through the last decades of the twentieth century. Tennant argues that New Zealand had its own distinctive trajectory of voluntary action and uses specific case studies, such as marriage guidance counselling of the 1950s and 1960s, to show the co-existing relationship that developed between the state and voluntary sector. Finally she suggests that *Voluntary action* was but one example of post-war discussions concerning the state and voluntary sector.

In examining the Australian response to *Voluntary action* in Chapter 12, Paul Smyth takes the view that independent voluntary effort was never taken seriously as an alternative to the state. Like others throughout this book, he argues that there has been some re-invention of the role of the voluntary sector in recent times that does not necessarily apply to the Australian context. As in the New Zealand example, Smyth contends that Beveridge's ideas in *Voluntary action* were not seen as offering a serious alternative to the role of the state in welfare. He takes us through the development of the voluntary sector since 1945, emphasising the shifts with a focus on the relationship between the state and voluntary sector. In Chapter 13, Peter Elson provides a Canadian perspective to Beveridge's *Voluntary action*, suggesting that it was initially ignored and that the ideas in it were taken up only later. He is highly critical of much of the voluntary sector in its response to social justice issues in Canada and stresses, as did Beveridge, that social conscience should at all times be a key attribute of voluntary action.

Conclusions

The situation that Beveridge set out to describe and analyse in 1948 has changed almost beyond recognition: the landscape in which voluntary action operates in the twenty-first century is now very different across all the countries surveyed in this collection. Beveridge himself would probably have found it difficult to come to terms with some of these social changes and the challenges they have thrown up – changes in the role of women and in sexual behaviour, the decline of deference and commodification of public services, the vast growth in various forms of popular culture (whose earlier manifestations he deplored) and the revolution in communications, shrinking distances and allowing experiences to be shared and compared. Others he would have found more familiar. The persistence of poverty, the giant that his 1942 report had set out to slay, both nationally and globally, would be one example – and one that he would undoubtedly find distressing.

Yet charities and voluntary organisations have proved capable of adapting to these changes, developing and expanding into different areas of activity and promoting and creating new forms of activity in order to do so. And there are other current means of addressing these issues through voluntary action which would seem thoroughly familiar to Beveridge, the role of philanthropy, for example – though Beveridge's warning about allowing the business motive to become too dominant looks prescient now. Volunteering remains a significant element in voluntary action. And then there is the role of the churches and other faith groups, with a presence in Britain on a scale that would astonish Beveridge. Beveridge, not himself a believer, was concerned that a decline in religion would have a destabilising effect on society, unless some form of substitute could be contrived. That is a debate that will undoubtedly continue, as religion continues to be a significant presence, even if in a greater variety of different forms.

The relationship with government was one of Beveridge's particular preoccupations and, although his prescriptions now look very dated, the principles he set down still have some relevance – in particular, his warnings about the need to preserve independence while seeking to build constructive relationships. In these and other ways, as the chapters in this volume demonstrate, Beveridge's report, despite all its weaknesses and omissions, still has resonance for today's world and lessons on which civil society can draw to address the problems of the twenty-first century.

Notes

1 Events have included a conference, 'Social security fifty years after Beveridge', held at the University of York in 1992, and the resultant book, J. Hills, J. Ditch and H. Glennerster (eds), *Beveridge and social security: an international retrospective* (Oxford: Clarendon Press, 1994).

2 *William Beveridge: a biography* (Oxford: Clarendon Press, 1977; 2nd edn, 1997).

3 See J. Kendall and M. Knapp, 'A loose and baggy monster: boundaries, definitions and typologies', in J. Davis Smith, C. Rochester and R. Hedley (eds), *An introduction to the voluntary sector* (London and New York: Routledge, 1995), pp. 66–95.

4 J. Kendall, *The voluntary sector: comparative perspectives in the UK* (London and New York: Routledge, 2003), p. 6.

5 See, for example, J. Kendall and M. Taylor, 'On the interdependence between politics and policy in the shaping of English horizontal third sector initiative', in B. Gidron and M. Bar (eds), *Policy initiatives towards the third sector in international perspective* (New York: Springer, 2010), pp. 189–212; C. Rochester, A. Ellis-Paine and S. Howlett, *Volunteering and society in the 21st century* (Basingstoke: Palgrave Macmillan, 2009); and P6 and D. Leat, 'Inventing the British voluntary sector by committee', *Nonprofit Studies*, vol. 1, no. 2 (2005), pp. 33–45; M. Lyons, *Third sector: The contribution of nonprofit and cooperative enterprises in Australia* (Sydney: Allen & Unwin, 2001); M. Tennant, *The fabric of welfare: voluntary organisations, government and welfare in New Zealand, 1840-2005* (Wellington: Bridget Williams Books, 2007); and Kathy L. Block, 'A comprehensive Canadian approach to the third sector: creative tensions and unexpected outcomes', in Gidron and Bar (eds), *Policy initiatives*, pp. 21–44.

6 Mitchell Library, Sydney (hereafter ML), Beveridge Papers, M2618, box 429, typescript of third De Carle Lecture, 'Voluntary action for social advance', April 1948.

7 W. Beveridge, 'Voluntary action for social advance', in *On and off the platform* (Wellington: Hicks, Smith & Wright, 1949), p. 63.

8 Beveridge, 'Voluntary action for social advance', in *On and off the platform*, p. 65.

9 Beveridge, 'Voluntary action for social advance', in *On and off the platform*, p. 3.

10 ML, Beveridge Papers, M2618, box 429, typescript of third De Carle Lecture, 'Voluntary action for social advance', April 1948, pp. 3–4.

11 Beveridge, 'Voluntary action for social advance', in *On and off the platform*, p. 64.

12 Beveridge, 'Voluntary action for social advance', in *On and off the platform*, pp. 70–1.

13 Editorial, 'Another Beveridge report', *The Times* (21 October 1948), p. 5; Lord Beveridge, 'Methods of social advance', *The Times* (21 October 1948), p. 5; 'Social welfare: Lord Beveridge on voluntary aid', *The Times* (21 October 1948), p. 2.

14 G. D. H. Cole, *Economic Journal*, vol. 59, no. 235 (September 1949), pp. 399–401. See also James H. S. Bossard, *American Sociological Review*, 1949, pp. 443–4; T. H. Marshall, 'Voluntary action', *Political Quarterly*, vol. 20, no. 1 (1949), pp. 25–36.

15 G. Finlayson, *Citizen, state and social welfare in Britain, 1830–1990* (Oxford: Clarendon Press, 1994), p. 260.

16 See Kendall and Knapp, 'A loose and baggy monster', pp. 66–95.

17 Harris, *William Beveridge*, p. 455.

18 Margaret Brasnett, *Voluntary social action: a history of the National Council of Social Service* (London: NCSS, 1969); Finlayson, *Citizen, state and social welfare*.

2

Voluntarism, the state and public–private partnerships in Beveridge's social thought

Jose Harris

In the short space of six years, between 1942 and 1948, William Beveridge wrote three landmark reports about the future of communal provision of social, economic and welfare services for the citizens of the United Kingdom. The underlying philosophy and rationale of these three reports spanned a very wide range of potentially conflicting policy positions, each of which still has resonance in debates about welfare services and the 'public' and 'private' sectors down to the present day. These underlying ideas ranged from a powerful evaluation of the importance of 'free choice', 'self-government' and 'voluntary action' in social welfare provision on the one hand, through to what appeared to be, on the other hand, an equal if not greater emphasis on the principle of 'universalism', which in turn seemed to require the directive and enforcing powers of the central state. In between lay a third position, which envisaged not merely extensive practical co-operation between the public and private sectors, but also a certain philosophical integration or 'incorporation' between the two spheres. In this chapter it will be suggested that the differing priorities in the three reports were partly a response to circumstances at the different moments when they were written; but that, more importantly, each of them reflected certain long-standing contradictory tensions about the respective roles of individuals, states and voluntary agencies in the thought of Beveridge himself.

The first and most famous of Beveridge's reports (the so-called Beveridge Plan) was *Social insurance and allied services* of 1942, which is often seen as a key foundation document for social welfare provision in any modern 'mixed economy', not just in the United Kingdom but also for much of the developed world. This report reviewed the working of earlier and existing social security arrangements in Britain and other countries, including both the means-tested Poor Law and Public Assistance system and the joint public-private contributory social insurance schemes that had been set up under the National Insurance Act of 1911. Beveridge concluded that both the Poor Law and the quasi-private contributory social insurance strands in Britain's historic public social welfare arrangements had failed to adjust adequately to modern needs. In their place he recommended a programme of comprehensive national health care, public maintenance of full employment, universal family allowances and universal subsistence-level contributory insurance, designed to cover the basic needs of all citizens 'from the cradle to the grave'. He acknowledged that the financial and actuarial aspects of the pre-war public–private partnership between state and voluntary insurance schemes had largely broken down, and needed to be replaced by a uniform national system of social security, directly managed by the state. But nevertheless he hoped to retain an important and socially creative role for self-governing voluntary organisations within the new state framework. This role would include both the encouragement of additional social insurance schemes over and above the statutory subsistence minimum and the non-statutory provision of ancillary caring, monitoring and personal services for the sick, the aged, the unemployed and other needy groups.[1]

Beveridge's second key wartime report, *Full employment in a free society* of 1944, likewise emphasised the continuing co-existence of public provision and private choice; but it nevertheless struck a very different balance between these two poles from the social insurance report of two years before. In *Full employment* Beveridge, developing his ideas under the influence of a group of young 'Keynesian socialists', for the first time envisaged that Keynesian-style fiscal and monetary management might achieve the levels of full employment and general economic prosperity required to finance the levels of welfare spending envisaged in the Beveridge Plan. But, if Keynesian remedies should fail, then he indicated that (in peacetime as in war) as much as 85 per cent of Britain's economic and financial institutions might need to come under direct or indirect central government control.[2] This was a prospect that Beveridge claimed to view with equanimity, since private enterprise, private ownership of property and private saving (as opposed to sacrosanct 'personal freedom') were no longer to be seen as part of 'essential British liberties' in the modern world. Indeed, the very notion that 'private ownership of the means of production' was an indispensable 'liberal principle' no longer had a place in the structure of modern progressive liberal thought. 'I regard myself as free a Briton as there is in the country', Beveridge told an audience of Fabians in 1943, 'and I have never owned any means of production at all in my life except a fountain pen'.[3]

Only three years further on, however, during a debate in the House of Lords on Labour's new national insurance legislation, Beveridge appeared to signal a further shift of emphasis in his views on the public–private divide. It did 'frankly send a chill to my heart', he declared, to hear that the management of social insurance and other social services was henceforth to be removed entirely from the sphere of self-governing friendly and collecting societies, and transferred lock, stock and barrel into the hands of public authorities.[4] This House of Lords speech anticipated the central theme of his third seminal social policy enquiry, carried out in 1946–47 and published as *Voluntary action: a report on methods of social advance* in 1948. Here Beveridge was once again highly critical of the government's recent social legislation, for doing away entirely with the unique public–private partnership arrangements between government, friendly societies and trade union schemes that had characterised British social security provision over the previous forty years.[5] Instead he set out a wide-ranging agenda that envisaged a continuing and even expanding role for voluntary, charitable, and mutualist organisations in the post-war world. It was a programme, moreover, in which voluntary agencies would work not just as supplementary or secondary bodies, but also as equal partners and innovators – and in some cases as active critics and rivals – of the new universalist 'social-service state'.[6]

Such a position, articulated by Beveridge in 1948, seems instantly recognisable as a prophetic forerunner of what many voluntary agencies see as their role, both national and international, in social care and provision in the present day. To many commentators in a newly 'socialised' post-war Britain, however, this was a vision that seemed at the time curiously quixotic and out of date. It seemed to fly in the face of the new realities of a centrally regulated economy, very high levels of post-war taxation, the dramatic decline in major local community associations (from 220 in 1938 to a mere 64 in 1947) and the onset of the new universalist social security system (the latter largely devised by Beveridge himself) that was now being implemented though the medium of central government. Pessimists and critics included some people who had themselves formerly been very active in voluntary movements, among them some very acute social observers such as Mary Stocks and Barbara Wootton, who believed that (useful as it had been in former times) the 'voluntarist' and 'self-helping' phase of human history was now irrevocably finished.[7] This was a view significantly shared by much of the British trade union movement, which would have nothing at all to do with Beveridge's Voluntary Action enquiry, even though the unions had warmly supported his reports on universal social insurance and full employment only a few years before. Indeed, in marked contrast to trade union movements in much of post-war western Europe, British trade unionists at this time largely dismissed participation in social welfare self-management schemes as not part of their proper social functions.[8] Social welfare voluntarism, of which the British trade unions had until very recently been among the outstanding pioneers, was now widely viewed by many labour activists at best as unnecessary and outdated, and at worst as trying to smuggle back a residual Lady Bountiful element into the new social-democratic welfare state.[9]

How can we explain the apparent shifts in Beveridge's own opinions on these issues between 1942 and 1948, which went in a direction that often appeared to run counter to that of many of his progressive contemporaries? These developments in Beveridge's own ideas may perhaps in part be explained by the transition from the context of a total war economy through to the very different circumstances of post-war reconstruction. But this explanation seems less than adequate, because the British economy was in many respects no less 'regulated' and state-controlled at the time of the Voluntary Action enquiry in 1947 than it had been in 1942 or 1944. And it also fails to explain why Beveridge's own thoughts on these issues – which in wartime had so dramatically captured the public imagination – now appeared rather to move *against* the fashionable spirit of the times. These shifts in Beveridge's social thought deserve closer attention from historians of voluntarism than they have so far received; so some relevant points and possible lines of explanation will form the focus of the rest of this chapter.

One important point is that the tensions in Beveridge's thought on such questions, between statism and voluntarism, public control and private initiative, were of much longer standing than a concentration simply on the mid-1940s might imply. Indeed, although most starkly spelt out in the rather abnormal circumstances of wartime, such seemingly conflicting vantage-points may be detected at many earlier stages in Beveridge's long career, both as a practitioner of progressive social and administrative reforms and as a social theorist. They had been present, for example, back in the early 1900s, when he had himself been a 'volunteer' on local community programmes, in his role as personal assistant to Canon Samuel Barnett, the founder and warden of the Toynbee Hall university settlement in London's East End. Even at that early date Beveridge had been constantly torn between admiration for Canon Barnett's saintly personal devotion to the London poor and a deep intellectual irritation at what he saw as the settlement movement's general failure to address the wider political economy of mass urban poverty.[10] A few years later Beveridge became an active participant in the Ruskinian Guild of St George, where he fully endorsed John Ruskin's view that moral exhortation to the poor without offering state help was disgusting and futile, but that state help *without* incentives to civic and personal improvement was equally degrading if not more so.[11] Similar tensions could also be seen in Beveridge's simultaneous attraction during that early period to both the Fabian Society and the Charity Organisation Society (COS). The COS was a body whose laissez-faire economic views he largely deplored; but he nevertheless admired and shared many of its members' convictions about the importance of developing an individual's personal civic and moral identity as a vital element both in social welfare and in the wider well-being of the state.[12] Likewise, Beveridge's visits to Germany between 1906 and 1908, first as a radical Fleet Street journalist and later as a special investigator for the Board of Trade, had left him with a lasting admiration for the many ways in which German public authorities incorporated labour leaders and trade unionists into the management of civic labour exchanges and state health insurance (although he was later to be rather less enthusiastic about the very limited democratic base of this incorporation).[13]

Equally conflicting themes had been apparent in many phases of Beveridge's subsequent career as a professional civil servant. At all stages he had passionately supported the principle of an idealised 'impartial state', but at the same time had regularly criticised and kicked against the state's deadening and unimaginative administrative procedures. As a senior official in the Board of Trade (from 1909 to 1916), and subsequently in the Ministries of Labour and of Food during the First

World War, Beveridge had constantly devised strategies that aimed to bring independent voluntary bodies into close co-partnership with public administration: a process that had involved the incorporation of friendly societies, trade unions, private individuals and large and small businessmen into the day-to-day execution of state policies.[14] He had gone on to pursue similar strategies during the later 1930s, when as chairman of the independent Unemployment Insurance Statutory Commission he had worked tirelessly to promote collaboration between the public and voluntary sectors. And, most famously of all, in the Beveridge Plan of 1942 he had stated the case for 'universalist' state insurance 'from the cradle to the grave'; but at the same time had also vigorously defended the limitation of state benefits to a flat-rate 'subsistence' minimum, so as to encourage both citizens and voluntary associations to continue making additional mutualist provision, in ongoing partnership with the 'social service state'.[15]

How is this apparent dichotomy, between passionate support for state provision and equally passionate support for welfare voluntarism and mutualism, to be reconciled, both in Beveridge's own thought and in ideas about social welfare more generally? Beveridge himself never acknowledged, or appeared even to notice, any inconsistency or tension in his own thinking about these issues; and he would almost certainly have denied that there was any contradiction between them. The reasons for this lay in the fact that his prime concern as a reformer and theorist of welfare was not with any particular model, either of social welfare management or of state power. Rather it lay with what he saw as the promotion of certain wider principles of good citizenship within a 'free society'. This is not to say that he was not genuinely concerned with the substantive issues of ill health, unemployment and poverty in old age. But his overriding concern was with devising social policies that did not reinforce the problems they were designed to solve, nor undermine incentives to personal independence, providence and good civic behaviour. The administrators of the English Poor Laws had for centuries been concerned with exactly the same kind of problems, to which they had responded often by subjecting the recipients of welfare payments to the crude though time-honoured penalties of shame, stigma, deterrence and withdrawal of civil rights. Beveridge's view, however, was that the opposite strategy was both more honourable and more effective. This was that independence, work-incentives, neighbourly fellow-feeling and identification with the interests of wider society could all be maintained and even enhanced, not by shame and deterrence, but by actively fostering the kind of 'personal service', communal 'solidarity' and 'neighbourhood visiting schemes' involved in friendly-society self-management. Such arrangements often involved some degree of eclectic compromise between apparently competing principles. 'Communal solidarity', for example, might entail a level of neighbourly intrusion into private lives that would have been deemed intolerable 'nosey-parkerdom' if practised by a public official. But it also meant, in Beveridge's view, that the personal needs of a sick, unemployed or disabled person could be met with a degree of flexibility and generosity when purveyed by a self-monitoring friendly society that would be practically impossible for a formal bureaucracy. Thus in certain circumstances a voluntary society could pay a sick or disabled worker *more* than his normal wage, in a way that would have been deemed dangerous or scandalous if allowed by a remote and impersonal public official.[16]

Another more 'metaphysical' element in this line of thought was the belief that insurance contributors, charitable volunteers and indeed citizens generally needed to feel that – not just as an abstract principle but as a matter of day-to-day neighbourly reality – they were part and parcel of the structure of the modern state.[17] Evidence for this view was writ large in Beveridge's journalistic writings, but it was also implicit in many of the more formal reports and memoranda that he wrote as a government adviser or public official. As a young Board of Trade official working on the introduction of unemployment insurance in 1910, for example, he had discussed with Winston Churchill the invaluable role of volunteers, unpaid officials and nonconformist ministers as the 'non-commissioned officers of democracy'. By this they meant that the fraternal, charitable and community-policing functions of individuals were the bedrock of what they saw as the unique combination of personal liberty and self-regulation that characterised early twentieth-century British society, by comparison with the much more heavily policed and state-registered systems common throughout Europe.[18] A similar concern to foster active voluntary participation in the management of state insurance was again apparent in Beveridge's work during the mid- and late 1930s, when he was chairman of the Social Insurance Statutory Committee; and, more explicitly, in the discussions of his Social Insurance Committee of 1942.[19] His enthusiasm for friendly societies reached its apogee, however, in the discussions of the Voluntary Action enquiry of 1947. 'As Aristotle said of Plato's Utopia', wrote Beveridge in his conclusion to the report of this enquiry, 'affection becomes watery when it is spread over too many and too diverse people. In this respect the friendly society movement has preserved an advantage over most other movements'.[20] And it was reflected also in his recommendation that voluntary agencies in the social welfare sphere should henceforth have their own representative in national government. This was to be a role mediated not through a formal administrative department, but through a minister who would act as their personal spokesman in cabinet and parliament (on a par with the responsibility in government exercised at that time by the Lord President of the Council, on behalf of universities and centres of scientific research).[21]

A number of questions about Beveridge's ideas on voluntarism remain unanswered, however, and deserve further consideration, in light of the great resurgence of interest in voluntary movements taking place at the present time. These questions may be identified as follows. Firstly, how 'realistic' was Beveridge's vision of voluntarism in relation to the wider social, economic and industrial structure of Britain in his own time; or was that vision even in the early to mid-twentieth century a dwindling relic of the ideas, values and social realities of an earlier age? Secondly, how representative were Beveridge's views on voluntarism? Did they reflect wider shifts and undercurrents in British public opinion, or were they always idiosyncratic and peculiar to Beveridge himself? And, thirdly, how far does Beveridge's personal vision of voluntarism, devised in response to problems and contexts of more than half a century ago (and sometimes much longer), have any relevance to the dilemmas and possibilities of voluntary action current in the first decade of the present century?

Possible answers to such questions can be only lightly touched upon here, but consideration of them may perhaps suggest some further lines of research for current historians of voluntary movements. As suggested above, Beveridge's interest in voluntary action, both as a medium of practical policy and as an ethical idea, was never at any time that of the kind of libertarian individualist for whom 'voluntarism' meant the polar opposite of management by the state. On the contrary, he saw voluntary action as part and parcel of the collective life of society, and as a means by which individuals could participate in, rather than differentiate themselves from, the wider public activities of the state. This approach was consistent with both the legacy of Comtean 'positivism' that he had inherited from his father (Henry Beveridge, the Indian judge) and the 'idealism' of T. H. Green that he had imbibed as a student at Balliol under the influence of Edward Caird.[22] Nevertheless, many historians of twentieth-century Britain have suggested that the gradual dwindling of this kind of 'liberal idealism', after the early decades of the twentieth century, mirrored the rise of a much more materialist, mass-production-based culture: a culture that (whether mediated through socialism or through competitive capitalism) spelt a lingering death to the voluntarist values, small-group cohesion and self-governing mutualism of the kind cherished by Beveridge. This perception of voluntarism as increasingly superannuated and passé has a persuasive air of plausibility about it – until we compare the British experience in the social insurance sphere with that of many parts of contemporary Europe. There we find numerous examples of recent or current national social security schemes, in which 'solidarism', self-government and the incorporation of occupational, religious and other subsidiary groups have continued to flourish into the first decade of the twenty-first century (and where Beveridge's role as a prophet of such 'public–private partnership' schemes is far more honoured than in Britain itself).[23] Such a comparative perspective at least calls into question whether Beveridge's model of small-group voluntarism within a wider state framework was really so inherently incompatible with mass production, materialism and advanced modernity as many British historical commentators have imagined: or whether perhaps the post-war collapse of voluntarism in Britain (and indeed its subsequent resurgence in many different forms) should be explained in some other way.

My second point, about the typicality or otherwise of Beveridge's views, particularly as expressed in his report *Voluntary action* of 1948, also invites further enquiry. As indicated above, this report evoked a public response quite different from the mass euphoria that had greeted Beveridge's *Social insurance* of 1942, and from the more muted but still widely favourable response to *Full employment in a free society* in 1944. Instead *Voluntary action* came out at a moment when the wider culture appeared to be relatively hostile to voluntarism, and even on Beveridge's own committee he was the only really strong enthusiast for it. As Barbara Wootton remarked at one of the committee's meetings, 'it was very difficult to re-enthuse collective fervour into a group that had lost it'.[24] This lukewarm response stemmed partly from the recent impact of wartime, when long-established charities and philanthropic bodies of all kinds had dwindled in funds and manpower, and partly from a widespread belief that the social legislation of the post-war Labour government (much of it adopted from Beveridge's own 1942 report) had rendered the traditional role of voluntary self-help schemes increasingly redundant. This crisis of confidence in voluntarism deserves more detailed discussion than is possible here, but a few speculative points may be raised on the basis of the evidence, both published and unpublished, submitted to the Voluntary Action Committee.

One point suggested by this evidence is that the post-war crisis of voluntarism was at least in part caused not so much by a decline in support for voluntarism *per se* as by a decisive turning-point in cultural, class and gender relations. This was a turning-point that had been provoked partly by the levelling impact of the war itself, and partly by certain developments within the voluntary sector that had taken place during the war period. Although the war had seriously undermined the financial viability of many older voluntary movements, including the friendly societies and the old-established 'endowment charities', it had also brought to the fore many newer ones such the Voluntary Aid Detachments, the Red Cross, the Women's Voluntary Service and the Citizens' Advice Bureaux, whose prime functions had initially been to help people who had been wounded, bombed, bereaved, rendered homeless and generally disrupted by war. In other words, far from destroying the voluntary ethos (as many commentators at the time were inclined to suggest), the war had generated a tremendous surge of both organised and more informal voluntary action – but of a kind largely unknown in Britain before, and with a quite different outlook and set of values from the voluntary movements of the Edwardian and pre-war eras.[25] Extensions of this discussion, including an Australian perspective, can be found in Chapter 4 of this book, by Frank Prochaska, and Chapter 6, by Melanie Oppenheimer.

One striking feature of the new volunteer movements was that they were predominantly female; another was that their primary aim was to give practical help (including nursing and home care) rather than to promote thrift and saving; and a third was that they reflected a class structure and outlook that were markedly different from those of voluntary movements earlier in the century, or even just before the Second World War. Far more than in the 1914–18 war, enemy bombardment and evacuation had brought into the voluntary services several millions of working-class and lower-middle-class women, together with a numerically much smaller but still significant contingent of women from the aristocratic and upper middle classes. Throughout the war many women from different class backgrounds had worked side by side on the same tasks, but an influential minority of upper-class volunteers had insisted on privileges inherited from an earlier era. Thus more than 5,000 women who entered the Voluntary Aid Detachment (VAD) service via the Red Cross had been granted 'officer' status and first-class travel expenses, even when performing tasks identical with those of other ranks, a fact that still deeply rankled with many women volunteers who submitted evidence to the Beveridge Voluntary Action enquiry several years later.[26]

Other reservations about 'voluntarism' expressed by witnesses to Beveridge's committee also had an implicitly 'class' connotation. Thus, there was an almost unanimous distaste for the very word 'charity', which had come to be widely perceived as deeply tainted with privilege, patronage, 'top-downism' and outdated moral values.[27] There were fears also about the takeover of the voluntary sector by a new professional 'social science salariat', recruited from university graduates in 'social administration', who were seen as having a vested interest in ensuring that social problems were never fully cured or resolved.[28] And similar passions were aroused by people who failed to recognise the 'citizenship' of the housewife, now portrayed as the most valuable and most numerous of the nation's conscripted 'volunteers'. Moreover, Beveridge's own enthusiasm for friendly societies and their putative role as the lower-class guardians of quintessential 'British liberties' (a theme to be discussed in detail by Daniel Weinbren in Chapter 5) was by no means widely endorsed. On the contrary, several members of his committee saw friendly societies as now largely redundant and 'suffering from gangrene', while, among witnesses to the enquiry, the friendly-society movement had come to be widely viewed as a distinctly 'unfriendly' element in British lower-class culture, associated with such negative functions as 'moral business', 'stopping malingering' and acting as 'social police'.[29]

Beveridge's personal understanding of the day-to-day business of voluntarism in 1948 appears therefore to have been not fully shared at the time among other participants in his enquiry, despite the fact that the men and women who gave evidence were well-nigh unanimous in their support for the general principle of 'volunteering'. One reason for this was this was that, for many 'volunteers' in 1946–47, the prime purpose of signing up to a voluntary society was to give 'practical help' in cases of emergency on the wartime model; whereas Beveridge himself, surprisingly perhaps for someone who had supposedly just invented the welfare state, seemed to be still excessively concerned with 'voluntarism' as a means of insuring people against a deficiency in 'saving' and shortfall in income.[30] And another slightly jarring element was the note of hostility adopted by some of Beveridge's advisers towards recent developments in mass popular culture, as though one of the main purposes of 'volunteering' was to divert citizens away from the dangerous counter-attractions of football pools, dog-racing, dance-halls and cinemas. This was an attitude that Beveridge himself, to his credit, dismissed as 'the last worst stage in totalitarianism'. But, nevertheless, even the title that he himself invented for the proposed government minister who was henceforth to represent voluntary movements in parliament (the so-called 'Minister-Guardian-for-Voluntary-Action') also had a slightly fustian and obscurantist ring, harking back, if not to Gilbert and Sullivan, then at least to a more paternalist and even patriarchal age.[31]

As so often in Beveridge's writings, however, there were certain passages in *Voluntary action* that struck a quite different note, and that seemed almost to be part of a wholly different report. These were the passages in which Beveridge forgot his rather nit-picking and negative expert advisers and instead linked voluntarism not to the immediate context of the later 1940s (an era with which he felt himself to be rather ill at ease and baffled) but to a much longer-term vista. This he saw as characterised by the continuous rise of the over-mighty state, using its control over public and private finance invisibly to regulate all aspects of human affairs, and by a global economy in which Great Britain no longer had any special privileges or resources in the world, other than the qualities of its own people. At such a time, voluntary action would once again come into its own, as a force that was able to 'do things which the State is most unlikely to do', that 'could pioneer ahead of the State and make experiments' and that could promote 'self-criticism' 'social invention' and 'social advance'. Such a setting, he predicted, would also once again bring to the fore the vital role of close co-operation between voluntary agencies and governments: a relationship that Beveridge portrayed as a peculiarly British invention, on a par with 'natural liberty', 'representative government' and 'the British Commonwealth of free and independent nations'.[32] It was in this context, where Beveridge's unusual and quirky institutional imagination came to the fore and where he forgot the depressing constraints of the later 1940s, that Beveridge's messages for the modern revival of voluntarist movements are most likely to be found.

Notes

1 William Beveridge, *Social insurance and allied services*, Cmd 6404 (London: HMSO, 1942), pp. 143–5, 147 (sometimes known as the Beveridge Report).
2 William H. Beveridge, *Full employment in a free society* (London: George Allen & Unwin, 1944; 2nd edn, 1960), pp. 123–207.
3 W. H. Beveridge, 'Freedom from idleness', in G. D. H. Cole et al., *Plan for Britain: a collection of essays prepared for the Fabian Society* (London: Routledge & Sons, 1943), p. 98.
4 House of Lords debates, 5th series, vol. 141, cols 1105–11.
5 A major reason for the ending of this partnership had been the massive expansion into the national insurance sector of commercial life assurance companies, whose costs in collecting premiums were very high and whose contribution to the friendly and 'self-governing' aspect of social insurance schemes was minimal. Beveridge was inclined to

overlook this trend in the discussions of his Voluntary Action committee in 1946–48; but his 1942 report had been deeply critical of the role of commercial insurance companies in subverting 'voluntary' social welfare. See Beveridge, *Social insurance and allied services*, pp. 277–80.

6 Lord Beveridge, *Voluntary action: a report on methods of social advance* (London: George Allen & Unwin, 1948), pp. 217–324.

7 J. Harris, *William Beveridge: a biography*, 2nd edn (Oxford: Clarendon Press, 1997), p. 457; Nuffield College, Oxford (hereafter NC), Chester Papers, Voluntary Social Services Inquiry (hereafter VSSI), 'Informal note of conversation with Mrs Stocks', box 29, file 3, memorandum 17 and memorandum 24.

8 On the post-war participation of continental trade unions and other corporate groups in social insurance schemes, see T. Lynes, *French pensions* (London: Bell, 1967); E. Jabarri, 'Pierre Laroque and the Origins of French Social Security, 1934–48' (D.Phil. thesis, Oxford University, 1999); G. Clark and N. Whiteside (eds), *Pension security in the 21st century: re-drawing the public–private debate* (Oxford: Oxford University Press, 2003).

9 The background to this shift in trade union thought, and how far it was a result of the inter-war depression, the rise of Marxism or some other factors, deserves more attention than it can be given here.

10 Harris, *Beveridge*, pp. 82–5, 94–7.

11 J. Harris, 'Ruskin and social reform', in D. Birch (ed.), *Ruskin and the dawn of the modern* (Oxford: Oxford University Press, 1999), p. 23.

12 Harris, *Beveridge*, pp. 106–9, 145–6.

13 *Morning Post* (5 October and 13 November 1907); W. H. Beveridge, 'Public labour exchanges in Germany', *Economic Journal*, vol. 18, no. 69 (1908), pp. 1–18.

14 Harris, *Beveridge*, pp. 168–256.

15 Beveridge, *Social insurance and allied services*, pp. 120–45.

16 *Tables showing the rules and expenditure of trades unions*, Cd 5703, compiled by W. H. Beveridge (London: HMSO, 1911).

17 W. H. Beveridge, *Insurance for all and everything* (London: Daily News, 1924).

18 British Library of Political Science, London School of Economics, Beveridge Papers, 'Winston Churchill as I knew him', X, 10, n.d.; Beveridge, *Voluntary action*, p. 294; cf. W. H. Dawson, *What is wrong with Germany?* (London: Longmans, Green & Co, 1915).

19 National Archives, Kew, Richmond, Surrey, CAB 87/76–80, Interdepartmental Committee on Social Insurance and Allied Services, 1941–42, minutes of evidence. Bodies consulted or giving written and oral evidence included the National Conference of Friendly Societies, the National Council of Women, the National Federation of Old Age Pension Associations and the National Association for the Blind, to name but a few.

20 Beveridge, *Voluntary action*, p. 294.

21 NC, Chester Papers, VSSI, first draft of *Voluntary action*, box 28, file 12, 19 November 1947; Beveridge, *Voluntary action*, pp. 313–14.

22 On the mixture of state control and syndicalist participation in the French social security tradition, see T. Lynes, *French pensions*, Occasional papers in social administration, no. 21 (London, 1967); E. Jabarri, 'Pierre Laroque and the origins of French social security, 1934–48' (D.Phil. thesis, Oxford University, 1999). On the influence of T. H.

Green and idealism, see M. Richter, *The politics of conscience: T. H. Green and his age* (London: Weidenfeld and Nicolson, 1964).

23 T. Lynes, *Paying for pensions: the French experience* (London: STICERD, 1985); L. Troiani (ed.), *Dopo Beveridge: riflessioni sul welfare* (Rome: Agrilavoro Edizioni Srl, 2003); Clark and Whiteside (eds), *Pension security in the 21st century*.

24 NC, Chester Papers, VSSI, minutes of sixth meeting, 28 May 1947, box 28; NC, Chester Papers, VSSI, box 29, memorandum 17.

25 W. H. Beveridge and A. F. Wells (eds), *The evidence for voluntary action* (London: George Allen & Unwin, 1949).

26 NC, Chester Papers, VSSI, 'Informal note of conversation with Mrs Stocks', box 29, file 3, memorandum 17, and memorandum 4.

27 NC, Chester Papers, VSSI, sixth meeting, 28 May 1947, box 28, file 2, L. When did the ancient and beautiful word 'charity' become tainted in English usage with overtones of patronage, miserliness and moral disapproval? A recent internet blog rightly cites Robert Louis Stevenson's reference to 'as cold as charity' (in his poem 'Christmas at sea', 1888) as evidence of its negative Victorian connotations, but wrongly ascribes the change to Dickens's *Oliver Twist*. It was after all not a voluntary charity but officials of the statutory Poor Law who starved and maltreated Oliver. There is an interesting conundrum here that historians of voluntarism may like to pursue further.

28 NC, Chester Papers, VSSI, Roger Wilson, 'Notes on the future of voluntary social work', box 29, file 2, memorandum 20; NC, Chester Papers, VSSI, 'Informal note of conversation with Mrs Stocks', box 29, file 3, memorandum 17.

29 NC, Chester Papers, VSSI, sixth meeting, 28 May 1947, box 28, file 2.

30 One possible reason for Beveridge's rather puzzling emphasis on friendly societies as the archetypal model of the voluntary sector (which, as he more than anyone had good reason to know, was no longer the case in the 1940s) was that research for the Voluntary Action enquiry had been funded by the National Deposit Friendly Society. This was an entirely non-profit-making body, but the society nevertheless clearly hoped that the enquiry would demonstrate the continuing importance of its social role.

31 NC, Chester Papers, VSSI, memorandum by Beveridge on 'Scope and objectives', 12 April 1947, box 29; Beveridge, *Voluntary action*, pp. 314–15.

32 Beveridge, *Voluntary action*, pp. 8–10, 21–3, 84, 150–2, 266–7, 302, 308–24.

3

'The night's insane dream of power': William Beveridge on the uses and abuses of state power

Nicholas Deakin

This chapter approaches the question of Beveridge's involvement with voluntary action from an oblique angle, drawing on an experience that he had in the 1930s when engaging in the rescue of academics exiled from Nazi Germany.[1] This experience apparently had no direct impact on the production of the report *Voluntary action*, and there are some reasons to suggest for this. However, my contention is that his concept of the state's role and both the potential for the abuse of state power and the means by which those abuses can be successfully confronted was strongly influenced by what he saw and heard during the extended rescue operation that he and like-minded academics mounted. My point of departure is the well-known final sentence of *Voluntary action*:

> So at last human society may become a friendly society . . . So the night's insane dream of power over other men, without limit and without mercy, shall fade. So mankind in brotherhood shall bring back the day.[2]

This last sentence may well now be the best-known part of the whole report; over recent years it has demonstrated its lasting attraction to radicals, conservatives and neo-liberals alike.[3] But what does it mean? Was Beveridge a *pentito* in old age, who had come to realise the risks attached to conceding too much to the power of the Leviathan state? Was he sulking at not having been given the personal power he expected to exercise in implementing the post-war settlement? Or was this simply a closing rhetorical gesture (of the kind to which he was prone), in part reflecting increasing anxieties about the general condition of the world after the Second World War – but also perhaps a lack of anything more telling to say? And if not signalling imminent danger in his conclusions to *Voluntary action*, upon what could Beveridge's expression of urgent concern about the misuse of power be based?

Beveridge and the state

It goes without saying that Beveridge had extensive experience during his long career of the British state and its functioning. In the introduction to his autobiography, *Power and influence*, he draws a distinction between these two 'alternative ways by which things get done in the world of affairs'. 'Power', he says, 'means ability to give to other men orders enforced by sanctions, by punishment or by control of rewards', while influence 'means changing the actions of others by persuasion, means appeal to reason or to emotions other than fear or greed'. By any test, he had had a fair experience of both by 1948, although he qualifies that experience by observing that 'since I came to manhood I have seldom been without influence. I have as seldom had "government", that is power and I have had it under limitations'.[4]

His own background provides a range of examples. In his Anglo-Indian childhood his ineffectual father had doubts about the exercise of power by the British imperial government in India, his more formidable mother (who had a lifelong influence on him) much less so. Or there is his own early career after university – reading for the bar but not practising there – and the search for an alternative route. The decision to go to Toynbee Hall as assistant warden ('the most difficult decision that I have ever been called on to make alone') set his feet firmly on the road to acquiring influence, first by using Toynbee as an observation post and a means of coming to grips with the social question, as a good Balliol man should.

Wider influence followed when he then took up the role of leader writer on the *Morning Post*; and when he acquired the skills required to promote new policy initiatives from his observation of the Webbs and their methods of permeation, after they had forgiven him his 'ugly manners' and taken 'the boy Beveridge' under their wing. This in due course brought him power, at first behind the scenes, through entrance into the civil service as promoter of employment exchanges. As he said at the time, 'Now I can write Blue Books!'[5]

Then came the First World War, by the end of which Beveridge was a permanent secretary. Some explicit power must have attached to that role, surely, even on a restricted scale. (We can ignore the customary disclaimers about responsibility attaching solely to ministers). But it is difficult to detect any 'insane dream of power' in his experience of the British state in the years up to and during the First World War. Although by the end of his time as a civil servant he declared himself disillusioned with state bureaucracy, he continued to tinker with schemes to reform it; and in retrospect, he was inclined to view war as a good opportunity to introduce into government the rudiments of comprehensive planning.[6] And while he remained ambivalent about politics and politicians (especially Churchill and Lloyd George) he does not seem to have nurtured fears of British statesmen exercising 'power without limit and without mercy'.

It is perhaps worth adding that Beveridge was perhaps unusual among contemporaries in being relatively untouched personally by the war itself, either directly

– he did not see the western front until after hostilities ended – or even indirectly. He lost no immediate relatives as casualties, which was unusual in his class and age group. Nor did he share the views expressed by many contemporaries about the dangers of a powerful Prussian state machine threatening tyrannical domination over Europe; Germany, he later opined, was 'more civilised than [our ally] Russia in 1914'.[7] So apparently there were no 'insane dreams' then.

The inter-war years

Beveridge left government for the directorship of the London School of Economics (LSE) in 1919, at Sidney Webb's invitation. There he expected to have power of an immediate kind; but his exercise of it was eventually compromised by a series of disputes, so there are perhaps no clear lessons about the exercise of power to be drawn there. He castigated himself in *Power and influence* for becoming too much absorbed in administration but as Harold Wilson subsequently commented, administration was exactly the thing he was not good at.

In his general attitudes towards state power and its exercise, Beveridge tacked during his LSE years across the political spectrum: first taking an increasing interest in free-market solutions to social problems, as reflected in his pamphlet *Insurance for all*; in the 1920s passing though a phase of thinking about going into politics as a Liberal; and then in his membership of the Royal Commission on the Coal Industry – a 'lost endeavour', as he put it subsequently.[8]

But after 1931 Beveridge became rapidly disillusioned with free-market approaches and tilted back towards valuing state intervention; this found practical expressing in his chairing of the Unemployment Insurance Statutory Committee and mending fences with unions. His changing views are reflected in the essays he published in the mid-1930s under the intriguing title of *Planning under socialism*, perhaps reflecting his closer relationship at this time with Beatrice Webb and her growing enthusiasm for the Soviet communist model.

Abuse of state power

But the experience from Beveridge's directorship of the LSE to which I particularly want to draw attention is that of helping academic exiles from Nazi Germany and his resulting first-hand encounter with totalitarianism and experience of what its full meaning could be. His response to the expulsion of academics from German universities was subsequently described by Lionel Robbins, not one of his fans, as 'Beveridge's finest hour'.[9]

Beveridge himself thought the episode of sufficient importance to provide his own accounts of what he attempted to do, first in *Power and influence* and later in a fuller version, *A defence of free learning*.[10] This later account, published in 1959, has serious limitations: it is idiosyncratic and extremely partial in both senses. But it leaves no doubt that Beveridge continued to regard the experience of dealing with the official policies of Nazi Germany as a vitally important episode, raising fundamental issues about the abuse of state power and means of addressing it.

The general story of the exiles from Nazi Germany is, of course a familiar one. But Beveridge's experience places it in a slightly different light, taking his engagement with this issue, together with that of his fellow-academics, as an example of citizen action taken outside the normal bounds of the state responsibilities, intended to address an acute crisis involving issues of principle. The form this action took, the limits within which it functioned and the extent of its effectiveness suggest some important lessons about voluntary action in twentieth-century Britain. But Beveridge's version of events needs supplementing and correcting, drawing on Ralf Dahrendorf's account in his history of the LSE and an important recent article by David Zimmerman, as well as on Daniel Snowman's classic *The Hitler emigrés*.[11]

The Academic Assistance Council

Beveridge happened to be in Vienna on academic business at the end of March 1933. There he had an accidental encounter with Lionel Robbins and the Austrian economist Ludwig von Mises (at the Hotel Bristol) and first heard the news of the first dismissals by the new National Socialist government of Germany of those academics 'with a high political profile, many of them Jews'. Beveridge was deeply affected by what he saw and heard and resolved to act immediately. As he subsequently told the story, he instantly realised what National Socialism meant in practice. On that same visit, he went to the cinema and saw newsreel film of Goebbels speaking – 'an ape possessed by a devil' – and travelled by train with a German professorial colleague and saw his terror of what might happen to him.[12] Beveridge was not alone in seeking to take immediate action: the Hungarian scientist Leo Szilard had reached the same conclusion and was trying to launch an international initiative to rescue threatened academics. But as it turned out it was Beveridge's intervention that proved to be decisive.

There is no doubt about the level of his passion. Beveridge was a devoted Germanophile. He spoke the language well; he had done field research there on unemployment policy before the First World War. As already suggested, he was not deeply affected by Prussian militarism. In 1914 he wrote to his mother that 'it goes all against the grain with me to go to war with Germany'.[13] He saw German literature and culture as a beacon of sophisticated civilisation. The Nazi traducing of those qualities was a gross personal offence to him.

Immediately upon his return from Vienna Beveridge went back to the LSE and established a committee within the school to take instant action to bring German academics to the school. But his ambitions went further than that. After some brisk canvassing a public appeal was made in May 1933, signed by forty-one leading academics, among them the cream of the British scientific establishment, including five

Nobel prize winners. Funds were raised, which in turn facilitated the setting-up of an Academic Assistance Council (AAC) under the wing of the Royal Society, with full-time staff. Walter Adams, subsequently himself to become director of the LSE, was secured as full-time secretary and was joined as assistant by Esther 'Tess' Simpson. Leo Szilard also worked there, briefly. The objective of the council, as described in a circular drafted by Beveridge, was to negotiate the safe passage of academic staff from Germany to take up posts in British universities.

The response of British academe to the appeal for funds and provision of posts for expelled academics was generous, with only a few exceptions. The LSE staff set an example by tithing themselves. But British industry, except for ICI (under the influence of Frederick Lindemann) and Courtauld, was not prepared to take an interest. Nor was the City of London. Beveridge's later lobbying of leading bankers produced no positive results.[14] An appearance by Albert Einstein at a mass meeting in the Albert Hall in October 1933 on his way through to exile in the United States gave the campaign much-needed wider publicity and secured additional funding. But the need remained acute. Beveridge turned to foundations; Rockefeller (previously so helpful in providing funding for the LSE) and Carnegie and did obtain some limited support from them. Otherwise the main institutional source of financial support was the Central Fund for British Jewry.

Beveridge's own role in all this was crucial. The AAC had been set up in classic British voluntary committee style, with a top hamper of distinguished names on the letterhead as members. Formally, Beveridge figured there as (joint) honorary secretary, providing oversight of Walter Adams and Esther Simpson, but the papers of the AAC show him taking part in a much wider range of activities. As David Zimmerman summarises it, he was the 'chief strategist'.[15] Inside the organisation, he was a very active member of the executive committee, which did the real business, often chairing its meetings. Still more significantly, he chaired the applications committee, which considered individual cases.

Outside, he worked tirelessly as propagandist for the cause. He was by this stage an experienced broadcaster and remained well-connected as a journalist, able to mobilise editorial contacts, particularly at the *Times*. He made a BBC broadcast from the Einstein meeting – and continued to use press and wireless contacts to put the case for support for the exiles. He went on speaking tours of universities to appeal for practical help. His speech in Birmingham in 1935 can stand as representative of these:

> Shadows of brutality and ignorance returning from the past lie across the world. The shadow does not lie on Germany alone. But the shadow looks deepest on Germany because in Germany before there was most light. The German people have been one of the great civilising forces of the world ... What is happening in Germany today is a challenge to us in Britain above all. It is a challenge not to be taken up by protests. Protests butter no parsnips. It is a challenge given by deeds not words – and must be met not by words but by deeds. It is a challenge given by deeds of hate; it should be met by deeds of charity.[16]

In a parallel Oxford speech given slightly earlier he went further in recognising the legitimate grievance that Germans may have felt about the Versailles Treaty. He said, 'I recognise the feeling of the German people that we have treated them unjustly and are responsible for their troubles. In a sense they feel they are only passing on a persecution'.[17] But his indignant response to Nazism was unwavering. When he appealed for support from the Rockefeller Foundation in 1934 its representatives reported that 'Sir William displayed an extraordinary bitterness towards the existing regime in Germany; he thought it might be pardoned in the eyes of the Lord but not in the eyes of man'.[18] All this suggests that the Nazis are strong candidates to be identified as the 'insane dreamers' of his conclusion to *Voluntary action*.

Sometimes this feeling led him to overreach himself, as in the attempt to try to rescue the library of the Frankfurt Institut für Sozialforschung. The resulting fiasco did considerable damage to his reputation in the LSE.[19] He was more successful with the attempt to get British academics to boycott a largely spurious anniversary celebration at Heidelberg University in 1936. And one of the AAC's outstanding early successes was the wholesale movement of the Warburg Institute from Hamburg to London. But any fleeting hope that the need for help would be temporary was dissipated by the passage of the Nuremberg laws in 1935.

Buttering the parsnips

The implementation of a longer-term programme of action raised a number of issues in connection with both strategy and tactics. In principle, should this be a campaign about the Nazi policy of dismissal of Jews and dissenters, seeking to change it by mobilising public indignation; or was it about addressing the circumstances of academic exiles and securing practical support for bettering them? Should there be appeals to general humanitarian principles or was this more specifically and particularly a matter of academic freedom and the 'Republic of Learning'?

Beveridge was never in any doubt: as he had frequently said on public platforms, 'protests butter no parsnips'. The job was to rescue individuals, and the practical need was for material assistance – in the form of jobs and financial support. And the grounds for doing so were specifically and solely the preservation of academic freedom. Hence, Beveridge refused invitations to speak on platforms where the Nazi regime was to be criticised, even in the company of an archbishop. He rejected a possible grant because it would involve making such public criticism: as his speeches to academic audiences indicated, he preferred to work behind the scenes to achieve the best possible outcome for fellow academics in distress. 'By remedial action we escape the need of making useless protests.'[20]

But who exactly were the beneficiaries of the AAC's work to be? 'Science and learning' was the overall category, meaning academics not just in the natural sciences but also in other disciplines, always providing that their academic expertise was transferable. The range of different disciplines among those eventually helped was impressive. But for a substantial block of the dispossessed, transferability was a major difficulty. Academic lawyers were a case in point: they were found in considerable numbers among German and later Austrian exiles, but their skills were of little use in a different legal context. An additional complication was the absence of any parallel organisation to the AAC dealing with the professions; indeed many British professional associations, most notoriously that of the doctors, were positively hostile towards the exiles, sometimes exhibiting the kind of pervasive anti-Semitism common at the time.

And then – excruciatingly painful – how were decisions to be made about whom to help? The principle was that established scholars should have priority – but how would 'established' be assessed? And what of those younger scientists showing ample promise but as yet little achievement? These were all problems with which the allocations committee, chaired by Beveridge, had to wrestle.

And then there was another issue which caused some difficulty from the outset. Was this an exercise focussed on Jewish academics, so prominent among the dispossessed, particularly after the passage of the Nuremberg laws, or was it more general? If the latter, how should the case be presented? The launching statement of the AAC had been clear that 'many who have suffered or are threatened have no Jewish connection'. In private, the Royal Society in particular took an even stronger line: nobody who signed the appeal and neither of the honorary secretaries should be a Jew.[21] One exception only was made to that rule. Appeal letters to possible funders stressed that the beneficiaries would be Jews and non-Jews alike. Beveridge insisted on this, and he himself made amendments to drafts to that effect. And Jewish organisations engaged in working to help the dispossessed were urged to treat the problem as a general one and not an issue for Jews alone. All this reflected the organisers' fears of anti-Semitism and the possible consequences of 'stirring it up' – an attitude perhaps explicable in the context of the time, but not readily excusable.

And by what methods should the cases be pursued? 'Buttering the parsnips', in Beveridge style, meant establishing cordial relations with Home Office bureaucracy from the Home Secretary downwards and later with the Foreign Office to allow academic refugees in as distinct category, and also with the Ministry of Labour, which was responsible for administering entry schemes. A lower public profile meant fewer obstacles in dealing privately with the bureaucracy. Here there is no doubt that Beveridge's tactics were successful; important concessions were secured in 1935, where the conditions of entry were relaxed in favour of particularly eminent German scholars. In his letter to the secretary, Walter Adams, the Home Office civil servant responsible wrote:

> I am sure you will be glad to learn that Sir John Simon, who has taken a personal interest in the work of the Academic Assistance Council since its beginning in 1933, has decided, after reviewing the whole position as set out in your letters under reply, that the conditions should be removed in all the cases mentioned in your letters.[22]

In sum, this was in many respects a classic 'great and good' exercise, catering for a limited group in peril, doing so by careful backstage diplomacy, avoiding making a public fuss and consciously omitting larger groups in equal danger. When Beveridge later went to see Sir Robert Vansittart to discuss tactics, he did so with a brief from Walter Adams urging him to make it entirely clear that the AAC's role was and should always be solely to deal with refugee scholars and scientists; there was no scope for expanding the area of concern to cover any other professional groups. This had been Adams's position from the beginning of his time as secretary in 1933. Jeremy Seabrook's description of this approach as 'elitist' is perhaps harsh, but fair. However, as an exercise in bringing influence to bear in the climate of those times it was a textbook success, given the deliberately restricted assumptions on which it was based.

In 1936, in recognition that the need was still growing and that similar issues were arising in other countries – Spain, Portugal and then the USSR – the AAC reconstituted itself as the Society for the Protection of Science and Learning (SPSL), inviting supporters to subscribe to support its work and to donate to an Academic Assistance Trust.

The 'cold pogrom'

After the outbreak of the Spanish Civil War the European situation deteriorated rapidly; Beveridge called this the 'period of troubled peace'. The number of cases dealt with by SPSL increased, and financial pressures on the organisation continued. Outside the United Kingdom, there had briefly been an alternative scheme in the United States – but this had ceased to be available after 1935, with American universities in the depression years reluctant to take on foreign staff. A parallel French attempt also eventually failed. Leo Szilard's notion of co-ordinated international effort did have some success (the New School in New York was one), but in general group schemes, apart from the Warburg, did not succeed. Efforts were made to involve the League of Nations, and a High Commissionership for refugees was created.

In 1937 Beveridge promoted and chaired an informal international gathering at his new base, University College, Oxford, to try to co-ordinate efforts with representatives from the United States and a number of European countries. It was generally agreed that the prospects were gloomy but that an international approach might pay dividends, provided that there were no politics involved, that the scheme would not be only for Jews and that scholars from countries other than Germany were included. The meeting concluded, rather ruefully, that 'the work is unavoidably expensive, compared with relief work for other classes of refugee'.[23]

Beveridge had himself attempted to raise funds through a broadcast appeal on the BBC ('This week's good cause'). He had hoped to persuade Winston Churchill to take this on but failed and in the event made it himself, raising over £1,000.

Beveridge was also closely involved in the recruitment of a new president for the SPSL after the death of Lord Rutherford. Beveridge wanted Stanley Baldwin, the retiring prime minister, but the AAC eventually settled for William Temple, the reforming Archbishop of York. Beveridge himself now relinquished the role of honorary secretary, although he continued his active engagement in AAC policy.

The crux year was 1938: by that year one third of the teaching staff of German universities had been dismissed. In March the Anschluss ended Austrian indepen- dence and led immediately to the dispossession and expulsion of large numbers of Jewish professionals and academics. In July 1938 the Evian conference, summoned by President Roosevelt to make an official attempt at international co-ordination on refugee issues, broke up without achieving any significant results. In October Hitler took over the Sudetenland under the terms of the Munich agreement. In the following month, the widespread destruction of Jewish property across the Reich during *Kristallnacht* left no further doubt about the regime's intentions. Then in March 1939 German troops entered Prague, setting off another wave of emigra- tion. This time the British government accepted some share of responsibility, moving from the attitude of cautious benevolence reflected in earlier exchanges to active support of refugees. Machinery was put in place to co-ordinate efforts – a Central Council for Refugees – and official funding provided. Unofficially, Lord Baldwin launched an appeal for charitable support. The SPSL became one in a range of organisations working in the field with official help, and by the end of 1938 had 830 cases placed, temporarily or permanently.[24]

Internment

After the outbreak of war in September 1939, the SPSL moved to Cambridge and Beveridge lost his direct connection with the organisation. He was already engaged in work for the government in London and took no active part in the next episode which involved the society. As a result of the war, refugee academics had (mostly) become categorised as 'enemy aliens', and after the fall of France in May 1940 something approaching a national panic broke out, in which all aliens were perceived as potential fifth columnists. Churchill's instruction to 'collar the lot' led to chaotic scenes as large numbers of Germans, Austrians and Italians (27,000 in all) were rounded up; among them were 530 of the SPSL's academic refugees, who were then either interned in the Isle of Man or sent overseas to Australia or Canada.[25]

The issue of internment as an abuse of power was immediately taken up in parliament by a cross-bench coalition marshalled by the formidable Eleanor Rathbone. One of the SPSL's most active members, Professor A. V. Hill, now sat in parliament as member for Cambridge University, and he succeeded in securing a concession from the Home Office; those refugee scientists capable of doing work of national importance would be released (17 July 1940). An appeal system was organised; the indefatigable Esther Simpson, acting for the SPSL, prepared the cases for the panels that had been established by the Learned Societies to rule upon the relevance of the detainees' skills and present applications to the Home Office. By December 1940 practically all the detained academics had been released.

Beveridge was only marginally involved by now, except in a purely honorific capacity (he had taken on the role of president), though he dealt with the internment episode at length in *A defence of free learning* with detailed case histories and concluded (as author rather than as participant) that this was a clear case of abuse of state power but through inefficiency rather than malice ('when a stupid decision is made in war, stupid men will make it worse in execution').[26]

More generally, Beveridge's very active engagement after 1933 with the refugee academic issue had eventually led him to a number of conclusions: first, that the successful provision of safe haven for refugees was an illustration of superiority of ideas over money; next, that informal charitable intervention was 'fleet of foot' but government was an essential partner – and could be drawn upon if the right approaches are made; and, finally, that the whole episode was a vindication of British values. Britain had served as exemplar of the academic virtues – the 'Republic of Learning', as A. V. Hill had called it, in action. And he found it significant that so many of the academic refugees stayed in Britain; although some went on to the United States, none returned to Germany. And he might have added – though he did not – that this was a classic example of the successful use of influence, as he defined it in his autobiography.

David Zimmerman also sees the whole episode as a striking example of the solidarity of British scientists, arguing that in bringing them together the campaigns transcended political differences in the scientific community: 'promoted by the SPSL's activities, the apolitical elite, conservatives and the Left joined in what had become a moral crusade'.[27] The evidence, he argues, does not support the theory advanced by Gary Werskey, in his *Visible college*, that the action taken was simply one consequence of the leftward shift during the 1930s among British scientists. But it is perhaps also worth pointing out that the AAC/SPSL was from the beginning by design not restricted to the natural sciences: if it had been, Beveridge would not have taken such a prominent role or become president – and the LSE would not have been a natural base for its activities.

Towards *Voluntary action*

Yet when he came in 1948 to write the report that became *Voluntary action* Beveridge did not find it necessary to refer directly to his experience with academic refugees. This might seem doubly odd, because at that same time he was also engaged in following up the cases of academics who might still be in displaced persons' camps: the letters written on his behalf from the secretary of the 'Voluntary Social Services Inquiry' are in the SPSL files.

There are at least two possible explanations for this. First is the scope of the academic refugee exercise, which was so narrowly and deliberately confined to one class of beneficiary. The interests and most of the needs of these beneficiaries lay clearly outside the range of the social service state, as Beveridge had defined it. And, secondly, there was the manner in which it was executed – sedulously avoiding public protest, working contacts in government and the press in order to achieve the desired outcome. In a sense, the whole exercise had been about setting up a functioning bureaucracy of rescue. If this was based almost entirely on volunteer effort, it remained very much activity taken within the peer group to benefit colleagues in undeserved distress. But at the same time, what were the appeals to the ethos of the 'Republic of Learning' about if not mutual aid, defined as one of the two great principles of voluntary action in his report and described in Chapter 1 of this book?

There were, of course, several of Beveridge's other recent activities and experiences that went into mix of influences on his drafting of *Voluntary action*. Obviously important were the first and second reports (*Social insurance* and *Full employment*), not just for their content but for the manner in which Beveridge approached the evaluation of what he initially termed 'Voluntary Social Services'. The format adopted was similar: the creation of a group of expert assessors, drawn in part from among those who had worked with Beveridge in the 1930s, the taking of evidence and then a text drafted by Beveridge himself with somewhat limited opportunity for comment or amendment. So it was logical for him to present the outcome at the time (although not subsequently) as his third report.

And there were some other influences that may also have been relevant. First, there was Beveridge's recent experience in party politics. It seems clear that he really intended to have a serious political career, building on popular adulation from his first and second reports and his status as a major public figure, able to command large audiences. His brief period in parliament as a Liberal MP provided him with a congenial platform for his views, and there are repeated references after 1945 to his disappointment at being deprived of it. He summarised his political credo for the 1945 general election in *Why I am a Liberal*. Some relevant distinctions are drawn there on the use and abuse of state power. Beveridge dissents sharply from Hayek in asserting the desirability of state intervention in the economy; the execution of a radical programme, he maintains, 'involves an extension of the responsibilities and functions of the state' – but only 'where it is necessary to cure evils that cannot be cured without them'. So 'Liberal radicalism avoids both the errors of both so-called individualists, who treat every liberty as equally important and of the collectivists who desire extension of state activity for its own sake'.[28]

Then there was planning. Beveridge was at one with most progressive thinkers of this period in propounding the importance of planning the post-war world, with population dispersal and control of the location of industry as some of the planners' main tools. But he went further than some in trying to ensure that these principles were applied in practice, through his work on creating and promoting New Towns – really the *locus classicus* of (benevolent) state planning in the period after the Second World War. Nobody fully committed to that cause could possibly be seen as a convinced sceptic about the uses of state power. Rather, this could be seen as an expression of his utopianism in the positive sense. Indeed, he went on to make a commitment of his own by living in one of the New Towns whose development commission he chaired, Newton Aycliffe.

Finally, there was his internationalism. He had been converted to the concept of federal union in Europe and lost few opportunities to advance the case for international co-operation. His concern for a better post-war settlement (remembering his critique of Versailles) led to the production of *The price of peace*, published in 1945, which Beveridge subsequently represented in *Power and influence* as his real 'third report'.[29] Rapid disillusionment with communism had followed the brief intellectual flirtation of the 1930s, when he had told Beatrice Webb that he would like to see communism tried under democratic conditions. Some of the concerns about totalitarianism and its recrudescence on the post-war world are to be found there, this time with the focus on the Soviet Union – as are anxieties about 'ultra-modern techniques' for influencing opinion.

The 'third report': some closing reflections

Voluntary action is certainly not now a 'forgotten text', as it once used to be described.[30] Rather it is a confused text, in which Beveridge steers an uncertain course, rejecting an extreme statist position but unable, despite some effort during the evidence-gathering and committee discussion, to provide a convincing alternative. The incoherence of the report is also reflected in his falling back on personal anecdotes and lives of the great praiseworthy philanthropists. There was and could be no master plan this time, merely an 'eight point program' with no thematic coherence. So what can the message be? It turns out to be a modest attempt to shore up what is good in mutual aid (the friendly societies, who had after all commissioned the report) and a tip of the hat to the possible supporting role of the state (the Minister-Guardian on University Grants Committee lines), topped with a dire but unspecific warning of worse to come. All this is quite superficial, but generally consistent with his civic republicanism, as Jose Harris sets it out in her biography.[31]

In some ways Beveridge himself seems not to have been convinced of the value of what he had done. It is surely odd that he was hesitant, as his correspondence shows, about initiating a debate on his own report in the House of Lords and then did not stay to the end to hear Lord Pakenham's conciliatory response, which is surely a better guide to Labour views at that time than Richard Crossman's posthumous confection.[32] And that behaviour was consistent with his own downgrading of the significance of the report in his later references to it. And yet over the past two decades the report has had a steadily growing influence. Perhaps that is because it contains something for everyone – a bran tub from which everyone can pull out a prize.

Devolutionists can point to the warnings about the limit to state action and the virtues of the locality as a basis for action, as the Conservative Party did in 2008–09, although Beveridge is surprisingly unforthcoming about local government as an alternative focus for activity.[33] Citizenship and its responsibilities (a New Labour theme) can also be readily identified as an emphasis in *Voluntary action* that is of continuing significance. Democracy must be made more efficient and equipped to exercise the wider power it now possesses. The electorate must be educated to take social responsibilities seriously and not be distracted by popular cultural entertainments. Civic education should be one vital role for voluntary action and another one filling the gaps left after the creation of the 'Social Service State'.

Then those concerned about the increased influence of business on voluntary and charitable action have their neat tag (the business motive is a 'good servant but a bad master'). Mutualism and brotherhood are there: 'methods of social advance', as Matthew Smerdon reminds us, is the subtitle of the report.[34] The volume of evidence, in some ways more valuable than the main report, shows mutualism in rapid decline but could also be used to suggest the potential for revival. The gap being left by the decline in organised religion and how it was to be filled was another Beveridge theme (he wrote as a non-believer). Lamentations on the right about the continuation of this process since 1948 – and concerns on the left about some implications of its possible reversal – are another illustration of the continued relevance of some of Beveridge's ideas, if not of the way in which he framed them in his report.

But finally, there is the question with which I began – the reasons for his passionate cry of alarm about the risks of totalitarian domination of civil society. Rationally, Beveridge always accepted the necessity of the existence of state power and sought to set limits on its exercise. 'Power, the stupid necessary mule', he said, 'should have neither pride of ancestry nor hope of progeny.'[35] But emotionally, he still saw it as a risk, and the refugee question crystallised this concern. Although he celebrated the achievement of British academia in the account he gave in 1959, he still regretted episodes like the 'tragic failure I had with Edith Speer, a brilliant administrator in the social field, whom I met when we were both thirty in Berlin and I had gone there to study labour exchanges and social insurance of which she was the master. She helped me then, but I failed to rescue her thirty years later'.[36] From such experiences he had accumulated enough first-hand acquaintance with the abuses of power, even if in this case the response that he was instrumental in organising fell outside the traditional boundaries of voluntary action. And, to end as he does on a positive note, that episode was also a moment when brotherhood (in this case the community of scholarship) did, to use his final phrase, succeed in 'bringing back the day'.

Notes

1 In preparing this paper I have been given access to the Beveridge Papers in the archives of the London School of Economics, where the papers of the Voluntary Social Services Inquiry (to give it the original title) are lodged. Also, by courtesy of the officers of that organisation, I was able to use the archive of the Society for the Protection of Science and Learning in the Bodleian Library, Oxford. This contains records of the deliberations of the committees of that organisation and a set of case files of individual scholars helped by the society. The catalogue of that archive by Nicholas Baldwin (1988) was of particular help.

2 Lord Beveridge, *Voluntary action: a report on methods of social advance* (London: George Allen & Unwin, 1948), p. 324.

3 See, for example, K. and J. Williams (eds), *A Beveridge reader* (London: Allen and Unwin, 1987); B. Knight, *Voluntary action* (London: Home Office, Centris Crown Copyright, 1993); F. Prochaska, *The voluntary impulse: philanthropy in modern Britain* (London: Faber and Faber, 1988); M. Smerdon et al., 'William Beveridge and social advance: modern messages for voluntary action', in B. Knight et al. (eds), *Building civil society: current initiatives in voluntary action: a special edition of the non-profit sector in the UK to mark the 50th anniversary of the publication of Voluntary Action* (West Malling: Charities Aid Foundation, 1998); F. J. Gladstone, *Voluntary action in a changing world* (London: Bedford Square Press, 1979); Conservative Party, *A stronger society: Voluntary action in the 21st century*, Responsibility Agenda, Policy Green Paper no. 5 (London: Conservative Party, 2008).

4 W. Beveridge, *Power and influence* (London: Hodder and Stoughton, 1953), p. 3.

5 J. Harris, *William Beveridge: a biography*, 2nd edn (Oxford: Clarendon Press, 1997), p. 167.

6 G. D. H. Cole et al., *Plan for Britain: a collection of essays prepared by the Fabian Society* (London: George Routledge, 1943).

7 W. Beveridge, *The price of peace* (London: Pilot Press, 1945), p. 34.

8 Beveridge, *Power and influence*, p. 221.

9 R. Dahrendorf, *LSE: a history of the London School of Economics* (Oxford: Oxford University Press, 1995), p. 286.

10 W. Beveridge, *A defence of free learning* (London: Oxford University Press, 1959).

11 Through the courtesy of the author and officers of the organisation that Beveridge was instrumental in creating, I was also able to see before publication a new history of that body, now called the Council for Assisting Refugee Academics (CARA), by Jeremy Seabrook.

12 Beveridge, *Power and influence*, p. 234.

13 Beveridge, *Power and influence*, p. 120.

14 D. Zimmerman, 'The Society for the Protection of Science and Learning and the politicization of British science in the 1930s', *Minerva*, vol. 44, no. 1 (2006), p. 39.

15 Zimmerman, 'The Society', p. 28.

16 Beveridge, *A defence of free learning*, p. 12.

17 London School of Economics (LSE), London, Beveridge Papers, box 9A/45 iii, 14 March 1935.

18 Dahrendorf, *LSE*, p. 289.

19 Harris, *William Beveridge*, p. 290; but compare Dahrendorf, *LSE*, pp. 290 ff.
20 Society for the Protection of Science and Learning (hereafter SPSL), Bodleian Papers, box 17/1, Beveridge speech notes.
21 Dahrendorf, *LSE*, p. 293.
22 SPSL, Bodleian Papers, box 3/1, as reported to the AAC Committee on 19 January 1935.
23 SPSL, Bodleian Papers, box 3/1, minutes of informal international meeting, Master's Lodge, University College, Oxford, 13 November 1937.
24 Beveridge, *A defence of free learning*, p. 39.
25 A good contemporary account of this episode is in Francois Lafitte's 'Penguin Special' *The internment of aliens* (London: Penguin Books, 1941).
26 Beveridge, *A defence of free learning*, p. 61.
27 Zimmerman, 'The society', p. 43.
28 William Beveridge, *Why I am a Liberal* (London: Herbert Jenkins, 1945), pp. 9, 33, 35.
29 Beveridge, *Power and influence*, p. 336.
30 Williams (eds), *A Beveridge reader*, p. 1.
31 Harris, *William Beveridge*, p. 488.
32 LSE, Beveridge Papers, boxes B6/36.
33 Conservative Party, *A stronger society*.
34 Smerdon et al., 'William Beveridge and social advance'.
35 Beveridge, *Power and influence*, p. 360.
36 Beveridge, *A defence of free learning*, p. viii.

4

The war and charity

Frank Prochaska

'The *Luftwaffe* was a powerful missionary for the welfare state', wrote A. J. P. Taylor over forty years ago.[1] Like many historians since, Taylor believed that the Blitz, and mass evacuation, triggered a social revolution in Britain, in which planning with a capital P came into full, luxuriant bloom. The impact of the Second World War on the flowering of state social policy has attracted such attention that its impact on charities and the voluntary work of the churches has been obscured. Historians of the welfare state have paid little attention to the effects of the aerial bombing on the morale, or the fabric, of the myriad charitable institutions that were in the forefront of the delivery of health and social services in Britain before the war. What was the impact of the war on what Beveridge called, in a lecture of 1942, that sense of 'Divine Vocation', in which the citizenry marked the brotherhood of man by serving one another with little thought of commercial gain?[2]

The Second World War, like the First, posed both a threat and a challenge to charitable agencies, sending out mixed signals to charitable campaigners. It offered them fresh opportunities but tested their resolve and their finances. As Richard Titmuss observed in his magisterial study of social policy, the Second World War provided many opportunities for people to be charitably useful, but it was, as he put it, 'much less romantic than the first'.[3] It was also longer, more uncomfortable and more physically demanding. In short, it required a much greater degree of adjustment in the personal lives of the British population than any war since the seventeenth century.

For charities, operating costs escalated, while wartime drives took away erstwhile subscribers. Yet institutions old and new were zealous in support of the British cause. Churches and charities responded to the emergency with improvisation and dedication, from looking after evacuated mothers to knitting socks for the Soviet army. Though rarely keeping up with demand, the public generously supported societies and funds set up for servicemen and their families. Indeed, war-related charities tended to do better than those concerned with domestic social need. Clearly the emergency made the imbalances in voluntary provision more apparent. The pressures on charities raised the long-standing charge that they did not have the depth, resources or co-ordination to deal with the 'challenge of circumstances'.[4] To an increasing number of citizens, the war exposed the patchy, decentralised nature of voluntarism, while making the alternative of central planning all the more attractive.

Manpower became a serious issue for many charities, for the continual calling-up of their personnel for the forces put them under enormous strain. It was estimated, for example, that the country needed between 37,000 and 67,000 trained nurses to cope with air raid casualties and to keep the voluntary hospitals running, but shortages were endemic and wastage rates high.[5] Meanwhile, the war effort drew heavily on churches and charitable institutions for recruits. For a start, thousands of clerics became chaplains to the forces. As the years passed and the casualties mounted, the war fractured parish life and dealt a blow to religious observance. As men went to the front, the women who filled their jobs had less time to give to those institutions that might otherwise have filled their idle hours. Many societies had to depend on part-time, untrained volunteers, who were too old or too young to serve on the front line. In a conflict of such dimensions, few charities were unaffected, from parish visiting societies to the Charity Organisation Society (COS), which underwent a general reassessment of voluntary policy during the war. With ever more distractions and rival centres of loyalty, charities had to adapt or decline.

Like earlier wars, the Second World War allied charity to national purpose, but also, as never before, to the priorities of government. As health and welfare shot upwards on the political agenda, the war not only exposed the shortcomings of charity but also pointed to the need for greater state assistance. As the government took over greater and greater responsibility during the emergency for housing, health and education, many voluntary institutions felt uneasy about their capacity to cope. The shift in the delivery of services to the state, which had been a feature of the inter-war period, accelerated during the wartime emergency. Whether they wished to or not, many charitable workers spent more and more of their time with the statutory services, or serving on care committees, pensions committees and trade boards. Many women left their parish institutions to join the Women's Voluntary Service (WVS), which was set up in 1938 to carry out a range of social services at the behest of government.[6] Recognising their financial constraints, the war made charitable institutions more and more amenable to partnerships, willing, as Charles Loch of the COS once put it, to take shelter with the state 'like creatures in a storm'.[7]

The shift to a war footing led to dramatic changes in charitable activity. Many urban institutions, among them asylums, orphanages and convalescent homes, closed or relocated to the provinces. This was especially true of those near the coast. In Broadstairs, for example, the Yarrow Home for Children, St David's Convalescent Home, the Metropolitan Convalescent Home and St Peter's Orphanage were among the local institutions that closed in 1939.[8] Meanwhile, churches and chapels saw their social services disrupted and congregations dwindle. As Donald Soper, the Christian Socialist Superintendent of the West London Mission, lamented:

'congregations evaporated, coffers depleted, subscriptions halved'.[9] Church member-ship in his own congregation at Hinde Street dropped from 180 in 1939 to 107 in 1947. Before long, the emergency resulted in many missions and other religious buildings being requisitioned by the authorities. During the Blitz, the West London Mission turned its buildings into bomb shelters and designated its hall as a rest and feeding centre. It was fortunate to escape with only modest bomb damage.[10]

There is no doubt some truth in the assumption that Total War reduced those social distinctions that were bound up with charity.[11] But arguably, the sheer phys-ical destruction of the war was more important in undermining charitable traditions than a rise in wartime egalitarianism. The First World War had not been kind to religion and philanthropy.[12] But the Second World War was much more unsettling. In communities across Britain, particularly urban communities, aerial bombing brought charitable proceedings to a sudden and deafening end, often eliminating local ser-vices that would be difficult to revive with the return of peace. The destruction of so many city missions, churches and chapels, homes and orphanages, hospitals and dispensaries, took a much heavier toll on religious and charitable institutions than has been widely recognised. Bombs destroyed thirty-eight of the missions run by the Ragged School Union, for example, which resulted in a dramatic decline in the society's charitable activities, not least district visiting, mothers' meetings and Sunday schools.[13]

Sunday schools had been centres of social work across Britain since the early nineteenth century. Like other charities, they often came to the rescue of needy families in times of personal calamity, illness, or bouts of unemployment. The schools commonly provided meals, clothing, shoes and holidays, and often boasted asso-ciated savings banks and sickness, burial and sports clubs.[14] The percentage of schools destroyed by bombing is unclear, but they suffered enormous damage during the Blitz, with a consequent loss of services and morale. Sheffield lost thirty-two schools in the first air raid. In London, bombs destroyed the headquarters of the Sunday School Union, causing the loss of its library and its publishing and business offices.[15] In the first year of the war the Church of England reported a massive decline in voluntary contributions to Sunday schools.[16] Meanwhile, the wartime relaxation of the Sunday observance laws made it more difficult to honour the Sabbath.

While the Sunday schools struggled to survive, government intervention intensified. The bombing often resulted in parishes shifting from charitable func-tions to activities geared to the needs of the emergency. Rooms in which Sunday school children, district visitors or mission workers met became recreation centres for servicemen or wards for air-raid casualties. With churches and chapels distracted, schools closed, staff missing and the parochial system in disarray, a crisis ensued. By the end of the war, the notion that Sunday schools served as nurseries of religious service was increasingly difficult to sustain, as were their traditions of social service. In the post-war years, the schools found it difficult to recover, a trend exacerbated by alluring alternatives to Sunday observance and changes in youth culture. By the end of the twentieth century only 4 per cent of the population attended Sunday school, significantly less than during the inter-war years, when the schools enrolled about 12 per cent of the population.[17]

As the destruction of many Sunday schools and city missions suggests, the Second World War took a much heavier toll of the infrastructure of Britain than the First. Contemporary memoirs, local newspapers and parish magazines tell the story of the physical and social effects of the air raids in graphic detail.[18] Nearly 4,000,000 houses – almost one third of the total housing stock – were damaged or destroyed in the bombing raids.[19] London was particularly hard-hit, though other cities, including Plymouth, Hull and Coventry, also suffered disproportionate losses. In the first three days of the war, 1.5 million people, including 827,000 school-children, retreated to the countryside.[20] The most destructive phase of the aerial bombardment that ended in June 1941 left about 2,225,000 people homeless. It also damaged or destroyed up to 4,000 schools, many of them religious institutions.[21]

The effect of the aerial bombing on district visiting societies, which were often attached to churches and chapels, missions and settlement houses was little less than catastrophic. This was not simply because of the physical damage to the societies themselves. District visitors were the pioneers of social work, but those who still turned up for their neighbourhood rounds after the onset of the bombing often found nothing but ruins, or families broken up by the evacuation of mothers and children. In 1939 there had been 60,000 district visitors at work in the Church of England alone, most of them women volunteers.[22] Tellingly, the church stopped providing statistics on the number of district visitors early in the war.

Importantly for the history of visiting – and Christianity – aerial bombing dev-astated a large number of churches and chapels, which hosted a wide variety of local charities. By 1942, over 1,000 Anglican places of worship, from parish churches to Lambeth Palace and Coventry Cathedral, had been destroyed or badly damaged, a number that rose in 1944 with the onset of flying bombs.[23] The devastation was so significant that it destabilised traditional parish life in the church and eventually required a new system of parochial organisation to be created.[24] The Methodists had, if anything, more to endure, for bombs destroyed or badly damaged 2,600 of their churches out of a total of 9,000 in Britain. Across the denominations, it was estimated that 15,000 ecclesiastical buildings, including churches, convents, and mission halls, suffered damage.[25] The number represented one building damaged or destroyed for every parish in England and Wales. The loss of spiritual and social capital, built up over the centuries, was immeasurable.

Whatever the effect of aerial bombardment on religious belief, it dealt a serious blow to religious observance and practical Christianity. It was not surprising that church attendance and visiting numbers fell during the war. As suggested, there were fewer clergymen available to perform services and oversee parish charities, as many of them had died or had commitments elsewhere. Many a churchman, having lost both his church and his congregation through air raids, 'found his life's work brought to a calamitous end'.[26] In the industrial cities, where the bombing was most acute, the supply of ordinands and curates in the Church of England dried up. In Birmingham, for example, the number of curates fell from 178 in 1939 to thirty-eight in 1948.[27] Even in the south of England, the number of curates after the war was only 60 per cent of pre-war levels. In 1914 there had been 20,000 Anglican clergy at work in England and Wales. By 1950 there were only 15,000, which meant only one parish priest for every 5,000 people in London, Liverpool and Manchester.[28] Social dislocation, lack of funds and cultural change contributed to the decline in religious commitment and denominational discipline, but there were also fewer churches to fill. Many of those destroyed were never rebuilt.[29]

As religious and charitable institutions collapsed into rubble, state planning blossomed. As suggested, wartime partnerships between charities and government departments increasingly enmeshed volunteers in bureaucratic regulation. The Emergency Medical Service, a centralised state agency empowered by the Ministry of Health, provided treatment for air-raid victims and transformed the hospital services. The war also saw the beginnings of the transference of voluntary social service to the local authorities.[30] Meanwhile, William Beveridge hammered home the persuasive thesis that unemployment was a problem of industry, not of personal character. His report *Social insurance and allied services*, published in 1942, called for a comprehensive social policy to tackle the evils of 'Want', 'Disease', 'Ignorance', 'Squalor' and 'Idleness'. It provided a blueprint for post-war reconstruction through government planning. Few now praised charitable agencies as a democratic safeguard or, as Stanley Baldwin put it in the 1930s, 'a means of rescuing the citizen from the standardizing pressure of the state's mechanism'.[31]

Partnerships between government and charitable agencies had expanded after the First World War, but as the Second World War persisted, a return to the inter-war relationships was no longer in vogue. Beveridge was by now a determined supporter of greater government control of the social services. As he famously put it in 1943, 'a people's war' required 'a people's peace'.[32] Social reconstruction offered the prospect of taking key industries into public ownership and nationalising the health and social services. A universal social security system promised to protect every citizen from destitution and want. The prospect of a vast expansion of state-directed health and welfare services created widespread disarray in the voluntary sector. What was the point of the material benefits of charity, now often described as demeaning, if cradle-to-grave social provision was on offer from the state, free at point of use?

What about medical provision and the charitable hospitals? As the war pointed to health as a national asset, it created and exposed deficiencies in health provision and its organisation. Medical costs mounted, but capital expenditure in a hospital or a nursing order, unlike a business, did not increase its earning power, but simply its spending capacity. One result of the First World War that had consequences for medical charities, and philanthropy generally, was the increase in levels of taxation on higher incomes. Inter-war taxation helped pay for the expansion of government services, while the voluntary sector struggled to make ends meet. In the depressed economic climate, legacies and large donations were harder to come by and charities had to turn to borrowing, to more elaborate appeals and to government assistance. In the straitened circumstances of the war years, an era of ever-greater patient demand, not least from the middle classes, the voluntary hospitals and related institutions were under enormous financial strain, which intensified calls for government action.[33]

Hospital provision had been a contentious issue for decades, but the Second World War turned it into a national issue. In the emergency, the public looked to government to provide assistance. It became imperative for the various medical charities to forge closer links with the military authorities and government departments. As elsewhere in the social services, greater professionalism and government regulation went hand in hand. While the war brought the future of nursing into question, the voluntary hospitals, which had struggled to retain their autonomy during the war, were so unsettled that a return to pre-war levels of fund-raising seemed impossible. Would the public respond with its traditional enthusiasm to future appeals to self-help after all the sacrifice the war itself demanded? Where were the contributions to come from? While the wealthy became poorer through taxation, the poorer classes began to expect welfare services provided by government, albeit at subsistence levels.[34]

The Second World War had more serious consequences for medical administration and nursing than the First because aerial bombardment damaged or destroyed so many of the nation's hospitals, dispensaries, nursing facilities and appeal offices. Scores of nurses were found dead or injured amid the rubble. Statistics on bombed hospitals are fragmentary, but by July 1941, in the London region alone, seventy-three voluntary hospitals had suffered bomb damage, most of them severely, with thousands of beds permanently lost.[35] The Dreadnought Hospital in Greenwich and the King Edward VII's Hospital for Officers near Buckingham Palace were rendered uninhabitable. St Thomas's, one of Britain's oldest Christian charities, lost 508 of its beds out of a total of complement of 682.[36] The renewal of German aerial attacks in 1944 damaged a further seventy-six London hospitals, both voluntary and municipal.[37] The Ministry of Information said the hospitals had been singled out for attack, though its analysis suggested that they did not receive more than their share of random bombs. Still, as Titmuss put it, London's hospital services 'were more seriously affected by losses of beds through damage than by the influx of casualties'.[38]

The King's Fund, which acted as a central board for the London voluntary hospitals, was a stalwart defender of voluntary principles in medical provision. Intriguingly, Beveridge had served on its propaganda committee in the 1930s. One of the fund's wartime tasks was to compile statistics on the number of bomb-damaged institutions in the capital. As a consequence, it was keenly aware of the problems ahead for hospital reconstruction. The figure made grim reading for the fund's officials, whose own operations were severely interrupted by the war. At St Bartholomew's the cost of the damage to the college alone was put at over £100,000.[39] After the raids of 1940–41, St Thomas's calculated its losses to be over £1,000,000, which turned out to be an underestimate.[40] The eventual cost of rebuilding the hospital was greater than the aggregate surpluses of all the 169 London charitable hospitals during the entire war.[41]

Clearly the bombing softened up the hospitals for post-war reorganisation, just when the strain of war was emptying the philanthropic purse. Arguably, the projected cost of rebuilding war-torn hospitals absolutely required government action. As a consequence of the destruction to hospital property, the Ministry of Health had difficult decisions to face. As early as 31 October 1940, a departmental minute questioned whether the hospitals would survive without ministerial intervention.[42] The large number of voluntary hospitals and dispensaries damaged or destroyed by German aerial attacks across the country placed an enormous burden on charitable finances and undermined morale in the voluntary hospital sector, weakening its negotiating position with government.[43] The King's Fund was particularly concerned about the tendency of people to assume that the state had become solely responsible for hospital provision.

Historians have long recognised that the Second World War triggered change in hospital affairs. While it did not alter the system during the conflict, it guaranteed that a major reorganisation was likely to take place at the end of it.[44] As the historian of the National Health Service (NHS) Charles Webster put it: 'It took a second world war to shatter the inertia of the established regime'.[45] In their analyses of the making of the NHS, historians have emphasised the deficiencies of hospital provision in the 1930s, the growing desire for fairness in public policy and the extension of government controls under the Emergency Medical Service. Disregarding the contradictory evidence, they have tended to exaggerate the growth in public support for state intervention during the war. Nor have they fully explored the implications in the sheer physical devastation to the hospitals by aerial bombardment. Principally, they have ignored the compromises it necessitated in the charitable sector. The mountains of rubble lowered morale across the charitable sector, and were a particular catastrophe to hospital voluntarists, who negotiated with the government from a position of weakness after the war because of the exorbitant cost of reconstruction.

Antagonism between charitable campaigners and state officials was particularly marked in the hospital sector, where valuable properties were at stake. It is worth remembering that the capital assets of Britain's voluntary hospitals were worth about £300,000,000 before the war.[46] Even after the bombing, the hospitals were worth a sum large enough to put a gleam in the eye of the Minister of Health and worth fighting over by benefactors and charitable campaigners, who raised the money to keep them open. To the more ardent hospital voluntarists, including not a few working-class supporters, the nationalisation of their independent 'local' hospitals would be an act of vandalism comparable to the dissolution of the monasteries. Sir Bernard Docker, Chairman of the British Hospitals Association, compared it to 'mass murder'.[47] The palpable loss of confidence in the recovery of the charitable hospitals based on flag days, subscriptions and contributory schemes made the situation seem dire indeed to hospital voluntarists. This loss of confidence was a significant factor in the voluntary hospital sector's eventual acceptance of a health service run and financed primarily by government. Would post-war health and social provision have looked any different had the bombing not been so devastating to the morale and infrastructure of the voluntary sector?

One cannot leave the subject of war and welfare without further reference to religion, which had been the principal engine of charity for centuries. Leading churchmen had become highly sensitive to the issues of poverty and unemployment in the inter-war years. As a consequence, many of them welcomed the expansion of government services.[48] Caught up in the enthusiasm for state planning, they felt that compulsory taxation was a more efficient way of promoting social justice than voluntary donations. Greater government spending, it might be said, was all the more alluring to churchmen because of the erosion of charitable tithes and contributions. As Christian funds and enthusiasm declined, the individualist argument against state intervention largely disappeared from public view. The evangelical conscience, which had been the cause of so much social change in the past, was largely exhausted by the war. Where it still flourished, it had, as often as not, been transformed into Christian Socialism, as in the case of the irrepressible Donald Soper, who called on government to remedy social abuse from his soapbox in Hyde Park.[49]

In 1941, William Temple, appointed Archbishop of Canterbury the following year, argued that the 'welfare state' (a term then coming into favour) was an expression of national benevolence. 'The State', he declared, '. . . is a servant and instrument of God for the preservation of Justice and for the promotion of human welfare'.[50] The wartime experience of religious leaders was further proof, if proof were needed, that the churches and the voluntary services could not cope without massive assistance from government. A report presented to the Lambeth Conference in 1948 titled 'The church and the modern world' neatly summarised the Anglican hierarchy's view of the government takeover of responsibility for education and welfare, a transformation that Archbishop Temple called 'epoch-making in its consequences'.[51] The report, which was a vital counterpart to the Beveridge Plan, applauded the government for its sensitivity to the needs of an industrial population and quickening the social conscience. In its analysis, it gave particular credit to the effects of war:

> Wars instead of delaying the process have hastened it by accustoming peoples to the mobilization of a nation's resources and manpower . . . The process is inevitable; it is

not likely to be reversed. None the less, it is presenting voluntary and free associations with new problems, and in particular is altering the boundaries of the respective spheres of Church and State.[52]

The report noted the 'delicate problem' presented by the 'omnicompetent' state to the Christian community. It warned of 'the natural bias of the State towards total-itarianism' and the need to promote local government and voluntary associations as a safeguard. 'Democracy', it declared, 'cannot work without the Christian qualities of self-restraint and discipline, and the training provided by Christian fellowship'.[53] But anxious to keep pace with social realities, the bishops passed a resolution at the Lambeth Conference in 1948: 'We believe that the State is under the moral law of God, and is intended by Him to be an instrument for human welfare. We therefore welcome the growing concern and care of the modern State for its citizens, and call upon Church members to accept their own political responsibility and to cooperate with the State and its officers in their work'.[54] In keeping with official opinion in the Church of England, the Archbishop of York, Cyril Garbett, declared that the welfare state embodied 'the law of Christ'.[55] Such opinions, un-exceptional at the time, were, to use Temple's words, 'epoch making' in the history of the church. They were also epoch-making in the history of British charity.

The shift of opinion in the church hierarchy was understandable given the level of social deprivation and a demoralised charitable sector. The bishops continued to see a need for voluntary agencies, working with the state services. But the Lambeth Conference resolution endorsing the welfare state dealt a serious blow to charity, particularly parish charity. For reasons of doctrine and limited resources, regular parochial visiting was consciously 'abandoned' in the Church of England. The loss to the community did not go unlamented. Cyril Garbett witnessed the process. As he observed: 'It is almost impossible to exaggerate the greatness of the loss when there is no regular pastoral visitation'.[56]

The reference to pastoral visitation was noteworthy. With their age-old links to women and religion, district-visiting societies suffered more than most charities in the post-war years. Visiting society after society collapsed for want of money, volunteers and purpose. Many visitors gave up and moved on, their enthusiasm for social engagement exhausted. Others stayed on in an altered role. Others still found employment in the state services. The transition 'from charity to social work' had been decisive. In 1960 there were nearly 40,000 employees in the state welfare services.[57] By this time, the number of district visitors, once numbering as many as 200,000, had been so dramatically reduced that official records no longer recorded their existence. Before long, organised visiting was so uncommon that many social workers did not realise that their forerunners were missionaries.

Swept up in the tide of nationalisation, churchmen discarded the parochial idealism that had motivated their forebears. They consoled themselves with the argument that the state had a 'moral and spiritual function' and was essentially

Christian.[58] They did not make an issue of the connection between the rise of state social provision and the decline of Christian observance and Christian charity, if only because they continued to believe that the state was acting on Christian principles. But as government took over primary responsibility for social welfare, the church was, as the historian Edward Norman put it, 'in practice disestablished'.[59]

The church's shifting views on social policy in the first half of the twentieth century, capped by its post-war approbation of the welfare state, played a more significant part in the decline of religious observance than might be imagined, if only because parish societies so often connected the citizenry, particularly women, to religious institutions. The decision to bow to the state was fashionable, perhaps irresistible, at the time; but it was to have unintended consequences. After all, it was the welfare role of religion that made it relevant to society. As long as the churches had an obvious social purpose, they retained an appeal to those with a sense of civic responsibility.[60] In relegating Christianity's historic charitable role to the sidelines, the churches estranged many traditional parishioners, especially women, who were so closely identified with philanthropic work. To paraphrase the Victorian philanthropist Josephine Butler, charity was the work of women, government the work of men. The Second World War signified the triumph of male legislators in social policy, leaving many female philanthropists in disarray and in search of a new role.

Many women, of course, continued to carry out charitable duties, but the maelstrom of war had cast women and girls from the service of the home and the local community. After the war, more and more of them reshaped their lives, as Callum Brown observes, 'within work, sexual relations and new recreational opportunities'.[61] As they entered the labour force it left them with less time for charitable work and church attendance, but with more money to enjoy new distractions elsewhere. Would women who had moved far from home during the war, who had taken up new employments and seen fresh opportunities, wish to return to voluntary work for disrupted charities? Once they had worked alongside men in the services, industry and agriculture, could those age-old beliefs in the differences between the sexes, which underpinned maternal culture, any longer satisfy or persuade? The growing national culture, secular and materialist, and traditional female culture, Christian and parochial, were increasingly at odds. Christianity and feminism, highly compatible to nineteenth-century women charitable campaigners, had diverged.

While the war accelerated the demands of women for lives beyond the home and the parish, it aroused greater expectations of social provision. In the new egalitarian context, many charities found it impossible to recover lost ground, especially as the war had promoted government benefits as a dutiless right. The post-war evolution of the welfare state in Britain reduced the demand for charitable services, especially among those institutions that provided medical or material benefits. Those savings banks and provident schemes, for example, which were still a feature of local charities in the inter-war years became outmoded in the face of increased state benefits and rising living standards. Those charities that carried on found it difficult to sustain their independence under the weight of post-war government pressures. Moreover, the acceptance of bureaucratic regulation had an underlying material-istic ethos that further narrowed discussion of voluntary activity to the relief of poverty. For many charities, state partnership meant that they would have to set aside their religious concerns in favour of secular social work.[62]

In an increasingly secular Britain that offered universal state benefits, competing voluntary agencies with religious leanings, local priorities and selective provision looked decidedly out of touch with post-war opinion. Government, not philanthropists, now largely dictated interpretations of social provision. Across the charitable sector, institutions collapsed or changed their priorities to suit a government agenda. Many of those that survived were transformed in ideological, professional and admin-istrative terms, which raised the issue of their independence. Parish charities, which had been so dependent on the work of women, suffered unduly; many simply disappeared. For them, like the voluntary hospitals, the Second World War and the social reconstruction that followed it was a calamity.

At the end of the First World War, the Girls' Friendly Society put its finger on the dangers to charity and religion when it reported on a society in which people were no longer buried in the same churchyard as their parents and grandparents.[63] The Second World War greatly propelled the dangers. In the increasingly mobile society, the age-old voluntary culture, often based on local subscriptions and parochial needs, could not survive intact. The hospitals, the visiting societies, the Sunday schools, the mothers' meetings and the array of other charitable institutions were institutional victims of cultural change and Christian decline. There was a degree of charitable adaptability to post-war circumstances. Indeed, state partnerships freed many voluntary bodies from former thankless tasks and sharpened their priorities. But in the heyday of state-directed health and social services after the war, chari-ties were relegated to the margins, being widely seen as providing amenities rather than essential services. As David Owen observed, they were now very much the 'junior partner in the welfare firm'.[64]

In what may be seen as the welfare equivalent of urban renewal, the war, com-pounded by post-war reconstruction, ravaged much of the historic fabric of the vol-untary services. But in the general enthusiasm for state entitlements and widening opportunities, few outside the voluntary sector noticed the loss of self-government and spiritual capital. And those who did notice were not much concerned by charity's decline. Perhaps wartime hardship had inured Britons to such suffering that they felt that personal service was ineffective. Increasingly they were content to exchange the burdens of self-help and individual responsibility for the rights and entitlements on offer from government. Though new charities formed – typically in areas beyond the competence of government – and old ones showed signs of resilience, an opinion poll in 1948 found that over 90 per cent of people no longer thought there was a role for charity in Britain.[65]

When Beveridge came to reconsider voluntary action in 1948, the outlook for the charitable services looked bleak. This was particularly noticeable on the job front. The growth of government services created a boom in public sector employment but losses to the salaried staff in the voluntary sector. Furthermore, the Labour Party was, with a few notable exceptions like Clement Attlee and Lord Pakenham, anti-voluntary.[66] To the public sector unions and large sections of the state bureaucracy, the word 'charity' was anathema.[67] The Ministry of Health, confident that voluntary traditions were no longer necessary to maintain an effective hospital service, directed that hospital fund-raising drives should cease and even had collection boxes removed from post offices.[68] A proper social democracy, argued Barbara Castle, a former Labour Minister of Health, should show 'a toughness about the battle for equality rather than do-goodery'.[69] The use of 'do-gooder' as a term of abuse encapsulated the transformation of values. It was a transformation to which Beveridge, a leading exponent of an impersonal, social service state, had made a significant contribution.

Did Beveridge have second thoughts? In the debate on voluntarism in the House of Lords after the war, he observed that 'Beveridge . . . has never been enough for Beveridge'. He paid effusive tribute to British voluntary traditions and worried about government control over the nation's social affairs. Some things, he noted, 'should in no circumstances be left to the state, or we should be on our way to totalitarian conditions'. But his much-quoted description of the voluntary sector as having a 'perpetually moving frontier' was ambiguous.[70] It was 'perpetually moving' because government now occupied so much of philanthropy's former terrain and had an appetite for more. In his book *Voluntary action*, Beveridge lamented the state's capacity to destroy 'the freedom and spirit . . . of social conscience'.[71] Was it a *mea culpa*?

Notes

1 A. J. P. Taylor, *English history 1914–45* (Oxford: Oxford University Press, 1965), p. 455.
2 Sir W. Beveridge, *The pillars of society and other war-time essays and addresses* (New York: Macmillan Company, 1943), p. 46.
3 R. M. Titmuss, *Problems of social policy* (London: HMSO, 1976), p. 348.
4 G. Finlayson, *Citizen, state, and social welfare in Britain 1830–1990* (Oxford: Clarendon Press, 1994), pp. 226–9, 243.
5 B. Abel-Smith, *A history of the nursing profession* (London: Heinemann, 1960), p. 161.
6 For a discussion of the Women's Voluntary Service (WVS), which sees it as an institution that upheld the continuities of class, see James Hinton, *Women, social leadership, and the Second World War* (Oxford: Oxford University Press, 2002).
7 Quoted in Finlayson, *Citizen, state and social welfare*, p. 279.
8 See www.stella-maris.org.uk/history1 (accessed 7 May 2010).
9 P. S. Bagwell, *Outcast London, a Christian response: the West London Mission of the Methodist Church 1887–1987* (London: Epworth Press, 1987), p. 113.

10 Bagwell, *Outcast London*, pp. 112–14.

11 For this point of view see, for example, D. Fraser, *The evolution of the British welfare state: a history of social policy since the industrial revolution* (London: Macmillan, 1973), p. 193.

12 F. Prochaska, *The voluntary impulse: philanthropy in modern Britain* (London: Faber and Faber, 1988), pp. 74–5.

13 *Shaftesbury Magazine*, vol. 97 (June 1945), p. 11.

14 On the social services provided by Sunday schools see T. Lacqueur, *Religion and respectability: Sunday schools and working-class culture 1780–1850* (New Haven: Yale University Press, 1976).

15 P. B. Cliff, *The rise and development of the Sunday School movement in England 1780–1980* (Redhill, Surrey: National Christian Education Council, 1986), chapters 15–16.

16 *Official year book of the National Assembly of the Church of England 1942* (London: SPCK), p. 272.

17 F. Prochaska, *Christianity and social service in modern Britain: the disinherited spirit* (Oxford: Oxford University Press, 2006), pp. 56, 68.

18 See, for example, S. Koa Wing (ed.), *Our longest days: a people's history of the Second World War* (London: Profile Books, 2007); A. H. Bell, *London was ours: diaries and memoirs of the London Blitz* (London and New York: I. B. Tauris & Co., 2008); P. Stansky, *The first day of the Blitz: September 7, 1940* (New Haven and London: Yale University Press, 2007); Mass-Observation Archive, University of Sussex, Falmer.

19 Titmuss, *Problems of social policy*, p. 330. See also John Stevenson, *British society 1914–45* (London: Allen Lane, 1984), p. 448.

20 N. Timmins, *The five giants: a biography of the welfare state* (London: HarperCollins, 1995), p. 31.

21 Titmuss, *Problems of social policy*, p. 331.

22 B. Heeney, *The women's movement in the Church of England 1850–1930* (Oxford: Clarendon Press, 1998), p. 27; *Official year book of the National Assembly of the Church of England 1941* (London: SPCK), p. 284.

23 *Official year book of the National Assembly of the Church of England 1942* (London: SPCK), p. 3.

24 *Official year book of the National Assembly of the Church of England 1944* (London: SPCK), p. 3.

25 G. Stephen Spinks, *Religion in Britain since 1900* (London: Dakers, 1952), p. 217.

26 Spinks, *Religion in Britain*, p. 224.

27 A. Calder, *The people's war: Britain 1939–1945* (New York: Pantheon Books, 1969), p. 479.

28 C. Garbett, *Church and state in England* (London: Hodder and Stoughton, 1950), pp. 278–9, 286.

29 On the issue of reconstruction see *The churches and war damage: payments for war damage to ecclesiastical buildings under section 69 of the War Damage Act, 1943* (London, 1944).

30 The experience of Bethnal Green was typical. See A. F. C. Bourdillon (ed.), *Voluntary society services: their place in the modern state* (London: Methuen, 1945), pp. 257–62.

31 *The Times* (27 October 1933), quoted in Elizabeth Macadam, *The new philanthropy* (London: George Allen & Unwin, 1934), p. 304.

32 Beveridge, *The pillars of society*, p. 119.

33 See M. Gorsky, J. Mohan and M. Powell, 'The financial health of voluntary hospitals in interwar Britain', *Economic History Review*, vol. 55, no. 3 (2002), pp. 533–57.

34 M. Stocks, *A hundred years of district nursing* (London: George Allen & Unwin, 1960), p. 145.

35 King's Fund, *Forty-fifth annual report* (London: King's Fund, 1943), p. 16; Titmuss, *Problems of social policy*, p. 331.

36 A. Gray and A. Topping, *Hospital survey: the hospital services of London and the surrounding area* (London: HMSO, 1945), p. 62.

37 F. K. Prochaska, *Philanthropy and the hospitals of London: the King's Fund, 1897–1990* (Oxford: Oxford University Press, 1992), pp. 136–8, 151.

38 Titmuss, *Problems of social policy*, p. 462.

39 V. C. Medvei and J. L. Thornton, *The Royal Hospital of Saint Bartholomew 1123–1973* (London: Longmans, 1974), p. 88.

40 London Metropolitan Archive, A/KE/325; Medvei and Thornton, *The Royal Hospital of Saint Bartholomew*, p. 186.

41 The total cost of war damage to the London hospitals is unclear. But the London Metropolitan Archive, A/KE/325, provides some useful detail on war-damage claims for the period up to October 1943. For the aggregate surpluses see King's Fund, *Statistical survey . . . for the year 1945* (London: King's Fund, 1946), p. 41.

42 Titmuss, *Problems of social policy*, p. 449, note.

43 King's Fund, *Forty-fifth annual report*, p. 16. See also G. C. Curnock (ed.), *Hospitals under fire* (London: George Allen & Unwin, 1941). On the issue of bomb damage and the formation of the National Health Service see Prochaska, *Philanthropy and the hospitals of London*, chapter 6.

44 B. Abel-Smith, *The hospitals 1800–1948* (London: Heinemann, 1964), p. 439.

45 C. Webster, *The National Health Service: a political history* (Oxford: Oxford University Press, 1998), p. 6.

46 National Archives, Kew, Richmond, Surrey, MH/80/24; see also MH/77/76.

47 Quoted in J. E. Pater, *The making of the National Health Service* (London: King's Fund, 1981), p. 122.

48 See J. Oliver, *The church and the social order: social thought in the Church of England 1918–1939* (London: Mowbray, 1968).

49 Bagwell, *Outcast London*, pp. 56–7, 127.

50 W. Temple, *Citizen and churchman* (London: Eyre & Spottiswoode, 1941), pp. 35–6.

51 Temple, *Citizen and churchman*, p. 31.

52 *The Lambeth Conference 1948: the encyclical letter from the bishops; together with resolutions and reports* (London: SPCK, 1948), part II, p. 17.

53 *The Lambeth Conference 1948*.

54 *The Lambeth Conference 1948*, part I, p. 32.

55 S. Mews, 'Religious life between the wars, 1920–1940', in S. Gilley and W. J. Sheils (eds), *A history of religion in Britain: practice and belief from pre-Roman times to the present* (Oxford: Blackwell, 1994), p. 471.

56 Garbett, *Church and state in England*, p. 279.

57 Ronald G. Walton, *Women in social work* (London: Routledge & Kegan Paul, 1975), p. 222.

58 Temple, *Citizen and churchman*, p. 36.

59 E. Norman, 'Church and state since 1800', in Gilley and Sheils (eds), *A history of religion in Britain*, p. 286.

60 J. Cox, *The English churches in a secular society: Lambeth, 1870–1930* (Oxford: Oxford University Press, 1982), p. 275.

61 C. Brown, *The death of Christian Britain: understanding secularization 1800–2000* (London: Routledge, 2001), p. 179.

62 See Macadam, *The new philanthropy*.

63 *Friendly Leaves*, vol. 44 (August 1919), p. 115.

64 D. Owen, *English philanthropy, 1660–1960* (Cambridge, Mass., and London: Harvard University Press and Oxford University Press, 1964), p. 527.

65 B. Breeze, 'The Return of Philanthropy', *Prospect* (January 2005), p. 53.

66 Prochaska, *The voluntary impulse*, p. 84.

67 This was particularly noticeable in the hospital sector. See Prochaska, *Philanthropy and the hospitals of London*, pp. 164–6, 193–4.

68 National Archives, HMC (48) 25A.

69 B. Castle, *The Castle diaries 1974–76* (London: Weidenfeld and Nicolson, 1980), p. 144.

70 House of Lords debates, 5th series, vol. 163, cols 95–6, 122, 23 June 1949.

71 Lord Beveridge, *Voluntary action: a report on methods of social advance* (London: George Allen & Unwin, 1948), pp. 10, 318, 320.

5

'Organisations for brotherly aid in misfortune': Beveridge and the friendly societies

Daniel Weinbren

> Friendly societies have been and are organisations for brotherly aid in misfortune and channels for the spirit of voluntary service as well as being agencies for mutual insurance and personal saving.[1]

Although Beveridge's characterisation of friendly societies as 'channels', as 'agencies' and 'for aid', was not adopted in subsequent analyses, many of which presented the societies in terms of wider developments such as welfare or social order or placed them on the periphery as proto-trade unions or unworldly insurance companies, it nevertheless has merit.[2] Beveridge's view of the societies as multi-faceted reflected the importance that he attributed to an idealised version of the friendly societies of his youth. Beveridge, born in 1879, was a young man when the societies were at their zenith, and the societies in which he showed most interest were the popular affiliated orders with quasi-autonomous branches.[3] There were between 4 and 6 million members in the 1870s and between 6.3 and 9.5 million members in 1910.[4] Legislation in 1911, based on the advice of Beveridge among others, gave the state greater control over health care and sick pay. A number of prominent friendly societies secured positions within the new system by becoming government 'approved societies', which administered the scheme. Beveridge presented this change in role as a 'marriage' to the state. Insurance and saving had long been of importance within the societies but rarely the only attractions. In the period after 1911 insurance became central to the societies which had gained approval. This led to tensions with civil servants, doctors and political parties and within the societies themselves. By 1911 people had found many other ways to engage in philanthropic and civic activities. Fraternal aid was less important as interest in the embodiments of fraternity, notably 'travelling brothers', inter-class relationships and male-only groups was reduced. The spirit of voluntary service and the traditions of reciprocity were further undermined by the legislation of 1911.

Beveridge's *Social insurance and allied services* (1942) was welcomed by the National Conference of Friendly Societies, which produced a poster stating, 'Sir William Beveridge says: – 'Voluntary insurance is an integral feature of the Plan for Social Security'.[5] In February 1943 the government announced that the approved status of friendly societies was to be abolished and that aspect of their work transferred to a Ministry of National Insurance. When Beveridge later reflected on his work, he listed all the elements of his report that the government accepted and mentioned only one element that had not become law: 'They have rejected my proposal to use the friendly societies as responsible agents for administrating State benefit'. He went on to refer to how

> The marriage of 1911 between the State . . . and the voluntary agencies . . . has been followed by complete divorce. The State, like a Roman father, has sent the friendly societies back to live in their own house.[6]

He later referred to 'the divorcement of State from Voluntary insurance' and to how the legislation of 1946 'divorced' the state and the societies.[7] Beveridge acknowledged that it would be difficult for the friendly societies to return to the *status quo ante*, again employing familial terms: they needed a 'spirit of service [and] to meet new needs by new methods in the old spirit of social advance by brotherly co-operation'.[8] He put a price on the divorce, arguing that the societies' income would fall by £2 million a year, that fewer people would join and more would leave.[9] He noted the 'decreasing interest of members in Societies' and argued that the societies needed to find new roles if they were to expand.[10] Nevertheless, he continued to see friendly societies as central.[11] He called for the restoration of the conditions in which the Victorian pioneers of social advance had worked:

> so that at last human society may become a friendly society – an Affiliated Order of branches, some large and many small, each with its own life in freedom, each linked to all the rest by a common purpose and by bonds to serve that purpose. So the night's insane dream of power over other men, without limit and without mercy shall fade. So mankind in brotherhood shall bring back the day.[12]

Just as the friendly societies, with names such as Druids, Anglo-Saxons and Ancient Britons, looked forward by referring to a long-gone golden age, so Beveridge looked forward with little reference to the immediate past, the period 1912–48. He took far more guidance from the period before the Liberal administration came to power, that is before he joined the Board of Trade and went on to advise Lloyd George. Beveridge's taxonomy, his yearning for the friendly societies to 'bring back the day' as a means of facing the next one, offered a route forward that was based on an account of the past. It illuminates his view of voluntary action as an element of the 'duty' which he felt 'humanity' required if it was to pick up the threads abandoned in his youth and 'resume the progress in civilization which had been interrupted by two world wars'.[13]

Mutual insurance and personal saving

Although the aims of different friendly societies included increasing temperance, promoting the Welsh language and supporting Freemasonry, a central element of their rationale was that they facilitated risk-sharing among members through the organised transfer of money.[14] They used pooled money to protect members against the consequences of being unable to work at their normal trade owing to problems such as injury or old age. In the event of the death of a member the family was offered support. Calculating the level of income required in order to ensure payments to sick members was difficult and, for many friendly societies for much of the nineteenth century, unsuccessful. However, this lack of actuarial acumen did not appear to deter recruitment, and indeed the imposition of mortality tables led some individuals and groups of members to leave. In the mid-1840s the Independent Order of Oddfellows, Manchester Unity Friendly Society (IOOFMU), one of the largest affiliated societies, required lodges (that is, branches) to provide information to the central officials about members in order to aid the creation of tables of benefits and contributions. It was argued that a large number of lodges had adopted unsustainable financial practices. Lodges representing a total of 16,000 members refused to comply. Many of them left to join a breakaway society, the National Independent Order of Oddfellows. Other friendly societies noted the bitter struggles over solvency and insurance and did not tackle the issue for many years, preferring to face the risk of financial instability rather than the risk of division. Despite the concerns about the costs of ensuring solvency, mortality tables were developed. Indeed, the historian of the IOOFMU dubbed the latter part of the nineteenth century 'a period which might be termed the dawn of actuarial science in the Manchester Unity'.[15] By the end of the century the IOOFMU was producing its own data, which were considered so sophisticated and accurate that they became the basis for government action on national insurance in 1911. It was by drawing on such data that the IOOFMU could see the changing age and health profile of the membership. Members were living longer, were making greater claims for sickness benefit and were having their funds drained by payments to those injured during the Boer War.[16] The IOOFMU leaders were thus able to make informed decisions about the society's commitments to its members when they debated and then campaigned for the introduction of state pensions. The increasing importance of this data was recognised by the Bishop of Winchester, who, in his address at a service held to mark the centenary of the IOOFMU, referred to 'your *principles* of financial stability and actuarial statistics'.[17]

The 1911 National Health Insurance Act focussed the approved societies on the administration of national insurance at a time when they were already finding it difficult to adjust to new expectations about health care and members who lived longer and made larger claims. As medication and the adoption of new techniques increased the cost of health provision, the main cost of the sickness of the breadwinner of a family changed from the loss of his income to the payment of medical bills. Commercial insurance companies adapted to the new patterns more adeptly than the friendly societies. Even without the 1911 Act the societies would have had to change. The legislation corralled them in ways which made adjustment more difficult. There were approved societies based on trade unions, approved societies based on friendly societies and also ones based on insurance companies. It was the last of these which were most successful.[18] They did not offer regalia, lodge nights, the election of officers or opportunities for members to become sick visitors. Insurance was only one of the attractions of the friendly societies, and this meant that they were not structured appropriately or as focussed as their commercial rivals. Many of those who have assessed the impact of this legislation have concluded that it led to an imbalance between the elements which, according to Beveridge, were the essence of the societies. In 1913, a year after it came into operation, the Secretary of the Charity Organisation Society and an honorary member of the IOOFMU, Charles Loch, wrote that the National Health Insurance Act was 'the death warrant of the friendly societies'.[19] In 1949, a year after the Act was superseded, Douglas Cole, a theorist of mutual aid, concluded that 'the friendly societies, including the Orders, despite their large membership, have ceased to count as a social force to anything like the extent to which they used to count in the Victorian era'.[20] Beveridge concluded that through the national insurance legislation that he had helped to plan and implement, friendly societies 'became more official and less personal. More of insurance agencies and less of social agencies'. He added, 'only a very few people appear to have joined a friendly society with the idea of participating in the social functions which it might provide ... to a large extent the assumption was that the main object of the friendly society was to administer national health insurance'.[21] A survey by Mass-Observation in the late 1940s reported that

> In the majority of spontaneous comments the friendly societies appear exclusively as a mechanism for 'putting by for a rainy day' ... there is a tendency among those who have been members of friendly societies for some considerable period to look back with regret to the time when the Society was very much more than a useful vehicle for 'a rainy day', when, through the provision of opportunities for social contacts it built up for itself a 'group' loyalty.[22]

The unpopularity of the friendly societies' administration of insurance may explain why Beveridge listed insurance and saving after brotherly aid and the channelling of the voluntary spirit. He held 'that the majority of the friendly society problems' arose from 'specialising purely in insurance'.[23] Subsequent analysis has often concurred. The legislation speeded the 'gradual abandonment of those aspects of mutuality and fellowship that had been the hallmark of friendly societies in Victorian Britain', according to Johnson, while Green argued that 'when national insurance was introduced it attended only to the material dimension and in separating the cash benefits from the moral and educational role of the societies destroyed their essence'.[24]

It was because the societies were associated with a complicated and unpopular insurance system that concern about the abolition of approved status was muted. The IOOFMU encouraged its members to lobby against the 'government's intention to abolish friendly societies', and Beacon Lodge, Penrith, produced a leaflet encouraging members with the words: 'Now is the time to make your effort to induce the government to utilise the existing machinery which has worked so effortlessly in the past'.[25] It called on members to write to their MPs.[26] If any members wrote making the case that the existing machinery worked 'effortlessly' they appeared to have had little impact. One account of the 1945 general election campaign mentioned that when Herbert Morrison (who became Leader of the Commons after the election) was asked, 'Are you aware that eight or nine million votes depend on Labour's attitude to friendly societies?' he gave 'no impression of being worried on this point'.[27] Similarly, James Griffiths, the Minister of National Insurance, provided no evidence of concern about the claim by Henry Goodrich, a Labour MP who was Parliamentary Agent to the National Conference of Friendly Societies, to expect demonstrations against the 1946 National Insurance Act.[28] In the nineteenth century insurance for working men had been less available, and there had been considerable interest in ceremony and ritual. By the mid-twentieth century there were many organisations that offered only insurance and others which focussed on sociable activities and which might be employed as vehicles for social advancement. There was less need to join an organisation which was a compromise between these functions.

Channels for the spirit of voluntary service

During the nineteenth century friendly societies had presented themselves as channels for the spirit of voluntary service. They 'intentionally organised themselves around notions of friendship, brotherly love, charity', and echoed and reinforced many charities' organisational models.[29] Some societies became charities, many made donations to charities, and in the case of societies with dominant patrons there was considerable overlap between the two categories. Some of the charity offered by societies was for members. A member of one of the larger, affiliated, friendly societies could appeal to the branch for help beyond that which was expected, and then to the region and finally to the national annual delegate meetings, which decided whether a member who made an appeal was worthy of additional charitable help from the society's funds.

For many friendly societies charitable activity was of great importance. The text of the IOOFMU's White Degree, an internal qualification which was required if a member was to rise through the ranks, began: 'The first point upon which our Order ordains to admonish you is no less than that of the first friendly duty to mankind – Charity'.[30] In 1886 the *Oddfellows Magazine* claimed, 'our primary object is to promote that spirit of brotherly love in our fellow creatures which is necessary for the well-being and success of any institution, no matter what its object'.[31] When the Druids held a concert at which the opportunity was taken to present 'an injured brother a sum of £40' or when £25 was given to a disabled member, the society ensured that news of its generosity spread. The Crewe Co-operative Industrial and Friendly Society ran a dental and sick benefit club for employees, and donated money to local people, famine relief in India, locked-out engineers in 1897 and the local hospital, to which it also recommended patients.[32] When IOOFMU members raised funds for the 1889 London dock strikers, the *Melbourne Oddfellow* commented, 'We glory in the manner in which the matter has been taken up in the lodges, as it is one of the fundamental principles of true Oddfellowship to assist their fellowmen in times of distress and tribulation'.[33]

Voluntary service involved maintaining relationships as members in turn gave, received and passed on 'gifts'. To friendly societies charity involved reciprocity. Benefits were sometimes referred to as gifts, and while, as the 1772 rule book of the Yarm Tradesman's Society indicated, fines could be imposed on a member 'who reflects upon his fellow for having received the gift of this society', there was an expectation that a recipient would reciprocate in due course. The term 'present' was used if there was no expectation of return. The Grand Master of the IOOFMU Rose of England lodge, Middlesbrough, was censored in 1848 'for going out to gather mushrooms while receiving the gifts of the lodge'.[34] Gifts were a mixture of altruism and selfishness, generosity and self-interest. Presenting benefits as gifts was a way of reminding members that they were obliged to the donor, the brethren of the society. Furthermore, because reciprocation could not be immediate, gifts were a means of maintaining a relationship.[35] Moffrey pointed out that 'the description of sick ailment as a "gift" and as funeral money as a "donation" lingered long after the system was changed to a definite benefit in the heading to the tables in the General Rules'.[36] The expectation of reciprocity extended to other gifts. Friendly societies often became patrons of hospitals in which treatment required a letter from a subscriber or governor. For example, between 1765 and 1814, sixteen friendly societies donated to Northampton General Hospital and thus secured places for their members. Through such activities the friendly societies were building on the neighbourly reciprocity, and gifts which required a return which were a familiar part of life in the United Kingdom.[37] Indeed, according to the satirical magazine *Porcupine* in 1880, the poor 'have a system of mutual assistance, a habit of helping each other, which prevents many of them ever becoming rich in anything but nobleness of character'.[38]

By the early twentieth century, and some have suggested earlier, it has been argued that gifting had died out as people ceased to be members of communities and became part of contractually organised, often urban, societies.[39] Cordery has suggested that friendly societies 'contributed to the diffusion of commercial values'. He saw the legislation of 1911 as part of a longer process of change, arguing that it 'represented another act in the drama of squeezing sociability'.[40] The legislation discouraged engagement, according to Whiteside, who has suggested that for many societies 'central regulation throttled the possibility of popular participation'.[41] Harris agreed that the legislation was a decisive step towards uniform central control and away from welfare, which was 'highly localised, amateur, voluntaristic and intimate in scale' while Deakin has concluded that by the 1940s the active involvement of the member-ship and effective accountability had 'almost entirely disappeared'.[42] Looking back in the 1930s, one observer claimed that 'an appreciable proportion of members of the old friendly societies . . . never had the slightest intention of drawing benefit and this type of member has now largely ceased to exist'.[43] Beveridge was not describ-ing that which he saw around him but his vision of both the past and the future. In 1947 a Mass-Observation report noted negative attitudes towards friendly soci-eties, even among the members, and that such attitudes were more pronounced among the younger people. The conclusion was that

> membership today is predominantly a passive one concentrating almost entirely upon payment of subscriptions and receipt of benefit. [This may] be related to the present centralising and impersonalising of friendly society organisation, useful enough in the interests of efficiency but perhaps not calculated to arouse much interest and enthusiasm among members.[44]

Writing in 1949, one observer noted that centralisation within the friendly societies had led to 'minority control and a façade of self-government', with the choice of representatives 'very largely in the hands of local officials'.[45] The gifting structure had helped to maintain relations between people. It had connected, pride, prestige, obligation and debt. The friendly societies had formalised the voluntary spirit in the nineteenth century, in that members who did not do their tasks could not rise through the ranks and could be fined. By the time Beveridge came to write his account, gifting was no longer seen as such an important means of survival.

Organisations for brotherly aid in misfortune

When he referred to 'brotherly aid' and 'brotherly co-operation' and stressed the importance of fellowship – ' "Friendly Society" is a better name and means a better thing than the "Frugality Bank" by which Jeremy Bentham wanted to replace it' – Beveridge was employing the language of the friendly societies.[46] However, there was less interest in a notion of fraternity as uniting men in civil discourse, transcending class and maintaining the dominance of male breadwinners within the home. At lodge level it was the offer of fraternity which helped to answer Frederick Eden's question of 1801 as to why a bachelor who wanted to protect himself against ill-ness should pay to bury his neighbour's wife.[47] If one assumed that the bachelor was driven by a desire to maximise his own material possessions, then impersonal transactions may have been his most efficient strategy. However, if he saw the money spent on burying a neighbour's wife as part of his engagement in community life it was not wasted. Such considerations may have weighed less heavily by the twentieth century. Throughout the nineteenth century, however, 'brotherly aid' extended beyond the lodge. Thousands of pounds were distributed to friendly societies' 'travelling brothers' as they sought work around the country and indeed the British Empire.[48] The average friendly society member in early Victorian society, if there was such a person, was a migrant to one of the new towns, where much employment continued to be seasonal and casual.[49] An early drinking pot of the Friendly Iron-Moulders Society is illustrated with a picture of a travelling moulder asking the foreman, 'Brother craft, can you give me a job?' and receiving the reply: 'If we cannot we will relieve you'.[50] By the late nineteenth century there were fewer itinerant workers within the United Kingdom. However, support was offered to travellers. In Norfolk in 1891 the Loyal Trafalgar IOOFMU lodge granted 'clearance' to Brother Hollis when he went to the United States, enabling him to draw on society funds while abroad, and in 1908 it made a sick payment to Brother Ward, who, although 'residing in Australia', had maintained his membership.[51] By the twentieth century migration, both internal and external, had slowed. Between 1931 and 1961 there was net inward migration to the United Kingdom. Meeting the needs of travelling brothers was no longer of such importance to the people whom the societies aimed to attract.

The friendly societies had gained popularity because they offered 'brotherly aid' which could reach beyond the grave. The provision for funerals and what were, in effect, pensions attracted those who feared the consequences of the 1832 Anatomy Act and the 1834 Poor Law (Amendment) Act. The pauperised could end their days in the workhouse, after which their bodies might be dissected and interned in paupers' graves,[52] and their next of kin were denied ownership of the corpse and many commemorative rites.[53] Some Poor Law guardians forbade mourners from throwing soil on the coffin, entering the cemetery or chapel or providing headstones. By contrast, article 12 of the South Shields 'sure, lasting and loving' Friendly Society laid down that members had to attend the funerals of deceased members, 'in proper order according to Seniority'.[54] Many societies' banners made clear their loyalty to the dead and the bereaved, featuring graveyard scenes with widows and children and references to late brothers. The inscription 'in memory of a brother departed' appears on a tombstone depicted on a banner of the Ancient Order of Foresters, while other banners bear reminders that those left behind would be well treated.[55] Many gravestones noted the occupant's membership of a friendly society. One IOOFMU gravestone noted that Thomas Fletcher provided '50 years of continued usefulness to the Order'.[56] However, interest in expensive funerals fell, and the prospect of a pauper's grave ceased to worry people in the ways that it had in the Victorian period. With the Local Government Act of 1929 the boards of guardians were abolished, workhouses were converted into hospitals, and the word 'pauper' ceased to be a legal term. The promises of eternal fraternity became less significant.

The notion of 'brotherly aid' was bolstered by the sense of fraternity stretching back in time. Many societies made references to their longevity and their roots in a mythic past, often using rituals to maintain and transmit multi-faceted, historiographies which linked a notion of trustworthy, vigilant fictive fraternity to mutuality, loyalty, trades, locality, empire and Christianity. Drama could be used to imply the ancient origins of the society both to critique and to aid its integration into current economic structures. Being open to a variety of interpretations, it could promote ethical reflection and recruitment and silence internal divisions. It was a means by which members could demonstrate respect and affiliation, satisfy emotional requirements, nourish relationships and strengthen social bonds. It was useful for checking on members' status, uniting members with a sense of exclusivity, instilling rules about confidentiality and ensuring that duties were distributed among members. Chase has argued that in the eighteenth century 'elaborate ritual, hierarchy and the language of brotherhood was one means by which the frontier of skill was defended', while Cannadine has pointed to the importance of late-nineteenth century civic ritual and pageantry.[57] These were part of a wider 'unprecedented honorific inventiveness' in the Victorian period, when the British saw themselves as

> belonging to an unequal society characterized by a seamless web of layered gradations, which were hallowed by time and precedent, which were sanctioned by tradition and religion.[58]

However, in his book describing his 1870 tour through Britain, the Austrian Liberal Josef Marie Baernreither contrasted the 'eccentric names' and the rituals of friendly societies with 'the thoroughly practical and sober objects of insurance against sickness and accident'.[59] Men who had a variety of other possible ways of spending their leisure time and other opportunities for ritual did not need to join the friendly societies to engage in fraternal bonding. In 1913 it was argued in the IOOFMU's *Oddfellows Magazine*, that initiation had the effect of 'creating a feeling of nervousness'. In the same year that society's Grand Master (that is, the annual national president) said that in some lodges 'ritual has fallen into utter disuse'.[60] By the mid-twentieth century, the attractions of joining an organisation such as the Nottingham Imperial Oddfellows (whose regalia included full-length medieval costumes) were less apparent to many people. Friendly societies realised that ritual and regalia alienated potential members. Beveridge's use of the term 'brotherly' evoked a period which seemed very distant by the 1940s.

During the nineteenth century, 'a large number of intelligent Europeans believed that much of what was happening in the world around them only happened because secret societies planned it'.[61] Secrecy was associated with gaining access to a higher truth, and in *The English constitution* (1867) Walter Bagehot suggested that while it might be reasonable to extend the franchise (most adults in the United Kingdom were not allowed to vote until the twentieth century), the nation should be ruled by the Cabinet, 'the most powerful body in the state', the meetings of which were 'not only secret in theory, but secret in reality'.[62] George

Simmel concluded that 'the role of the secret in social life' offered 'the possibility of a second world alongside the manifest world; and the latter is deeply influenced by the former'. He also noted that secrecy could be associated with power and jealousy and that 'British parliamentary discussions were secret for a long time; and as late as under George III, press communications about them were persecuted as criminal offences, explicitly as violations of parliamentary privilege'. In the nineteenth century friendly societies helped to secure social acceptability through offering symbols, allegories and access to sacred truths. As Simmel argued, there was a 'peculiar attraction of formally secretive behavior . . . that what is denied to many must have special value'.[63] By the 1920s the need for secrecy and passwords was reduced; secrecy was perceived as a cause of the First World War and was contrasted with the 'open diplomacy' promoted within Woodrow Wilson's Fourteen Points.

In the nineteenth century many within the friendly societies saw a need to present fraternity as a means to cross class boundaries. Initially, the societies may have been a means to reconstruct an idealised version of the fraternity between masters and men in the craft workshop. Later in the century some friendly societies welcomed patronage because it was associated with respectability and financial and organisational acumen. A trustee of a friendly society with about 500 members noted: 'We are a plain lot of uncultivated agricultural labourers [who need] 10 or 20 per cent of middle class to keep [us] straight'.[64] The Collingbourne Kingston Friendly Society's banner features a symbolic figure representing labour clasping hands with a representative of capital. Gentry-financed friendly societies existed throughout the nineteenth century in many areas.[65] Many female friendly societies were dominated by patrons.[66] Employers also saw the benefits of having an interest in men's associations. In 1870 there were about eighty friendly societies sponsored by railway companies.[67] By the twentieth century, however, there was a greater interest in class-based politics, and for some of those whom the societies sought to attract, accommodation with wealthier people appeared unnecessary and even counter-productive.[68]

Whereas there may have been a heightened preoccupation with gender difference and female inferiority among men in the early years of industrialisation, by the twentieth century, when the societies were seeking to attract women, their attachment to male-only rituals and habits may have alienated women.[69] Victorian working-class masculine self-respect demanded the exclusion of women, and membership strengthened male control over the domestic income. One Preston Oddfellows lodge forbade 'members sending their money . . . by women and children', thus reminding members of their status.[70] In 1902 a select committee was told that a man earning thirty shillings would give his wife twenty-five shillings and would keep the rest for 'his private spending money and for his Oddfellows'.[71] This world was disappearing, and the friendly societies recognised the need for change. In 1945 a special conference on reconstructing the IOOFMU emphasised that 'every lodge should be built like the nation, upon the basis of the family and be encouraged to have men, women and juvenile members'.[72] By contrast, Beveridge's account, in looking forward, built upon a notion of secure gender roles, undisturbed by total war.

In making his case, Beveridge offered a view as to why there had been a reduction in interest in friendly societies since 1945. Although he downplayed both the tensions between the elements he identified and the exclusion of poorer women, preferring to focus on the absence of the middle class, he did present an interpretation which recognised that rituals, rules, reciprocity, funds and social functions were linked and were reliant on members' enthusiasm for recruitment and retention.[73] Presenting friendly societies as the intersection of where brotherhood, charity and insurance met, he pointed to the direction that the IOOFMU subsequently took about half a century later. It had about a million members in 1910 and still had that number in 1945. From the late 1940s, however, membership plummeted, despite attempts to amend its investment strategy. It was only when it decided to focus on improving 'the quality of life of our members by meeting their social and welfare needs' that membership rose again. A former Grand Master argued in 2008 that the IOOFMU had gone 'back to our roots as a mutual, caring Society, but with an up-to-date twist'.[74] The Oddfellows is still an agency for saving and mutual insurance; it has its own credit union, and is still a channel for the spirit of voluntary service; sick visitors are now called welfare development officers; and it is still an organisation for brotherly (and sisterly) aid in misfortune in that it raises money for charity and provides care to members. Beveridge's hopes for the future of voluntary action and 'the spirit of voluntary service' were built upon his conceptualisation of the past. It was because he had a sophisticated understanding of the development and roles of friendly societies and recognised their integration within communities that he did not present them simply in terms of insurance administration. Rather, as the concluding sentences of *Voluntary action* quoted earlier indicate, for Beveridge they were models for human society.

Notes

1 Lord Beveridge, *Voluntary action: a report on methods of social advance* (London: George Allen & Unwin, 1948), p. 62.

2 The categorisation of friendly societies is considered in D. Weinbren, '"Imagined families": research on friendly societies', *Mitteilungsblatt des Instituts für die Geschichte der sozialen Bewegungen*, vol. 27 (2002), pp. 117–36, and in D. Weinbren and B. James, 'Getting a grip – the roles of friendly societies in Australia and the UK reappraised', *Labour history*, vol. 89 (2005), pp. 87–104.

3 By 1939, 80 per cent of friendly society members were in five affiliated orders. Beveridge, *Voluntary action*, p. 79.

4 P. H. J. H. Gosden, *The friendly societies in England* (Manchester: Manchester University Press, 1961), estimated that there were 'over four million' members in

1872; B. B. Gilbert, *The evolution of national insurance in Great Britain: the origins of the welfare state* (London: Michael Joseph, 1966), pp. 165–6, plumped for 4.25 million members in the early twentieth century; P. Johnson, *Saving and spending: the working-class economy in Britain, 1870–1939* (Oxford: Oxford University Press, 1985), p. 55, argued that this figure was 'too high'; D. G. Green, *Working-class patients and the medical establishment: self-help in Britain from the mid-nineteenth century to 1948* (Aldershot: Gower, 1985), p. 31, proposed that there were 9.5 million in 1910. Voluntary membership of the societies grew by 25 per cent between 1910 and 1937 according to W. Beveridge and A. F. Wells (eds), *The evidence for voluntary action* (London: George Allen & Unwin, 1949), p. 111. For a discussion of the number of friendly society members, see B. Harris, *The origins of the British welfare state: society, state and social welfare in England and Wales, 1800–1945* (Basingstoke: Palgrave Macmillan, 2004), pp. 82, 194, and also E. P. Hennock, *The origin of the welfare state in England and Germany, 1850–1914: social policies compared* (Cambridge: Cambridge University Press, 2007), pp. 166–81.

5 A copy of the poster is held by West Lothian Council. See www.scran.ac.uk/database/record.php?usi=000-000-502-929-C&scache=2fp6o1o2di&searchdb=scran (accessed 2 January 2009).

6 The allusion was to the Roman custom of women being handed over to their husbands by their fathers on marriage; in the event of a divorce, the conclusion of this business arrangement, the wife and some or all of the dowry was returned to the protection of her father.

7 Beveridge and Wells (eds), *The evidence*, p. 109; Beveridge, *Voluntary action*, p. 83.

8 Beveridge, *Voluntary action*, pp. 80–3.

9 Beveridge and Wells (eds), *The evidence*, pp. 110–11.

10 Beveridge and Wells (eds), *The evidence*, p. 272.

11 He addressed the annual general meeting of the National Deposit Friendly Society in June 1947 and acknowledged its 'public-spirited help' in *Voluntary action*, p. 15.

12 Beveridge, *Voluntary action*, pp. 323–4.

13 Beveridge, *Voluntary action*, p. 14.

14 These examples refer to the Philanthropic Order of True Ivorites, the Independent Order of Rechabites and the Masonic Benefit Society.

15 R. W. Moffrey, *A century of Oddfellowship: being a brief record of the rise and progress of the Manchester Unity of the Independent Order of Oddfellows from its formation to the present time* (Manchester: Oddfellows, 1910), p. 64.

16 J. C. Riley, *Sick not dead: the health of British workingmen during the mortality decline* (Baltimore: Johns Hopkins University Press, 1997).

17 Moffrey, *A century*, p. 177. Italics mine.

18 M. Heller, 'The National Insurance Acts 1911–1947, the approved societies and the Prudential Assurance Company', *Twentieth Century British History*, vol. 19, no. 8 (2008), pp. 1–28.

19 *Charity Organisation Review*, vol. 33, no. 328 (June 1913). For Loch's initiation as an honorary member see *Oddfellows' Magazine* (February 1901), p. 61.

20 G. D. H. Cole, 'Review of Lord Beveridge, *Voluntary action*: a report on methods of social advance', *Economic Journal*, vol. 59, no. 235 (1949), p. 400.

21 Beveridge, *Voluntary Action*, pp. 78–9; Beveridge and Wells (eds), *The evidence*, p. 20.

22 Mass-Observation findings cited by Beveridge and Wells (eds), *The evidence*, pp. 17–18.

23 Beveridge and Wells (eds), *The evidence*, p. 273.

24 Johnson, *Saving and spending*, p. 68; D. Green, 'The friendly societies and Adam Smith Liberalism', in D. Gladstone (ed.), *Before Beveridge: welfare before the welfare state* (London: IEA Health and Welfare Unit, 1999), pp. 24–5.

25 *Odd Fellows Magazine* (January 1945), p. 5.

26 *Odd Fellows Magazine* (December 1945), pp. 248–9.

27 Davenport Hall, Catford, 1945, recalled in A. Brownjohn, 'Like 1945', in N. Jackowska (ed.), *Voices: from 'arts for Labour'* (London and Sydney: Pluto, 1985), p. 66.

28 *Odd Fellows Magazine* (December 1945), pp. 244–6.

29 N. Doran, 'Risky business: codifying embodied experience in the Manchester Unity of Oddfellows', *Journal of Historical Sociology*, vol. 7, no. 2 (1994), p. 134.

30 *The complete manual of Oddfellowship* (Manchester: IOOFMU, 1879), p. 94.

31 *Odd Fellows Magazine* (February 1886), p. 38.

32 F. Edwards, 'The treatment of poverty in Nantwich and Crewe 1730–1914' (MA dissertation, Keele University, 1990), pp. 487, 491, 501–6, 523.

33 D. G. Green and L. G. Cromwell, *Mutual aid or welfare state: Australia's friendly societies* (Sydney: George Allen & Unwin, 1984), pp. 61–2.

34 1772 rule book of the Yarm Tradesman's Society and Rose of England Lodge, Manchester Unity, minute book 1842–72, October 1848, quoted by J. J. Turner, 'Friendly societies in south Durham and north Yorkshire c1790–1914: studies in development, membership characteristics and behavior' (Ph.D. dissertation, University of Teeside, 1992), pp. 328, 329, 360.

35 This notion was widespread. For example, in Ireland farmers refrained from paying off their debts to suppliers in order to maintain a state of mutual indebtedness. C. M. Arensberg, *The Irish countryman: an anthropological study* (Gloucester: Peter Smith, 1937); A. O'Dowd, *Meitheal: a study of co-operative labour in rural Ireland (aspects of Ireland)* (Dublin: Comhairle Bhealoideas Eireann, 1981).

36 Moffrey, *A century*, p. 40.

37 For examples from London, Preston, the Potteries, Rhum, rural Perthshire, Wales and elsewhere see D. Weinbren, 'Supporting self-help: charity, mutuality and reciprocity in nineteenth-century Britain', in B. Harris and P. Bridgen (eds), *Historical perspectives on charity and mutual aid: European and American experiences since 1800* (London: Routledge, 2007), pp. 72–3.

38 *Porcupine* (29 May 1880), p. 138.

39 See, for example, K. Polanyi, *The great transformation: the political and economic origins of our time*, 2nd edn (Boston: Beacon Press, 1957), chapters 4–5; J. R. Gillis, *A world of their own making: myth, ritual, and the quest for family values* (New York: Basic Books, 1996), p. 79; G. Stedman Jones, *Outcast London: a study in the relationship between classes in Victorian society* (Oxford: Oxford University Press, 1984), pp. 256, 257, 259.

40 S. Cordery, *British friendly societies, 1750–1914* (Basingstoke: Palgrave, 2003), pp. 14, 174.

41 N. Whiteside, 'Private provision and public welfare: health insurance between the wars', in Gladstone (ed.), *Before Beveridge*, p. 41.

42 J. Harris, 'Political thought and the welfare state, 1870–1940: an intellectual framework for British social policy', *Past and Present*, vol. 135 (1992), p. 116; N. Deakin, 'Voluntary inaction', in R. Whelan, *Involuntary action: how voluntary is the 'voluntary' sector?* (London: Institute of Economic Affairs, 1999), p. 29.

43 V. A. Burrowes, 'On friendly societies since the advent of national health insurance', *Journal of the Institute of Actuaries*, vol. 63, no. 3 (1933), pp. 307–82.

44 Mass-Observation Archive, University of Sussex, Falme, Report 2506, Mass-Observation, *A report on the friendly societies* (Mass-Observation, 1947), pp. 22–3.

45 J. A. Lincoln, 'Problems of friendly societies', in Beveridge and Wells (eds), *The evidence*, p. 270.

46 Beveridge, *Voluntary action*, pp. 62, 82, 83.

47 F. M. Eden, *Observations on friendly societies for the maintenance of the industrious classes during sickness, infirmity and old age* (London: J. White, 1801).

48 D. Weinbren, *The Oddfellows, 1810–2010: Two Hundred years of Making Friends and Helping People* (Lancaster: Carnegie, 2010).

49 M. Gorsky, 'The growth and distribution of English friendly societies in the early nineteenth century', *Economic History Review*, vol. 51, no. 3 (1998), p. 503. On casual labour see G. Stedman Jones, *Outcast London* (Cambridge: Cambridge University Press, 1970); J. H. Treble, 'The seasonal demand for adult labour in Glasgow, 1890–1914', *Social History*, vol. 3, no. 1 (1978), pp. 43–60.

50 This emblem is reproduced on the endpapers of R. A. Leeson, *Travelling brothers: the six centuries' road from craft fellowship to trade unionism* (London: Paladin, 1980).

51 B. Stibbins, '"A highly beneficial influence": friendly societies in Norfolk in the nineteenth century, with particular reference to north Norfolk' (MA dissertation, University of East Anglia, 2001), p. 41.

52 R. Richardson, *Death, dissection, and the destitute*, 2nd edn (Chicago: University of Chicago Press, 2001).

53 J. Strange, '"Tho' lost to sight, to memory dear": pragmatism, sentimentality and working-class attitudes towards the grave, c1875–1914', *Mortality*, vol. 8, no. 2 (2003), p. 153.

54 Articles of the South Shields Friendly Society, 1794, and *Newcastle Courant* (10 January 1801), quoted in R. Colls, *The pitmen of the northern coalfield: work culture and protest 1790–1850* (Manchester: Manchester University Press, 1987), pp. 215–16.

55 D. Weinbren, 'Beneath the all-seeing eye: fraternal order and friendly societies' banners', *Journal of Cultural History*, vol. 3, no. 2 (2006), pp. 167–91.

56 J. M. Clarke, *London's necropolis: a guide to Brookwood cemetery* (Stroud: Sutton, 2004).

57 M. Chase, 'A sort of corporation (tho' without a charter): the guild tradition and the emergence of British trade unionism', in I. A. Gadd and P. Wallis (eds), *Guilds and association in Europe, 900–1900* (London: Centre for Metropolitan History, 2006), p. 190; D. Cannadine, 'The transformation of civic ritual in modern Britain: the Colchester oyster feast', *Past and Present*, vol. 94 (1982), pp. 128–9. By the early years of the twentieth century it was recognised that Edwardian men were more likely to join 'processions dominated by advertising for private companies and state agencies'. See J. M. MacKenzie, *Propaganda and empire: the manipulation of British public opinion, 1880–1960* (Manchester: Manchester University Press, 1984).

58 D. Cannadine, *Ornamentalism: how the British saw their empire* (New York and London: Oxford University Press, 2001), pp. 4, 85, 99, 105.

59 J. M. Baernreither, *English associations of working men* (London: Swan Sonnenschein, 1889), p. 221.

60 *Odd Fellows Magazine* (July 1914), pp. 282–93.

61 J. M. Roberts, *The mythology of secret societies* (London: Secker & Warburg, 1972), pp. 1–2.

62 W. Bagehot, *The English constitution*, ed. with introduction and notes by Miles Taylor (Oxford: Oxford University Press, 2001), p. 13.

63 *The sociology of Georg Simmel*, trans., ed. and with an introduction by Kurt H. Wolff (New York: Free Press, 1950), pp. 330, 332.

64 Stibbins, 'A highly beneficial influence', p. 46.

65 M. Fisher and D. Viner, '"Go thou and do likewise": the Ebington Friendly Society (1856–1920) and its banners', *Folk Life*, vol. 37 (1998–99), pp. 64–79; J. Cooper, *The well-ordered town: a story of Saffron Walden, Essex 1792–1862* (Saffron Walden: Cooper, 2000), p. 183; D. Neave, *Mutual aid in the Victorian countryside* (Hull: Hull University Press, 1991), pp. 1, 48–9, 68, 95, 97; N. Mansfield, *English farmworkers and local patriotism, 1900–1930* (Ashgate: Aldershot, 2001), pp. 47, 48, 198, 205; A. Fisk, *Mutual self-help in southern England 1850–1912* (Southampton: Foresters Heritage Trust, 2006), p. 135.

66 D. Weinbren, 'The social capital of female friendly societies', in M. F. Cross (ed.), *Gender and Fraternal Orders in Europe, 1300–2000* (Basingstoke: Palgrave, Macmillan, 2010), pp. 200–22.

67 W. G. Rimmer, *Marshalls of Leeds, flax spinners, 1778–1886* (Cambridge: Cambridge University Press, 1960), pp. 104–5, 194, 216–17; S. Cordery, 'Mutualism, friendly societies, and the genesis of railway trade unions', *Labour History Review*, vol. 67 (2002), pp. 265–7; J. Benson, 'Coalowners, coalminers and compulsion: pit clubs in England, 1860–80', *Business History*, vol. 44, no. 1 (2002), pp. 47–60; C. Bradbury, 'The impact of friendly societies in north Staffordshire', *Staffordshire Studies*, vol. 13 (2001), pp. 130, 134. On the dominance of the employers in a Wigan-based society see *The Lancashire and Cheshire Miners' Permanent Relief Society: report of the 33rd AGM, 1906* (Wigan: Wall and Sons, 1906), p. 9.

68 This notion is discussed in M. Savage, *The dynamics of working-class politics: the labour movement in Preston, 1880–1940* (Cambridge: Cambridge University Press, 1987).

69 J. Tosh, 'What should historians do with masculinity?', *History Workshop Journal*, vol. 38 (1994), pp. 186–7.

70 S. D'Cruze and J. Turnbull, 'Fellowship and family: Oddfellows' lodges in Preston and Lancaster c1830–c1890', *Urban History*, vol. 22, no. 1 (1995), p. 40.

71 *Report from the Select Committee of the House of Lords on betting 1902*, p. 147, quoted in R. McKibbin, 'Working-class gambling in Britain, 1880–1939', *Past and Present*, vol. 82 (1979), p. 170.

72 *Odd Fellows Magazine* (November 1945), pp. 208, 209.

73 Beveridge and Wells (eds), *The evidence*, pp. 271–3.

74 Quoted in Weinbren, *The Oddfellows*, p. 291.

6

Beveridge in the Antipodes: the 1948 tour

Melanie Oppenheimer

During the first half of 1948, while the report on voluntary action was in press, William Beveridge and his wife Janet toured New Zealand and Australia. Beveridge was invited to New Zealand by its oldest university, the University of Otago in Dunedin, to deliver the first De Carle lectures.[1] This invitation was quite the antidote to a freezing and generally depressing British winter, one of the coldest on record, through which Beveridge and his team of inquiry assessors and research assistants (including his wife, Janet) worked to complete his third report, *Voluntary action*. With the manuscript and the supplementary volume, *The evidence for voluntary action* completed, the thought of leaving behind food rationing, queues, strikes and a mood of quiet despair for an all-expenses-paid round-the-world trip for himself and his wife was too good to pass up.[2] A keen traveller, Beveridge had not before been to New Zealand, and to include a visit to Australia, which he had last visited at the age of three in 1882, and where he had many cousins, was an opportunity not to be missed.[3] Beveridge was also interested in these two 'British nations', and he was keen to assess their development since the war and to 'see people, to ask them questions, to get to know them'.[4]

Following a 'depressing' debate in the House of Lords on the 'economic situation', Beveridge and his wife left cold and wintry London in late February, arriving in Wellington on Sunday 11 April.[5] There they were met by the New Zealand Labour Prime Minister, Peter Fraser. His connections with the voluntary sector through voluntary organisations such as the Smith Family and Plunket Society, and an interest in social security (Fraser had played a key role in New Zealand's 1938 Social Security Act) as well as world government, a current pet topic of Beveridge's, meant that the two men had much in common.[6] Spending exactly one month in New Zealand, the couple then flew across the Tasman Sea, arriving in Sydney on 11 May. After a punishing schedule travelling through three states in three weeks by road, rail and boat, the Beveridges left Fremantle in Western Australia, disembarking in London on 6 July.

Overall it was an extraordinarily productive but quite exhausting trip for the septuagenarian (Beveridge turned seventy en route to New Zealand on 5 March). In a manner reminiscent of a bygone era, Beveridge travelled with a suite of suitcases and trunks full of books and papers, preparing his varied lectures and talks while on board ship. He also managed to co-author two books on his return to England. Covering essentially the same material, *Antipodes notebook* was released for the British market, and *On and off the platform: under the Southern Cross* was published in Australia and New Zealand.[7] The title of the latter book reflects the Beveridge's continuous and sometimes relentless round of speaking engagements, broadcasts and interviews, or as Janet later remarked, plenty of 'singing for our supper'.[8] This chapter explores the Beveridge's 1948 Australasian visit and his impressions of the two countries, and reflects on his responses to Australia and New Zealand in the immediate post-war period. It also examines some of the ideas contained in the report *Voluntary action*, in terms of Beveridge's view that 'we are the same kind of people in the same boat'.[9]

Beveridge in New Zealand

During the Antipodean tour, Beveridge spoke on a number of wide-ranging themes that reflected both his areas of special interest and the expectations of his host countries. Between 13 and 21 April, Beveridge presented the four De Carle lectures on topics selected by him in consultation with the university, which determined the order. His first lecture, 'Economic position of Britain', was on a topic dear to the hearts of New Zealanders, and focussed on how Britain was coping in the uncertain post-war period. The second De Carle lecture, 'Public action for social advance', dealt with his 1942 report and its aftermath. Then came 'Voluntary action for social advance', or 'Beveridge is not enough', delivered on 19 April and based on his most recent and as yet unpublished report.[10] Reflecting Beveridge's concern with the tenuous post-war new world order, his fourth De Carle lecture was entitled 'Necessity for world government'. Beveridge was inundated with requests and invitations from a range of organisations, and other engagements included a speech in Wellington on Anzac Day, 25 April, on the topic of 'Security and liberty'. This was followed by a lecture organised by the Institute of Public Administration in Wellington on the topic of 'Planning a new town', with his final public lecture, 'First things first', delivered on 6 May at the Auckland University College.

Weighed down by his notoriety as the British economist who created the welfare state, Beveridge was somewhat surprised at the reaction to some of his lecture topics. He later wrote in *Antipodes notebook* that he 'experienced an intriguing difference of view . . . between the things which audiences in Australia and New Zealand most wanted to hear from me, and the things which I most desired to say to them'.[11] This was clearly apparent at a question and answer session in Dunedin, as Beveridge explained:

> Almost the first question asked was: What is the most important problem now facing New Zealand? I gave as my answer: 'The same problem as that which faces every country in the world – how to make peace secure and abolish war'. I did not

think at the time that this answer went down at all well: I was expected to say 'housing' or 'more secondary industries' or 'how to keep people on the farms' or, of course, something about social security, or hospitals. After this answer, I was asked why I had ceased to be interested in social problems.[12]

Although Beveridge found this exchange disconcerting, it is perhaps not surprising that the main interest in New Zealand was in hearing him, as the eminent and world-famous economist and author of what was then termed the 'Beveridge Plan', discuss the new British social security system and the current economic situation in Britain.[13] Beveridge painted a dire picture of Britain, making clear the very real threat of financial economic collapse. The possible consequences for countries like New Zealand, whose economy was intertwined with Britain's, was recognised and editorialised in newspapers such as the *Otago Daily Times*.[14]

Despite the intense media interest and the hectic schedule, the Beveridges clearly enjoyed New Zealand, its people and especially the abundance of food. Lady Beveridge bought up crates of fresh fruit, causing considerable disquiet for the New Zealand shipping company and the Prime Minister's office when they were delivered to the hold of the ship returning the Beveridges home. Not only was the fruit taking up precious space needed for the ship's supplies, but it was in excess of the amount permitted by the Board of Trade.[15] But this was an administrative aside. The Beveridges were feted and treated like royalty wherever they went, with one leading lawyer and soon-to-be politician, John Marshall, describing in his memoirs how he was able to sit 'beside, and metaphorically at the feet of, the father of the Welfare State and the high priest of modern liberalism'.[16] Tours were organised, including a side-trip to Queenstown 'through incredibly beautiful country over unbelievably thrilling roads', as Janet wrote breathlessly.[17] On the way to Rotorua, they witnessed a volcanic eruption at Ruapehu, which made them realise that not all of New Zealand was a replica of 'home' with lush scenery, verdant farms and British stock. Their experiences of Maori hospitality and the traditional hakka, which Janet later explained 'was almost too close to the exalted seats in the front row allotted to us', reinforced the cultural differences between Britain and its smallest and quaintest dominion.[18]

Beveridge in Australia

After the highly successful, well-organised one-month tour of both the North Island and the South Island of New Zealand, the Beveridges arrived in Sydney. First impressions were not promising, as Janet later noted:

It might have been any modern city anywhere which had developed in haphazard stages, the overhead electric trams still filling the inadequate roadways . . . Man, it seems, can never pause to consider before he builds it what a city should be like, but each time rushes on with a headlong development, committing in Australia the same mistakes as other great prosperous money making communities have made.[19]

Despite being accommodated at the Australia Hotel – *the* hotel of Sydney at the time – the Beveridges found the city noisy and distracting. To make matters worse, they discovered on arrival that their Australian itinerary was not yet confirmed, despite lengthy correspondence with government officials and the Australian Prime Minister, Ben Chifley.[20] Perhaps their bad humour had something to do with the rigour of the New Zealand tour. It was suggested that Beveridge was 'a little tired though he would not want to admit it', and that he wanted to meet with politicians and people of influence 'particularly Parliamentarians' rather than undertake rounds of 'formal speaking engagements', which were very tiring.[21] But there were other forces at work that possibly coloured their first impressions of Australia.

Beveridge's tour coincided with the political upheaval caused by the calling of a referendum by the federal government. In order to wrestle away permanent control of rents and prices from the six state governments, the federal Labor Prime Minister, Ben Chifley, was attempting to create a national system under Commonwealth control. During the Second World War the federal government, under the Labor Prime Minister, John Curtin, had temporarily assumed this responsibility to prevent war profiteering and control inflation. But a permanent change required constitutional amendment. This is a notoriously difficult thing to achieve in Australian politics, and since 1901, of forty-two proposals put forward to the people to change aspects of the constitution, only eight have been success-ful.[22] The consequence for Beveridge was that all the Australian politicians whom he particularly wanted to meet and engage with were preoccupied. Even federal parliament in Canberra was in recess to focus on the referendum. The combin-ation of local politics and world events, for example, the ending of Britain's man-date over Palestine and Donald Bradman's famous 1948 cricket tour, dominated the newspapers. Beveridge's tour of Australia was thus inadvertently and completely overshadowed.[23]

On their first night in Sydney, the Beveridges had intended to relax and take in a film. Instead they accompanied their Australian host and minder, Dr Lloyd Ross, to the Sydney Town Hall for the referendum campaign launch. Ross was well known in Australian history circles as a writer and labour intellectual, journa-list, trade unionist, one-time member of the Communist Party and later the Director of Public Relations in the Department of Post-War Reconstruction. He was assigned to accompany Beveridge, arrange his itinerary and generally make sure everything was in order. The fact that Australia was completely focussed on a referendum on prices and rents for the entire duration of Beveridge's visit was unfortunate but unavoidable.

As Lloyd Ross was involved in the referendum, the Beveridges were thrown into the cut and thrust of Australian politics when Ross invited them to attend the opening of the 'Yes' campaign at the Sydney Town Hall, where Prime Minister Ben Chifley and his deputy, Herbert 'Doc' Evatt, were to speak. Beveridge was given a first-hand account of Australian federalism at work. He was bemused at the idea of compulsory voting in Australia and struggled with the concept of six separate price-fixing authorities (the states). It was also reported in the press that Beveridge privately believed that neither prices nor rents should be controlled, which resulted in those publicising the 'Yes' case, the Labor government, shuddering 'at the possibility of such an authority stating this view in public'.[24] He later confided that he was pleased not to have been pressed to make a decision, as all Australian adults were compelled to do through compulsory voting, because he could not vote either 'yes' or 'no'.[25]

After that hastily arranged introduction, a round of speaking engagements followed, including an address sponsored by the United Nations Association and Federal Union on world government, as well as recorded talks for ABC Radio.[26] Despite a quiet weekend in the country, the Beveridges appear not to have enjoyed their Sydney visit. When asked about how she supported her husband in his political career, Janet Beveridge told an interviewer that she found 'electioneering much less strenuous than visiting Sydney!'[27]

Things picked up once they arrived in Canberra. As guests of the Governor General, the former Labor leader William McKell, the Beveridges enjoyed the rustic tranquillity and quieter pace of the capital city. They met diplomats and picnicked with students from the University College and members of the United Nations Association.[28] Unfortunately there were few politicians to be found, and Beveridge did not see the parliament in action, as 'all members of the Cabinet were moving about the country stirring up the voters'.[29] Presumably he was referring to Chifley, whom he met again briefly in Canberra as he flew in from Brisbane on his way to Tasmania.[30]

The Beveridges were even more impressed with Melbourne, 'a gracious city with gracious people'.[31] Perhaps it was because they felt more at home attending the theatre (they went three times to see Sir Laurence Olivier and Lady Olivier playing Shakespeare on tour with the Old Vic Theatre Company) or because Beveridge attended an Aussie Rules football game. They certainly spent 'less time on the platform', rather holding informal meetings with key Australians such as the industrialist Essington Lewis, Dr Clunies Ross from the Council of Scientific and Industrial Research (CSIR) and top bureaucrats from Social Services and the Housing Commission.[32] Beveridge was also awarded an honorary degree of Doctor of Laws by the University of Melbourne. His acceptance speech was laced with humour when he responded by saying that he was proud to receive the degree (his first from the southern hemisphere) 'as it brings my list of honorary degrees into double figures . . . I am beginning to have something like a reasonable batting average'.[33]

Most of the Australian lectures and broadcasts were based on topics delivered earlier in New Zealand. But Beveridge did venture out with a couple of new speeches, such as 'Leisure for housewives', recorded in Melbourne on 29 May and broadcast across Australia on 14 June.[34] In this illuminating speech, Beveridge spoke about unpaid female domestic labour, and how married women were officially described as 'unoccupied' unless they worked for money outside the home. He described how he had drawn attention to this problem in his 1942 report, *Social insurance and allied services*, and how it was time to change the way unpaid domestic labour was viewed. Beveridge was highly critical of the current British Labour government's 1946 National Insurance Act, which excluded the work of housewives, viewing women as 'non employed persons' or adult dependants. On numerous occasions throughout the tour, he mentioned the tendency to 'underestimate the importance of work that was not done for pay, the most striking example being the housewife and mother'. This was, he argued, fundamentally an issue of 'social justice as a condition for effective citizenship'.[35] Beveridge suggested that as in Britain, the housewife in New Zealand and Australia did 'not receive the substantial consideration which the importance of her work to the community should command'.[36]

It was on the final leg of Beveridge's Australian tour, in Adelaide – arguably the most British of Australian cities especially in the late 1940s – that Beveridge seemed most comfortable. Maybe it was due to the fact he was on his way home, that his work 'on the platform' was almost done. In Adelaide, he not only met up with his cousins but felt most connected with his audience, whom he described as 'the largest, most attentive and most intelligent audience he had faced on his Australian tour'. In Adelaide, as in New Zealand, Beveridge seemed to find people who responded to him and his ideas. They turned up in droves to hear him speak, and the city press responded by giving him the largest and most consistent newspaper coverage of his Australian tour.[37] But overall there can be little doubt that the extraordinary circumstances of the prices referendum, which the government lost, had an impact on Beveridge's tour in Australia.[38]

Voluntary action in New Zealand and Australia

Beveridge made a number of observations about the two societies – these British social laboratories of the new world – that help us better understand voluntary action in the Australian and New Zealand context. In planning the tour, Beveridge mentioned that he was most interested in finding out what these British societies in the southern hemisphere were really like – and to compare and contrast them with those of Britain. Compared with the current post-war austerity of Britain, Australia and New Zealand appeared as lands of plenty, with shops full of stock and food in abundance. However, Beveridge was shocked at the shortage of housing in both countries, especially as there had been no war damage.[39] He also commented on the general shortage of labour – unfilled job vacancies hovered around 26,000 in New Zealand and 100,000 in Australia – and said that both countries could and should expand their migration programmes, not focussing exclusively on British migrants but also attending to the displaced persons scattered in camps across Europe.[40]

Beveridge noted that this shortage of manpower was tied up with the lack of shipping and had a knock-on effect especially in areas of domestic service and the hospitality industry generally. The Beveridges were concerned about the lack of domestic servants and appalled at the rigidity of workplace regulations, especially in New Zealand, where restrictions on restaurant hours and meal times meant 'the traveller who was delayed on the road would go hungry', something that happened to them on a couple of occasions.[41] They were also highly critical of industrial relations and of the power of the trade unions over the statutory restrictions on work and conditions, the level of strike action and the lack of coal production. Beveridge argued that when there was a demonstrated acute shortage of labour, it was counter-productive to have New Zealand's five-day working week or Australia's forty-hour week, recently introduced on 1 January 1948.

Beveridge was aware of the social welfare developments of Australia and New Zealand in the first decades of the twentieth century, and he had made special reference to the New Zealand scheme, especially its provisions for old-age pensions, in his 1942 report.[42] His second De Carle lecture was a detailed comparison of the social services of Britain and New Zealand. He later added a section on Australia for publication in *On and off the platform*. Each country used different terminology – Britain used 'national insurance', New Zealand 'social security', and Australia 'social services', and the schemes varied accordingly (see Chapter 11), but the underlying premise of public action was the same. Beveridge painted a picture of the two 'British communities' with an 'incessant . . . cross-fertilization of ideas' leading the world as they developed what he called 'public action for social advance'.[43] In 1938, Beveridge argued, New Zealand had gained the lead with its Social Security Act, and Britain was only now catching up. Ten years later he could boast that 'the two British communities of New Zealand and of Britain, at opposite ends of the earth, each have Social Security now developed further than any other country'.[44] The new British social security plan (which was similar to New Zealand's in terms of having no means test) would help 'to lift human life a step higher and to put a floor below inequalities'.[45]

Beveridge believed that Australia lagged behind New Zealand and Britain, notwithstanding the introduction of the 1947 Social Services Consolidation Act. Australia used a means test and appeared to be spending proportionally less on social welfare than either New Zealand or Britain. And as Beveridge observed at first hand with the referendum on prices, Australia had its federalist system, which complicated matters, especially in the area of health and hospitals. Although the Commonwealth government was successful in a referendum on social services in 1946, it still had to negotiate and co-operate 'with each of the separate States to whom in general the hospitals belong'.[46] These issues were not lost on the Australian public, and some newspapers picked up on these comparisons between the British and Australian systems of social security, drawing special attention to the lack of a means test in Britain, where social security benefits were available for all, irrespective of savings or property, which encouraged those over sixty-five to continue working without penalty. Beveridge was strongly opposed to the concept of a means test, believing that the state must not interfere with the individual's capacity to prepare for old age. An editorial in the newspaper *The Sun* supported Beveridge's view and argued that in Australia the means test effectively penalised thrift and punished old-age pensioners who wanted to work.[47]

Beveridge continually warned that social security was only the first step. 'It dealt with', he argued, 'the distribution of purchasing power, a financial operation that was far from solving all their problems or from making the kind of society they wanted . . . and much depended on the voluntary action of individuals as a means to social advance'.[48] Beveridge neatly weaved together these two concepts – of public and voluntary action – on many occasions during his visit. But while there was strong interest in his views on public action, there was not the same response to the theme of 'Voluntary action', the topic of his third De Carle lecture. Beveridge did not repeat it, nor did he record a broadcast in Australia. Rather, he continually made links to voluntary action in other speeches. The original typed text of his New Zealand lecture 'Voluntary action for social advance' and that later published in *On and off the platform* are a succinct distillation of the contents of the larger report and are very useful for comparisons between Australia, New Zealand and Britain. There are also interesting differences between the original speech and the published version.[49]

Beveridge began his lecture 'Voluntary action for social advance' by explaining to his audience how he came to write the report *Voluntary action* (as outlined in Chapter 1 of this book). He then went on to explain what he meant by voluntary action – that it included self-help, mutual aid and philanthropy. Beveridge noted that in the Antipodes, the friendly society movement, a key part of self-help and mutual aid, was proportionally smaller than in Britain, with 620,000 and 83,000 members in Australia and New Zealand respectively as opposed to Britain's eight million members. In relation to the size of the population, for example, New Zealand's membership should have been around 300,000. 'Consumers' Co-operation' or co-operatives, with nine and a half million members in Britain, were another form of mutual aid that was even smaller in Australia and New Zealand. The co-operative movement never reached the heights of Britain, although recent research by the Australian Labor historians Balnave and Patmore on the Rochdale consumer co-operatives indicates that retail co-operatives were a feature in rural and working-class areas such as coal-mining districts in Australia, with around 120,000 members.[50] Never establishing a close relationship with the labour movement (unlike Britain), the movement fell into abeyance in the post-war period, although in New Zealand the Labour government of Peter Fraser was particularly sympathetic to consumer and producer co-operatives, especially with new state housing initiatives in the Hutt Valley. It was argued in 1949 that both Australia and New Zealand 'were too prosperous to afford a live and active consumer co-operative movement'.[51]

It was a different story, however, with trade unionism, which was, according to Beveridge, 'the most important of all our forms of voluntary association'.[52] Trade unions were proportionally the same size in Australia and New Zealand as in Britain, but their activities were quite different. In Britain, trade unions offered many benefits similar to those of the friendly societies and were the pioneers in unemployment insurance. In Australia and New Zealand, however, Beveridge observed, the trade union movement offered fewer mutual-aid-type benefits for its members, preferring to concentrate on industrial arbitration, wages and conditions.[53]

The second major component of voluntary action was philanthropy, which was strong in both New Zealand and Australia. 'Philanthropy is not patronage nor condescension', Beveridge was at pains to point out, but rather consisted of citizens assisting those less fortunate in their communities. The two countries had their share of philanthropic pioneers although no charitable trusts, an integral component of philanthropy in Britain.[54] In his lecture, Beveridge made special mention of the Plunket Society as an outstanding achievement. 'I would be as proud of it as New Zealand's going to war', he declared triumphantly.[55] The visitors were also impressed with what voluntary organisations like the Country Women's Association (CWA) did for rural women and children in Australia with their rest rooms and baby clinics, 'an essential part of the social system operating for the benefit of the community'.[56]

Beveridge's 1948 observations on voluntary action are supported by recent studies, such as Margaret Tennant's study of New Zealand *The fabric of welfare*, as well as my own research on the Australian context, that explore the complex interrelationship between the state and voluntary action in terms of philanthropy and mutual aid.[57] As early as 1944, Lloyd Ross was highlighting the value of voluntary action in post-war Australia to his boss Dr Nugget Coombs, Director of Post-War Reconstruction. As he wrote to Coombs:

> It is not sufficient to plan merely for economic policy – due consideration should be given to ensuring the fullest opportunity for people as individuals and as members of a community carrying on those activities . . . there has been a great expansion of group activity during the war for patriotic and social purposes, and there is widespread demand for continuance of this activity into the peace.[58]

Ross believed that a partnership between the government and voluntary groups was crucial to the success of Australia's post-war reconstruction. He believed that governments had a responsibility to support local community voluntary organisations to achieve their aims, and it was through voluntary groups that the 'full needs of the people are satisfied'. Reflecting Beveridge's voluntary action theories, he continued, 'a government can build a community centre, but only the people in the community can make it work and live. A government can build a library, but the people borrow the books'.[59]

Just as Beveridge recognised the role of the Second World War as important for voluntary action in Britain with the rise of organisations like the Women's Voluntary Service (WVS) and the Citizens' Advice Bureaux, so too had Ross identified an 'awakening of citizenship' in Australia in the wake of the war. These two prominent organisations, established in Britain during the war, were also formed in Australia. I have noted the impact of civilian volunteering in my detailed studies on the Australian home front and, at the same time, I acknowledge Prochaska's differing view of the destructive effect of the war on voluntary activity (see Chapter 4).[60] Lloyd Ross, too, wanted to harness this voluntary spirit, but it required an active government presence to assist with planning and finances. He spent considerable time and energy developing his ideas through his Community Activities Section of the Department of Post-War Reconstruction. Discussion groups were established, and Ross travelled around Australia giving talks on the subject, with the ABC assisting with publications and broadcasts.[61]

There is little evidence, however, to ascertain how Beveridge's third report, *Voluntary action*, was received in Australia. Beveridge sent a copy to Lloyd Ross in late 1948, hoping that he would 'find something of interest to read in it and perhaps to say about it'. Although Ross read the book 'with considerable interest and enthusiasm' and said that he was reviewing it for the *Australian Quarterly*, I have not been able to find the review. It seems it was never published.[62] Even if Ross never completed his review, he clearly understood what Beveridge was saying about voluntary action. He knew what Beveridge meant when he used the Greek myth of Scylla and Charybdis to explain how voluntary action was integral to fostering 'a working partnership between the state, individuals and voluntary action'.[63] As outlined by Deakin in Chapter 3 above, Beveridge saw voluntary action as negotiating between the laissez-faire of free markets and totalitarianism.[64] To Beveridge voluntary action was a necessary buffer between states and markets: 'the business motive is a good servant but a bad master, and a society which gives itself up to the dominance of the business motive is a bad society'.[65]

Conclusion

William and Janet Beveridge arrived back in London on 6 July 1948 to a nation in crisis, with the first battle of the Cold War – the Berlin airlift – underway. The new National Health Service and national insurance scheme were introduced the previous day.[66] *Voluntary action: a report on methods of social advance* was published three months later in mid-October, but as outlined in Chapter 1, despite reasonable reviews it did not have the impact in the United Kingdom of Beveridge's earlier reports. Beveridge's Antipodean tour, however, allowed him the time and distance to reflect on his report *Voluntary action*, and to write a neat distillation of his ideas on voluntary action for his third De Carle lecture. When delivering this lecture in New Zealand, he said:

Beveridge has shown you what the State can do to get freedom from want, and the State is doing it. Thus nothing that the State or any public authority can do can make the kind of society in which you live; only voluntary action can do what is necessary ... I have tried in this book [*Voluntary action*] to describe the chief voluntary action of Britain in the past in order that Britain must make certain that it is preserved in the future in one way or another.[67]

Beveridge's ideas, briefly articulated through this chapter, are demonstrated in more depth in Chapters 11 and 12 below, where the role, influence and impact of Beveridge and voluntary action in New Zealand and Australia respectively in the second half of the twentieth century are discussed by Margaret Tennant and Paul Smyth.

Sixty years later, in 2010, we know that 'Beveridge is not enough'. Using Anthony Giddens's analogy of the three-legged stool, we know that there has to be a balance.[68] We know that a well-functioning democracy needs the state, the economy and civil society to be in balance, in accord with each other, with no individual part dominating, bullying, strangling or taking the others for granted, for otherwise society falls apart. Clearly, through the pages of *Voluntary action*, Beveridge knew that too. But in 1948 the state was in the ascendancy in all three countries, and the proponents and voices of voluntary action were muted for a generation.

Notes

1 The university lecture series were made possible by a generous endowment from Miss Edith de Carle, who died in 1946. The De Carle Distinguished Lectureship continues today.

2 J. and W. Beveridge, *Antipodes notebook* (London: Pilot Press Ltd, 1949), p. 6.

3 W. Beveridge, *Power and influence* (London: Hodder & Stoughton, 1953), pp. 355–6.

4 National Archives of Australia (hereafter NAA), Canberra, A461/8 748/1/839, cablegram from Australian High Commission, London, No. 41, for Prince Minister from Beasley, 13 February 1948, Visit – Beveridge, Lord; and Beveridge, *Antipodes notebook*, p. 3.

5 Beveridge, *Antipodes notebook*, p. 7.

6 Peter Fraser has been called one of New Zealand's greatest prime ministers. Representing the New Zealand Labour Party, he held the position from 1940 to 1949. For his role in social welfare and voluntary action and that of his wife, Janet Fraser, see M. Tennant, *The fabric of welfare: voluntary organisations, government and welfare in New Zealand, 1840–2005* (Wellington: Bridget Williams Books, 2007). He played a key role in the establishment of the Social Security Act 1938. See T. Beaglehole, 'Fraser, Peter 1884–1950', *Dictionary of New Zealand biography*, www.dnzb.govt.nz/dnzb/ (accessed 25 October 2008).

7 Beveridge, *Antipodes notebook*, and W. and J. Beveridge, *On and off the platform: Under the Southern Cross* (Sydney, Wellington and Melbourne: Hicks, Smith & Wright, 1949).

8 Beveridge, *On and off the platform*, p. 151.

9 Beveridge, *Antipodes notebook*, p. 138.

10 A subtitle suggested by Beveridge himself. Beveridge, *On and off the platform*, p. 63.

11 Beveridge, *Antipodes notebook*, p. 84.

12 Beveridge, *Antipodes notebook*, p. 85.

13 *New Zealand Herald* (12 April 1948), p. 6; *New Zealand Herald* (1 May 1948), p. 10. Margaret Tennant also makes this observation on Beveridge's visit to New Zealand in her book *The fabric of welfare*, pp. 129–32.

14 *Otago Daily Times* (15 April 1948).

15 I would like to thank Margaret Tennant for this story. See Archives New Zealand, Wellington, EA 1 PM 59/3/305, Pt 1, correspondence New Zealand Shipping Company to Prime Minister's Office, 15 May–3 June 1948.

16 Quoted in Tennant, *The fabric of welfare*, part III, p. 247, n. 57.

17 Beveridge, *On and off the platform*, p. 123.

18 Beveridge, *Antipodes notebook*, p. 39. See also Mitchell Library (hereafter ML), Sydney, Beveridge Papers, newspaper clippings, MS2618, *Rotorua Post* (5 May 1948).

19 Beveridge, *Antipodes notebook*, p. 46.

20 See ML, Beveridge Papers, M2618, letter from Chifley to Beveridge, 24 April 1948, and letter from Beveridge to Chifley, 6 May 1948. See also NAA, Canberra, A461/8 748/1/839, Prime Minister's Department, Visit of Lord Beveridge, 9 April 1948. In April, the Prime Minister's Department prepared a detailed brief involving state premiers, the Minister for Labour and National Service and the Director-General of Social Services, whose suggestions included an inspection of a number of industrial sites as well as discussions on all aspects of social security. The suggestions also included visits to the Commonwealth Aircraft Corporation, Fishermen's Bend and General Motors Holden in Melbourne, as well as heavy industries in and around Sydney.

21 NAA, Canberra, A461/8 748/1/839, cable from Minister for External Affairs, Wellington, to New Zealand High Commissioner, no. 101, for McKenzie and Shanahan, Canberra, Wellington, 9 May 1948.

22 The writ was issued on 12 April 1948, and polling day was called for 29 May 1948. The campaign officially started on 11 May, the day the Beveridges arrived in Sydney. Each state had different regulations until Gough Whitlam introduced the Trade Practices Act in 1974 and Bob Hawke the Prices Surveillance Act in 1983, both of which were designed to protect consumers and promote competition. Since 1995, an independent federal authority, the Australian Competition and Consumer Commission, has overseen the Acts.

23 See, for example, *Sydney Morning Herald* (12 May 1948).

24 *Sunday Sun* (23 May 1948), p. 22.

25 Beveridge, *On and off the platform*, p. 11. Beveridge said he could not have voted 'no' because he believed that there should be uniform prices across the nation, not based on state boundaries, but he also could not have voted 'yes' as that would have appeared to favour increased state controls.

26 See *The Sun* (14 May 1948), p. 7.

27 'Personality parade', *The Sun* (14 May 1948), p. 11.

28 *Canberra Times* (19 May 1948), p. 4.

29 Beveridge, *On and off the platform*, p. 146.

30 Beveridge, *On and off the platform*, p. 11.
31 Beveridge, *On and off the platform*, p. 150.
32 See ML, Beveridge Papers, M261, printed itineraries.
33 *The Argus* (29 May 1948), p. 1.
34 *The Sun* (18 May 1948), p. 7; Beveridge, *Antipodes notebook*, pp. 86–7. 'The Crusade for World Government' was broadcast from Sydney on 16 May; in Canberra, Beveridge talked about social security; and in Adelaide, the economic position of Britain. See also NAA, Sydney, SP300/1, box 30, ABC – Talk Scripts – General, 1948, 'Leisure for house-wives', Monday 14 June 1948, 3LO 7.15–7.30pm.
35 *New Zealand Herald* (7 May 1948), p. 8.
36 Beveridge, *On and off the platform*, p. 193. Perhaps coincidentally, as part of the ABC's programme 'The nation's forum of the air', a live discussion on the topic 'Should the housewife receive a wage?' was held on Wednesday 2 June and broadcast on 30 June 1948. See NAA, Sydney, SP369/3, vol. 4, no. 11.
37 See *Advertiser* (2–4 June 1948).
38 With the exception of that of Adelaide, one can detect a bland indifference in the Australian press. *The Bulletin* had one small extract published on 26 April 1948, p. 11, but nothing very exciting or in depth. The Adelaide coverage was more extensive, probably reflecting Beveridge's personal and well as his political connections with the city.
39 Beveridge, *On and off the platform*, p. 199.
40 This was already happening. One of the politicians Beveridge met in Melbourne was Arthur Calwell, Australia's first Minister for Immigration, who had introduced the Displaced Persons Scheme in 1947.
41 Beveridge, *On and off the platform*, p. 201.
42 *Executive summary of Sir William Beveridge's report on social insurance and allied services*, November 1942, Cmd 6404 (London: HMSO), www.sochealth.co.uk/history/beveridge.htm (accessed 5 November 2008). See also appendix F, 'Some comparisons with other countries', in William Beveridge, *Social insurance and allied services*, Cmd 6404 (London: HMSO, 1942), pp. 287–93.
43 Beveridge, *On and off the platform*, p. 42.
44 Beveridge, *On and off the platform*, p. 43.
45 *New Zealand Herald* (7 May 1948), p. 8.
46 Beveridge, *On and off the platform*, p. 61. The division between state and Federal governments over health issues continues to this day and is highly contentious.
47 Editorial, *The Sun* (20 May 1948), p. 3. Reporting on Beveridge's lecture on social security at the University of Melbourne, the Melbourne *Argus* led with the quote 'social security means only that everybody can buy bread before anybody can buy cake'. *The Argus* (29 May 1948), p. 1. This was amended in a similar talk given later in Adelaide, where he was quoted as saying 'the State provides the bread, and the individual provides the cake'. See *Adelaide Advertiser* (2 June 1948), p. 3.
48 *New Zealand Herald* (7 May 1948), p. 8. This detailed newspaper report reveals that Beveridge managed to talk about all his pet issues during the address and question time afterwards, including a mention of world government and the unpaid labour of housewives.
49 See ML, Beveridge Papers, M2618, box 429.

50 Indeed in his speech Beveridge stated that New Zealand had no co-operatives at all, so they were not obvious to him. N. Balnave and G. Patmore, '"Practical Utopians": Rochdale Consumer Co-operatives in Australia and New Zealand', *Labour History*, no. 95 (November 2008), pp. 1–14.

51 *Common Wealth* (October–December 1949), p. 2, quoted in Balnave and Patmore, '"Practical Utopians"', p. 11.

52 ML, Beveridge Papers, M2618, box 429, typescript 'Voluntary action for social advance', p. 7.

53 Beveridge, *On and off the platform*, p. 69.

54 Beveridge, *On and off the platform*, p. 72.

55 ML, Beveridge Papers, M2618, box 429, typescript 'Voluntary action for social advance', p. 9. The Plunket Society, formed in 1907 to assist mothers and babies, is the most successful and famous voluntary organisation in New Zealand. For its history, see L. Bryder, *A voice for mothers: the Plunket Society and infant welfare, 1907–2000* (Auckland: Auckland University Press, 2003); M. Oppenheimer, '"Hidden under many bushels": Lady Victoria Plunket and the New Zealand Society for the Health of Women and Children', *New Zealand Journal of History*, vol. 39, no. 1 (April 2005), pp. 22–38; and P. Mein Smith, *Mothers and king baby: infant survival and welfare in an imperial world, Australia 1880–1950* (Basingstoke and London: Macmillan Press, 1997).

56 Beveridge, *On and off the platform*, p. 148.

57 See Tennant, *The Fabric of welfare* and M. Oppenheimer, *Volunteering: why we can't survive without it* (Sydney: UNSW Press, 2008).

58 National Library of Australia (hereafter NLA), Canberra, Papers of Lloyd Ross, MS3939/10/1, extract from a report on the work of the Ministry of Post-War Reconstruction, Community Building, undated (c.1944/45), p. 9.

59 NLA, Canberra, Papers of Lloyd Ross, series 10, Department of Post-War Reconstruction, 1944–49, Community Activities Section, MS 3939/10/5, talk by Lloyd Ross, 27 April [c.1945].

60 See *All work, no pay: Australian civilians in war* (Walcha: Ohio Productions, 2002).

61 For further details of Lloyd Ross and his ventures into voluntary action, see M. Oppenheimer, 'Voluntary action and welfare in post-1945 Australia: preliminary perspectives', *History Australia*, vol. 2, no. 3 (December 2005), pp. 82.1–16.

62 ML, Beveridge Papers, 1921–62, M2617, 66, box 427, letter to Lord Beveridge, 4 February 1949.

63 Beveridge, *Voluntary action*, p. 10.

64 Beveridge, *On and off the platform*, p. 78.

65 *Voluntary action*, p. 322.

66 Indeed, the Beveridges would have arrived back on the momentous day itself except for the martial-law problems with the Suez Canal that delayed them. See Beveridge, *On and off the platform*, p. 7.

67 Type script 'Voluntary action for social advance', pp. 11, 15.

68 A. Giddens, *The third way: renewal of social democracy* (London: Polity Press, 1998).

7

Voluntary politics: the sector's political function from Beveridge to Deakin

James McKay

The voluntary sector is a major player in British politics.[1] Taken cumulatively, its role in training citizens, shaping agendas, influencing governments and delivering services means that it has a right to be considered one of the country's most important political actors. However, the importance of this role is often overlooked, with unfortunate consequences for understanding the nature and extent of voluntarism, on the one hand, and politics, on the other, in contemporary Britain. This chapter seeks to argue for 'voluntary politics', and approaches the task in two ways. Firstly, it will discuss the representations of the political role of the sector in the post-war decades, concentrating on the years between the publications of Beveridge's *Voluntary action* in 1948 and the Deakin Report in 1996.[2] This period has been chosen as a coherent era in voluntary politics. At its start, the establishment of the welfare state under the Attlee government was a decisive turning point in the history of voluntarism, albeit one that can be exaggerated, with much borrowed from what came before.[3] At its end came the era of New Labour and the Compact, marking a major re-evaluation on behalf of government of the socio-political significance of the voluntary sector, and an intention, at least, to give the sector a greater consultative role in the design and implementation of policy.[4] Two themes of the sector's contribution to politics emerged strongly in these years: that it acted as a pioneer of new forms of social welfare, and that, through building up what is now called social capital, it supported the working of the democratic system. Although important, these two functions do not cover the entirety of the sector's political role, and it should also be acknowledged as a direct political actor (or, more properly, an agglomeration of these) helping to fill the void left by the long retreat of the political parties.

Secondly, the chapter considers another interaction between voluntarism and politics, the policing of the political activities of charities, through a review of the annual reports of the Charity Commissioners for England and Wales. Through this, it is shown that the idea that charities are non-political is hard to sustain, being dependent upon a reading of politics that is both narrow and fluid. More broadly, the social implications of their work mean that charities clearly have a political role, which in turn means that their status is frequently politicised. Overall, the chapter will argue that a political function for the voluntary sector clearly exists, albeit as a minority concern for most organisations, and that this function is broader, and more important, than is often allowed for. In doing so, it will not seek to artificially impose a political character onto the sector as a whole, but rather attempt to emphasise that politics, broadly conceived, is one of the many concerns of an extraordinarily diverse collection of causes and organisations.

Three key reasons for the neglect of voluntary politics during the period can be identified. Firstly, the understanding of what constitutes politics in relation to the voluntary sector has conformed to a particularly narrow, if widely recognised, interpretation of the term: 'politics', in this context, denotes party politics and the formal legislative process, with its narrow range of constitutionally sanctioned actors, rather than referring to a broader notion of the political, capable of embracing all those seeking to influence society in some (or any) way, and thus lead us all the way from the politician, via the pressure group, to the protestor and beyond. It is within this more diffuse concept of the political that the sector's influence can be best detected, yet it suffers for contradicting the Westminster–Whitehall paradigm more commonly employed. Secondly, it would be misleading to suggest that political influence is the first concern of the sector as a whole: in the main, the needs and interests of its beneficiary groups are clearly prioritised above wider socio-political engagement (notwithstanding those two goals not being mutually exclusive). Finally, and relating back to the two previous points, there is the effect of terminology. 'Voluntary sector', for example, conjures up an image of professionalised organisations, dedicated to service delivery, and much of the contemporary academic work related to the sector addresses issues of management, funding and performance – central concerns to professionalised organisations. Less-favoured and perhaps more old-fashioned terms, such as 'voluntarism' and 'voluntary action', meanwhile, are more open to possibility and diversity, albeit suffering from the imprecision this brings in its wake. This chapter uses the terms 'voluntarism', 'voluntary action' and 'voluntary sector' interchangeably, and in doing so understands them to encompass social movement organisations, non-governmental organisations and pressure groups, among others. It will also consider charities, a specific legal subset of voluntarism. Cumulatively, these three elements, the definition of politics, the prioritisation of politics, and the terminology of voluntarism, have meant that an important, if minority, function of the voluntary sector, its exercise of political and socio-political influence, has struggled to get the attention it deserves.

The political function of the sector

In his 1948 report, Beveridge presents an image of voluntary action as socially pioneering, with its relationship to the state as part-alternative, part-counterweight and part-complement:

> Voluntary Action is needed to do things which the State should not do, in the giving
> of advice, or in organizing the use of leisure. It is needed to do things which the State
> is most unlikely to do. It is needed to pioneer ahead of the State and make experi-
> ments. It is needed to get services rendered which cannot be got by paying for them.[5]

The role of social leadership is particularly attributed to a select group of pioneering figures within philanthropy, 'the few', as Beveridge calls them (and the potted
biographies of a selection of whom make up an entire chapter of the report): 'There
is always a need for the few – dynamic individuals wholly possessed by this spirit.
They call it forth in others; they create the institutions and societies through which
it acts; they lead by their example'.[6] However, the leadership function of voluntary
action is not simply a matter of inspired individuals. There is a general sense in the
report that within society there is simply so much to do, that one cannot, and should
not, rely solely upon the state; voluntarism is required to ensure the adequate provision of social goods. Furthermore, in his discussion of the friendly societies and
their exclusion from the administration of national insurance under the 1946 Act,
Beveridge goes significantly beyond this notion of complementarity, with his fears
of state incompetence, in comparison to the capabilities of voluntarism, coming
through clearly:

> Will the State be able to create a machine capable of doing what the affiliated orders
> did in the most difficult of all forms of social insurance, of combining soundness with
> sympathy in the administration of cash benefits to the sick? . . . The present rulers of
> the State have lightheartedly taken on a task without as yet having shown understanding
> of its nature.[7]

That said (and even given Beveridge's famous invocation of voluntary action as a
counterpoint to totalitarianism),[8] it would be excessive to claim that he conceptualised it as having a political function *per se*: the notion that there are political implications to voluntary action floats through the text, but the point is never
deliberately made.[9]

Insofar as a political function has been attributed to the sector, it has largely been
done in one of two ways: the contribution of voluntarism to what would now be
called 'social capital', and the pioneering of new forms of social goods and services.
In the case of social capital, Pamela Paxton has pointed out that the theory has a
long and varied ancestry in the literature on democracy and association, with
contributions from writers as diverse as Montesquieu and Habermas.[10] The pre-
cise meaning of the term is of course subject to authorial construction: Bourdieu,
for example, uses it in a way that emphasises social distinction, in concert with economic and cultural capital. Others within the field (whether or not they use the
term) take their lead from the grassroots practicalities famously emphasised by
Tocqueville's *Democracy in America*, and focus on the social skills, relationships and
inclinations, honed in associational life, which serve to support democratic participation, and thus legitimate the political system more generally.[11] In their classic 1960s

study of political culture in Europe and the United States, Almond and Verba high-lighted the significance of high levels of voluntary association to the successful functioning of the democratic system: 'Voluntary associations are the prime means by which the function of mediating between the individual and the state is performed . . . Membership in voluntary associations gives him a more structured set of political resources, growing out of his varied interests'.[12] The importance of the vibrancy of associational life to successful democracies was further emphasised (both in celebration and in warning) by Robert Putnam in the 1990s, and has recently been highlighted in the British context by John Garrard.[13] This line of thought can indeed be seen as a continuing theme for those concerned with voluntarism in Britain. In 1949, during a House of Lords debate on voluntary action, Lord Nathan observed of what he called the 'voluntary services':

> They have been schools in the practice of democracy; in the way in which they have been conducted, they have underpinned many of our democratic organisations, and they have afforded a debating ground where men and women of varied upbringings and different outlooks may find a common basis for associating together and may learn once more how much we are all members one of another.[14]

In a passage in the contribution of voluntarism to a pluralistic political system, the 1978 Wolfenden Report also notes that 'The principal benefits attributed to the voluntary sector in this sense relate mainly to its potential as a means of enabling widespread direct public participation', providing the public with 'experience and skills that enhance their capacity to contribute in roles they fill in other sectors of society'.[15] Moreover, the theme continues in the current century: a 2002 United Kingdom government review of charities and the wider not-for-profit sector remarked that a key aim for the sector was to help it build 'social cohesion and inclu-sion by involving citizens', while a recent white paper from the United Kingdom Department for Communities and Local Government praises local participation for leading to 'increase[d] knowledge about how to influence local decisions'.[16]

The second main representation of the political function of the voluntary sector has been to identify and cater for new needs in society, making use of its advantage of greater flexibility over the state to act as a sort of social pioneer. In this way, the coming of the welfare state served to renew the mission of voluntarism, to act as the vanguard of social care despite recent concerns that the rise of statutory provision was an essentially negative development for voluntarism, in supplanting its social role.[17] In a Commons debate in 1975 on the financial plight of voluntary organ-isations, the Labour MP Frank Hooley remarked that they 'have played a pioneering and experimental role that has often been extremely important in alerting the public to social and political problems over many decades'.[18] A few months later, the Labour Prime Minister, Harold Wilson, picked up the theme, arguing that 'the Welfare State ... does not eliminate the need for private charity, it enhances it, it releases it for those purposes to which it and it alone can make the vital contribution'.[19] Similar sentiments, albeit somewhat less optimistic after the chastening experience of Thatcherism, can also be found in the Deakin Report:

> When tides of change sweep through society as a whole, the contours of voluntary action also shift. When the state advances, the voluntary sector adjusts its role accordingly. When the state retreats and the market advances, as has happened in most advanced Western democracies over the past decade, voluntary organisations adapt their mission, taking a more prominent role in what has come to be called 'the mixed economy of welfare'.[20]

Both the social capital and social pioneering functions are clearly important, yet at the same time they are perhaps best seen as implicitly, rather than explicitly, political. The socio-political context of the later twentieth century suggests that they do not form the sum of voluntarism's political contribution. A further aspect to voluntary politics comes in response to the retreat of the political party. Britain, in common with the rest of the industrialised West, has long been experiencing a crisis of its representative democracy. Combined membership of the two main political parties, which stood at around three million in the early 1960s, halved by 1980, and then halved again by 1998, continuing to fall steadily thereafter – a trend that can be broadly seen across the industrialised world.[21] As people turned away from political parties, electoral participation also fell, with average turnout in OECD states falling by eight percentage points since 1970.[22] In Britain, these two trends came together to mean that governments were elected with declining levels of support from the electorate as a whole, threatening the legitimacy of the political system. Against this backdrop, some scholars have argued that the nature and function of the political party changed over the twentieth century, with an increased emphasis within inter-party competition on competence and managerialism, at the expense of substantive policy difference and mass participation.[23] The role of the party as a dominant forum for citizen action is thus compromised, and this leads to the emergence of pressure groups (often from within the voluntary sector) taking on the vacated role of articulating policy alternatives.[24] This systemic change has taken place in conjunction with wider social changes triggered by rising levels of affluence, education and technological innovation, having the effect of replacing an essentially passive electorate with a more engaged active citizenry, as individuals prioritise the pursuit and support of their own idiosyncratic values above simplistic and deferential support for class-based political blocs.[25]

    This explicitly political contribution of voluntarism has been highlighted by Brian Harrison.[26] It can be illustrated with reference to the rise of environmentalism, and the crucial role played by the voluntary organisations (in this context, more commonly labelled pressure groups, social movement organisations or non-governmental organisations) that make up much of the environmental movement. Scholars have noted the startling rise of the environment up the political agenda in the period since the 1970s, with credit often being attributed to the work of environmental organisations in achieving this policy saliency.[27] The emergence of organisations with environmental concerns became increasingly pronounced in the period since the late 1960s, with the formation of groups such as the British Trust for Conservation Volunteers (1970), Friends of the Earth (England and Wales) (1971), the Life Style Movement (1974), Greenpeace UK (1977) and the Green Alliance (1979). A particular burst of activity came in the years 1989–91, which saw the establishment of more than a dozen environmental bodies, ranging from 'traditional' conservation groups like Plantlife International (1989) and the Bat Conservation Trust (1990), to those organisations specifically dealing more generally with the impact of humanity on the environment, such as Tourism Concern (1989), the Rainforest Foundation UK (1989) and the Optimum Population Trust (1991), as well as groups at the forefront of the United Kingdom transport controversies of the 1990s, such as Earth First! (1991) and Alarm UK (1991). That this organisational peak (along with the steady growth in the previous two decades) preceded a high point of political saliency for the environmental issue within the Labour and Conservative parties (seen at the 1992 general election), and that it came following the historic peak of British public concern with environmentalism at the end of the 1980s, is suggestive of the role such organisations play in articulating emergent political concerns, acting as an indirect channel between the citizenry and the political elite.[28] As concerns over emergent issues develop, people come together to form proselytising groups in order to express and explore them, and in doing so, pressurise the political elite to act. Voluntary action is therefore a key political actor, through the articulation of new priorities.

None of the preceding should be taken as a claim that the voluntary sector has adopted the mantle of political leadership. The Deakin Report rightly argued that the sector could not be seen as coherently political, and attempts to cast it 'as a kind of standing "people's opposition" [would] founder on the wide range of organisations that exist for quite different reasons . . . voluntary organisations in modern societies march to the sounds of an infinite number of different drummers – and not necessarily all in the same direction'.[29] Equally, evidence from the Charity Commission can be taken as suggesting that political action is low down in the priorities of the sector as a whole.[30] That said, one does not need to provide evidence of a unified political programme, or find a politicised majority, to argue for the sector's influence in this area: the role of the sector in providing a non-party, political public space is crucial, as Helen McCarthy has argued for the inter-war period.[31] As a recent report notes, 'Campaigning is neither the only course of action available to civil society, nor uniformly the best . . . But [it] remains a distinctive reminder of popular sovereignty, and the power of unity collective social action can generate'.[32]

Politics and charities

Charities form a particular, privileged sub-set of the voluntary sector. In recognition of their pursuit of certain objectives, specified by law, they accrue the considerable financial (and reputational) benefits that come with charitable status.[33] One of the costs that come with these benefits is the requirement to ensure that their activities are non-political. Overseeing this requirement was (and is) the responsibility of the Charity Commissioners for England and Wales.[34] Therefore, by examining the role of the commissioners, through their annual reports, one is able to access a significant interaction between voluntarism and politics. Here, politics was narrowly defined as seeking to influence political parties and/or the legislature, as a way of securing changes in (or maintenance of existing) law and policy. A line was also drawn between propaganda (not permissible) and education (permissible), provided of course that such education did not simply focus on informing the public of one particular set of political principles.[35] Therefore, a charity might quite properly submit comments to a government consultation exercise, or provide MPs with information pertaining to a forthcoming debate, but would be on much more treacherous terrain if seeking to promote its own changes in the law, and would need to ensure that it was acting in a way 'merely ancillary' to its (non-political) charitable purposes. Ultimately, if charities were to 'stray into the field of political activity', the charity's trustees would be acting in breach of trust, bringing with it the potential for legal proceedings to recoup funds improperly spent.[36]

There was no shortage of justifications for such restrictions to be placed upon charities, in return for the benefits their status provided. A principal argument turned on it being impossible to judge whether proposed changes in law and policy would be in the public interest, as any benefits that might accrue would be speculative at that point.[37] The process by which charitable definitions had been developed over the centuries, through the accumulation of case law, also brought with it constitutional implications – specifically, that in deciding upon such cases, the judiciary would be in danger of compromising its impartiality, and, more generally, that to allow charities to pursue political objectives would be to undermine the role of the legislature.[38] Understandably, given the narrow drawing of what constituted 'political', it was also argued that such activity would inevitably associate charities with political parties.[39] Perhaps most persuasive, however, was the argument that in engaging politically, charities risked the public goodwill and privileges upon which their collective future depended. The Charity Commissioners made the following comment in their report for 1969:

> . . . we think it should also be borne in mind that if charities step outside the sphere of activities to which the law confines them they may not only prejudice the support they receive from some people, who could resent the new activities, but they may also eventually endanger the privileged position which charities as a whole have been accorded by the state.[40]

Charities benefited from, even depended upon, the public's 'spontaneous desire to give', but this desire in turn rested upon the understanding that recipient causes were uncontroversially good, in a way in which (party) political causes could never hope to be.[41] As the Deakin Report noted for the wider voluntary sector, 'if the sector wishes to continue to be judged favourably in "the court of public opinion", it needs to be aware that its claims to virtue will not go unscrutinised'.[42]

For all the justifications, attacks upon the restrictions were not unknown. One of the most strident came from Ben Whitaker in 1976, in his minority report that emerged out of the Goodman inquiry into charity law. In stark contrast to the consensus-orientated traditionalism of the majority report, Whitaker was driven to sweep away the contradictions cluttering up charity law, even those legitimated by 'dead hands from the grave'.[43] This involved both redefining charity as 'the prevention and relief of deprivation' (with the proviso that benefits provided should be available to all) and abolishing the political restrictions.[44] These were only partly applied in any case, Whitaker argued, with religious organisations at liberty to promote their 'beliefs and propaganda' with the benefit of public subsidy, while the same was denied their secular competitors.[45] However, this was not a proposal based upon righting an injustice, but rather ensuring the efficacy of the sector, it being 'not only the right but in fact the duty of charities in many areas to act as political pressure groups . . . The days of confining charities to pouring soup into faulty old bottles should be consigned to the past'. Given the spending power of the state, the best way for charities to secure their objectives was to lobby the Leviathan: using the example of the British government's £20 million cut in overseas aid in 1966, Whitaker pointed out that this was a sum greater than the total spending of Oxfam since its formation in 1942, and raised the suggestion that if, instead of providing assistance, 'Oxfam concentrated on education, propaganda and political pressure in Britain . . . vastly more "poverty, distress and suffering" would be relieved overseas'.[46]

Complementary cases have been made elsewhere. Eleanor Burt, in a 1998 article, argued that 'Voluntary organisations can fulfil their responsibilities as part of the fabric of modern democratic society only if the current restrictions governing political activity are ended'.[47] Similarly, during the 1975 Commons debate on voluntary organisations, Frank Hooley identified the political restrictions on charities as the 'major defect' in the regulatory regime: subject to oversight, tax advantages should be available to all voluntary organisations 'which have an important contribution to make to our social life in putting forward ideas, studies and thoughts'.[48] The Charity Commissioners reported that the regulations brought complaints from the sector, both from registered charities feeling they were too restrictive, and from organisations with 'a political bias', protesting against decisions not to register them.[49] The restrictions were also 'a frequent issue in the evidence submitted to the [Deakin] Commission'.[50]

In response to these criticisms, the Charity Commissioners protested that they were only doing their job. Their role was to see that the current law was adhered to: changes to the law were the responsibility of the legislature, and its interpretation was down to the judiciary. During their report for 1971, the commissioners felt it necessary to point out that their guidance was 'simply a statement of what we understand the present law to be ... the law is, of course, what it is, and we cannot change it by saying it means something different'.[51] The law clearly stated that 'no organisation whose objects include a political purpose can be accorded charitable status'.[52] Further, in enforcing this, the commissioners insisted that they should not be seen as taking sides: 'Our task is not one of social, moral or political judgement: the question is not whether the activities in questions should be carried out, but whether they can properly be carried out by a charity'.[53]

Enforcing the political restrictions was clearly a task taken seriously by the commissioners. Perhaps the foremost example of this was action taken against the international development charity War on Want. During the late 1970s, the organisation sought 'to move away from the traditional forms of relief and to concentrate on overcoming the causes of poverty', through research, campaigns and publications exploring the social, political and economic roots of the problem. In the course of this shift, the commissioners felt that the charity undertook activities that 'lay outside the legitimate scope of the charitable field', and were thus incompatible with charitable status.[54] Subsequently, a separate, non-charitable body, WOW Campaigns Ltd, was established, but this failed to solve the problem. In 1981, War on Want (rather than its campaigning arm) launched an anti-poverty campaign in Labour party colours, with support from party members and trade unionists. This, the commissioners felt, went 'well beyond what was permissible'. The charity responded by explaining it was 'experiencing teething troubles' in its working relationship with WOW Campaigns, and assured the commissioners that it 'would refrain in future from impermissible political activities'.[55] This was by no means the only example of the commissioners enforcing the political restrictions. Other high-profile cases included investigations into Oxfam (in 1978 and 1991) and a long-running process focussing on the commissioners' refusal to register the Amnesty International Trust.[56] Despite the impeccably progressive nature of these causes, the commissioners were clearly politically even-handed in their defence of principle. In 1982, they found against the British Atlantic Committee (BAC) for having issued leaflets designed to counter the arguments of the Campaign for Nuclear Disarmament, which resulted in BAC deciding to establish a non-charitable arm for such purposes.[57] In 1976, the commissioners found in favour of the Family Planning Association (FPA), in the face of an attack on the FPA's charitable status launched by the parliamentary all-party Family and Child Protection Group.[58]

With the commissioners defining 'politics' as seeking to influence parties or parliament, charities were subject to a fluid system. Legislative action was assumed (perhaps erroneously) to turn controversial subjects into broadly accepted elements of British socio-political life. Accordingly, new laws transformed previously forbidden activities into perfectly proper charitable endeavours. This was true of the FPA, whose stance that advice on contraception should be provided to unmarried men and women was deemed problematic until the passing of the 1967 National Health Service (Family Planning) Act, which accepted 'such a service for unmarried people as being for the benefit of the community', and thereby expanded the commissioners' notion of what was permissible.[59] A similar process can be seen with race relations. Charity case law from the 1940s suggested that promoting racial harmony was not a charitable objective. However, by the 1980s the commissioners were confident that 'the question . . . [was] no longer a political one as legislation had been passed in an attempt to enforce good race relations'. Ultimately, this came back to the public benefit argument. Political objects could not be charitable, as public benefit was seen as impossible to judge. In cases such as these, however, 'The nation, through Parliament, has already decided that it is for the public benefit and the matter has ceased to be political'.[60] As well as the boundary between permissible and impermissible activities being subject to change, the commissioners admitted that the rules were not applied evenly to all organisations. In their report for 1973, mention was made of the complaint of some bodies which had been refused registration because their objects were too political, that the same could be said about bodies safely on the register. This, the commissioners explained, was a result of a government decision during the passage of what became the 1960 Charities Act, to treat existing charities 'sympathetically' when they came to register under the new regime. Because of this, 'Many organisations . . . were in fact registered without too close a scrutiny of their objects' and, once on the register, were given 'the benefit of the doubt'.[61]

Given the nature of their work in dealing with often sensitive social issues, it is perhaps inevitable that the work and privileged status of particular charities should in itself be politicised from time to time. The 1981 War on Want case, discussed above, was itself triggered by complaints from MPs.[62] Five years earlier, the commissioners commented that they 'continue to receive some complaints about the activities of a few charities which are alleged to be engaging in political activities or propaganda . . . Most of the criticisms received recently have related to family planning, abortion and anti-smoking'.[63] The issue reached a particularly high political salience in 1983, when the Attorney General issued guidance to student unions reminding them of their duty not to use their charitable funds for political purposes. This came shortly after one student union had approached the commissioners asking for guidance on the legality of their printing 'leaflets for distribution to students urging them to vote for a particular political party in the forthcoming General Election'.[64]

Conclusion

The voluntary sector has a major and multi-faceted political role, which includes pioneering new causes and services, nurturing the development of social capital and direct political intervention. Even in the case of supposedly non-political charities, there are also clear political dimensions, notwithstanding the narrow drawing of 'politics' under charity law: their role is politicised, and the list of things they can and cannot do can be shown to have been both historically fluid and unevenly applied.

However, in order to grasp fully the political contribution of the sector, the best thing might be not to break it down into its component parts, but rather to broaden out one's concept of the political, and embrace in its entirety the rolling, heterogeneous social and political challenge that the sector poses. Exemplified by, but by no means restricted to, the 1960s, this looks to the sector's championing of what has been called 'do-it-yourself politics'.[65] The leading example is perhaps the work of the poverty lobby within the context of the rediscovery of poverty.[66] Here, new organisations such as Shelter (1966), Crisis (1967), the Child Poverty Action Group (1965), Gingerbread (1970) and the Disablement Income Group (1965) drew attention in different ways to the failings of the welfare state, and set about fixing them. This is a pattern that can be seen time and again in the history of the sector. On issues as diverse as environmentalism, homelessness, racial equality, gay rights, single parenthood and older people, to name just a few, the sector played a crucial role in shaping the social and political agenda, often leaving politicians running to catch up. To neglect this, to allow it to be obscured by the Westminster–Whitehall political paradigm, not only does an injustice to the breadth of the sector's role in British life; it also does an avoidable injury to our understanding of the diversity of politics in the twentieth century.

Notes

1 This chapter emerges out of the work of the Leverhulme-funded project 'Non-governmental organisations in Britain, 1945–1997' at the University of Birmingham (www.ngo.bham.ac.uk), grant number F00094AV, Principal Investigator Professor Matthew Hilton. I would particularly like to thank my colleague Jean-François Mouhot for his assistance.

2 W. Beveridge, *Voluntary action: a report on methods of social advance* (London: George Allen & Unwin, 1948); Commission on the Future of the Voluntary Sector, *Meeting the challenge of change: voluntary action into the 21st century. The report of the commission on the future of the voluntary sector* (London: NCVO Publications, 1996).

3 G. Finlayson, 'A moving frontier: voluntarism and the state in British social welfare', *Twentieth-Century British History*, vol. 1 (1990), pp. 183–206; D. Marquand, *Britain since 1918: the strange career of British democracy* (London: Weidenfeld & Nicolson, 2008), p. 107.

4 J. Lewis, 'New Labour's approach to the voluntary sector: independence and the meaning of partnership', *Social Policy and Society*, vol. 4, no. 2 (2005), pp. 121–31.

5 Beveridge, *Voluntary action*, pp. 301–2.

6 Beveridge, *Voluntary action*, p. 154.

7 Beveridge, *Voluntary action*, p. 84.

8 See Chapter 3 above, by Nicholas Deakin.

9 Beveridge, *Voluntary action*, p. 10.

10 P. Paxton, 'Social capital and democracy: an interdependent relationship', *American Sociological Review*, vol. 67 (2002), p. 254.

11 Alexis de Tocqueville, *Democracy in America* [1835, 1840], trans. H. Reeve, ed. H. S. Commanger (Oxford: Oxford University Press, 1946). See especially chapters 11 and 25.

12 G. Almond and S. Verba, *The civic culture: political attitudes and democracy in five nations* (Princeton, NJ: Princeton University Press, 1963), pp. 300–1.

13 For the importance of associational life to democracy, see R. Putnam, *Making democracy work: civic traditions in modern Italy* (Princeton, NJ: Princeton University Press, 1993), pp. 91–9. For his account of the crisis of association in recent United States history, see R. Putnam, 'Bowling alone: America's declining social capital', *Journal of Democracy*, vol. 6 (1995), pp. 65–78. See also J. Garrard, *Democratisation in Britain: elites, civil society and reform since 1800* (Basingstoke: Palgrave, 2002), pp. 5–7, 9.

14 House of Lords debates, 5th series, vol. 163, cols 89–90, 22 June 1949.

15 Committee on Voluntary Organisations, *The future of voluntary organisations: report of the Wolfenden Committee* (London: Croom Helm, 1978), p. 29.

16 Prime Minister's Strategy Unit, *Private action, public benefit: a review of charities and the wider not-for-profit sector* (London: Prime Minister's Strategy Unit, 2002), p. 32; Department for Communities and Local Government, *Communities in control: real people, real power* (London: Department for Communities and Local Government, 2008), pp. 44–5.

17 Cf. F. Prochaska, *Christianity and social service in modern Britain: the disinherited spirit* (Oxford: Oxford University Press, 2000), pp. 150–2.

18 House of Commons debates, 5th series, vol. 895, cols 372–3, 8 July 1975.

19 Harold Wilson speaking to the National Council of Social Services, 10 December 1975. Quoted in Lord Goodman, *Charity law and voluntary organisations: report of an independent committee of inquiry set up by the National Council of Social Service, under the chairmanship of Lord Goodman, to examine the effect of charity law and practice on voluntary organisations* (London: National Council of Social Service, 1976), p. 10.

20 *Meeting the challenge of change*, p. 15.

21 P. Mair and I. van Biezen, 'Party membership in twenty European democracies, 1980–2000', *Party Politics*, vol. 7, no. 1 (2001), pp. 5–21; R. Katz, P. Mair et al., 'The membership of political parties in European democracies, 1960–1990', *European Journal of Political Research*, vol. 22 (1992), pp. 329–45.

22 C. Hay, *Why we hate politics* (Cambridge: Polity, 2007), p. 13.

23 R. Katz and P. Mair, 'Changing models of party organization and party democracy: the emergence of the cartel party', *Party Politics*, vol. 1, no. 1 (1995), pp. 5–28; M. Blyth and R. Katz, 'From catch-all parties to cartelisation: the political economy of the Cartel Party', *West European Politics*, vol. 28, no. 1 (2005), pp. 33–60.

24 Katz and Mair, 'Changing models of party organization', p. 23.

25 R. Inglehart, *The silent revolution: changing values and political styles among Western publics* (Princeton, NJ: Princeton University Press, 1977), pp. 3–18.

26 B. Harrison, 'Civil society by accident? Paradoxes of voluntarism and pluralism in the nineteenth and twentieth centuries', in J. Harris (ed.), *Civil society in British history: ideas, identities, institutions* (Oxford: Oxford University Press, 2003), pp. 88–9. Harrison's analysis is, it should be noted, considerably less sanguine than that presented here.

27 See, for example, H. A. van der Heijden, 'Political opportunity structure and the Institutionalisation of the environmental movement', *Environmental Politics*, vol. 6,

no. 4 (1997), pp. 25–6, and N. Carter, *The politics of the environment: ideas, activism, policy*, 2nd edn (Cambridge: Cambridge University Press, 2007), pp. 1–2.

28 Assessments of political saliency are drawn from the data of the work of the Comparative Manifestos Project. See Ian Budge et al., *Mapping policy preferences: estimates for parties, electors and governments 1945–1998* (Oxford: Oxford University Press, 2001), and Hans-Dieter Klingermann et al., *Mapping policy preferences II: estimates for parties, electors, and governments in Central and Eastern Europe, European Union and OECD 1990–2003* (Oxford: Oxford University Press, 2006). Assessments on public concern are drawn from MORI's regular 'most important issue' polling; see www.ipsos-mori.com/researchspecialisms/socialresearch/specareas/politics/trends.aspx (accessed 13 May 2010).

29 *Meeting the challenge of change*, p. 15.

30 During 1993, of those investigations conducted by the commission which substantiated initial concerns, only 3 per cent dealt with political activities: Charity Commission, *Report of the Charity Commissioners for England & Wales for 1993* (London: Charity Commission, 1994). More generally, its 1978 report felt that the legal restrictions on political activity would present 'no difficulty to the very great majority of charities'. *Report of the Charity Commissioners 1978* (London: Charity Commission, 1979).

31 H. McCarthy, 'Parties, voluntary associations and democratic politics in interwar Britain', *Historical Journal*, vol. 50, no. 4 (2007), pp. 891–912.

32 P. Hilder, J. Caulier-Grice and K. Lalor, *Contentious citizens: civil society's role in campaigning for social change* (London: Young Foundation, 2007), p. 7. The phrase 'civil society' is of course multi-faceted, but in this context was used in a way that was congruent with concepts of voluntarism and social action.

33 The list of admissible charitable purposes, until the 2006 Charities Act, was ultimately derived from the list in the preamble to the 1601 Statute of Charitable Uses, as developed through case law, and rationalised into four 'Heads of Charity' by Lord Macnaghten in the 1891 Pemsel case. See *Charity law and voluntary organisations*, pp. 7–8.

34 The current regime, it is worth pointing out, is considerably more liberal than that described in this chapter, with an emphasis upon the range of political activity that charities can legitimately undertake. See Charity Commission, *CC9: Speaking out: guidance on campaigning and political activity by charities* (London: Charity Commission, 2008).

35 *Report of the Charity Commissioners 1981* (London: Charity Commission, 1982).

36 *Report of the Charity Commissioners 1969* (London: Charity Commission, 1970).

37 *Charity law and voluntary organisations*, p. 41.

38 A. Dunn, 'Charity law as a political option for the poor', *Northern Ireland Legal Quarterly*, vol. 50, no. 3 (1999), pp. 298–9.

39 *Charity law and voluntary organisations*, p. 44.

40 *Report of the Charity Commissioners 1969*.

41 The phrase comes from *Charity law and voluntary organisations*, p. 7.

42 *Meeting the challenge of change*, p. 35.

43 *Charity law and voluntary organisations*, p. 143.

44 *Charity law and voluntary organisations*, p. 145.

45 *Charity law and voluntary organisations*, p. 146.

46 *Charity law and voluntary organisations*, pp. 148–9.

47 Eleanor Burt, 'Charities and political activity: time to re-think the rules', *Political Quarterly*, vol. 69, no. 1 (1998), pp. 29–30.

48 House of Commons debates, 5th series, vol. 895, cols 372–3, 8 July 1975.

49 *Report of the Charity Commissioners 1973* (London: Charity Commission, 1974).

50 *Meeting the challenge of change*, p. 87.

51 *Report of the Charity Commissioners 1971* (London: Charity Commission, 1972).

52 *Report of the Charity Commissioners 1991* (London: Charity Commission, 1992).

53 *Report of the Charity Commissioners 1978*.

54 *Report of the Charity Commissioners 1978*.

55 *Report of the Charity Commissioners 1981*. A further major investigation followed a decade later, identifying 'many grave deficiencies in the administration of the charity', including misleading accounts, failure to recover money owed to the charity by related organisations and 'other serious failings of management and financial control'. *Report of the Charity Commissioners 1991*.

56 For details of the Oxfam cases, see *Report of the Charity Commissioners 1978* and *Report of the Charity Commissioners 1991*; for Amnesty, see *Report of the Charity Commissioners 1978* and *Report of the Charity Commissioners 1981*.

57 *Report of the Charity Commissioners 1982* (London: Charity Commission, 1983).

58 *Report of the Charity Commissioners 1976* (London: Charity Commission, 1977).

59 *Report of the Charity Commissioners 1969*.

60 *Report of the Charity Commissioners 1983* (London: Charity Commission, 1984).

61 *Report of the Charity Commissioners 1973*.

62 *Report of the Charity Commissioners 1981*.

63 *Report of the Charity Commissioners 1976*.

64 *Report of the Charity Commissioners 1983*.

65 Jim Radford's phrase, quoted in S. Rowbotham, 'Introduction', in H. Curtis and M. Sanderson (eds), *The unsung sixties: memoirs of social innovation* (London: Whiting & Birch, 2004), p. x.

66 See T. Evans, 'Stopping the poor getting poorer: the establishment and professionalisation of poverty NGOs, 1945–1995', in N. Crowson, M. Hilton and J. McKay (eds), *NGOs in contemporary Britain: non-state actors in society and politics since 1945* (Basingstoke: Palgrave Macmillan), 2009, pp. 147–63.

8

Youth in action? British young people and voluntary service, 1958–70

Georgina Brewis

Introduction

One of the most significant changes in volunteering policy and practice in Britain in the sixty years since William Beveridge published *Voluntary action* has been the growth in organised volunteer schemes for young people, particularly overseas volunteer programmes. Beveridge noted that participation in voluntary activities should start young, suggesting, 'service *of* youth should be directed into service *by* youth'.[1] Such encouragement places Beveridge in a long tradition of advocacy of voluntary service as part of education, which continues today.[2] In particular, since the late 1990s the British government has sought to encourage 'active citizenship' through citizenship education in schools and numerous new schemes to promote domestic and international volunteering by young people. Indeed, a review produced for the Commission on the Future of Volunteering, which reported in 2008, suggests that 'the current weight of expectation about the contribution [volunteering] can make to individual development, social cohesion and addressing social need has never been greater'.[3]

Although researchers have shown interest in youth volunteering, overseas service and the 'gap year' in recent years, this growing literature lacks a rigorous historical interpretation of young people's service at home or abroad.[4] This chapter is intended as a contribution to this literature and suggests that voluntary service by young people has been presented as a palliative to perceived societal ills at a number of periods in modern British history.[5] The chapter will identify and discuss key features of what has been called a youth 'volunteer boom' in the period 1958–70.[6] It begins by examining continuities and changes in patterns of youth volunteering before and after the Second World War. It then discusses the context in which new models of volunteering emerged and were presented as safe and constructive outlets for members of a post-war generation perceived to be a threat to the established order.[7] The chapter ends with a discussion of the challenges facing youth volunteering in the 1950s and 1960s, particularly the underlying tension between effective service and educative function.

Service by youth: continuities and changes

In 1966 the MP Frank Judd concluded that the previous decade had seen a change in emphasis from 'service for youth to service by youth'.[8] The emphasis on new forms of community and overseas service in the 1960s has led the continuities with pre-war voluntary action to be underplayed. From the late nineteenth century secondary and higher education in Britain was underpinned by an ethic of service. In an era in which most people did not receive post-elementary schooling, the service ideal drew on the Platonic notion of educated talent in the service of society.[9] In the period 1890–1914 new-found anxieties about adolescence were reflected in the formation of youth organisations which enlisted large numbers of middle- and upper-class young people in the service of others. Participation in voluntary service was felt to have an educative function for young people and to bring opport- unities for self-realisation and character development.[10] Schools and colleges involved students in a wide range of activities under a broad heading of 'social service', which included practical support for missions, clubs and settlements in working-class districts of towns and cities. In addition, dozens of independent social service leagues and guilds for young people flourished, although such groups as the Girl's Realm Guild of Service, Time and Talents, the Girls' Diocesan Association, the Agenda Club and the Cavendish Association have been largely forgotten. The formation of a range of boys' and girls' clubs, brigades and uniformed associations opened new opportunities for the tens of thousands of mainly young people who volunteered as brigade officers, club leaders and instructors. It was largely through this array of voluntary associations, rather than any formal citizenship education, that students at schools, colleges and universities were made aware that the privi- leges of education carried social obligations. Indeed, the many social study circles and clubs which accompanied practical service may be seen as an early form of cit- izenship education. After the Second World War, despite the new provisions of the welfare state, many such older traditions of service continued. Throughout the 1950s and 1960s traditional voluntary activities continued in many schools and colleges, while opportunities for service remained with the cadets of the St John Ambulance or Red Cross and as volunteers for the Scout and Guide Associations or the Boys' Brigade.[11] Likewise older causes such as settlements and missions retained support into the 1960s, although the nature of young people's support was changing. For example, in 1968, pupils at 121 girls' schools across the country continued to support the Union of Girls' Schools for Social Service Settlement in Peckham, established in 1896.[12]

Developing patterns of service

Despite these continuities, the late 1950s and the 1960s were marked by significant developments in youth volunteering as young people began to seek new expressions for the service ideal. For example, the demand for service opportunities was partly met through the expansion of work-camps as a strand of European reconstruction in the decade following the Second World War. Work-camps were a form of service developed in the inter-war period in which volunteers – often from different countries – worked as a group to complete a practical project.[13] After about 1955 voluntary associations which organised work-camps – including International Voluntary Service (IVS), the National Union of Students (NUS) and the United Nations Association (UNA) – reported a significant increase in applications for service at home and on the European continent.[14] Typical work-camp activities included building and decorating projects, gardening, fruit picking and farm work. At the same time, some of these groups began to extend their work to developing countries, in line with a new recognition that current and former European colonies needed skilled manpower alongside capital investment.[15] In 1957 Britain was supplying 2,500 technical assistance experts to developing countries, and the novel suggestion that some middle-level roles might be filled by young volunteers was gaining acceptance.[16] IVS, for instance, began to send skilled volunteers on development projects to Ghana.[17] In 1958 two experimental schemes sent small numbers of school-leaver volunteers to other parts of the British Commonwealth, one run by the British Council and the other by the newly formed Voluntary Service Overseas (VSO).[18] VSO had been founded by Alec Dickson of the Royal Commonwealth Society and drew financial support from Inter-Church Aid (later Christian Aid) as well as public funding through the Colonial Development and Welfare Fund.[19] Dickson, who was well known by the late 1950s for his colonial citizenship and leadership training schemes, identified a desire among British youth for 'adventurous service' in places of real need.

Alongside this growing interest in overseas volunteering was an emphasis on new forms of 'community service' by young people in Britain.[20] Service was a central component of the Duke of Edinburgh's Award Scheme, started in 1956.[21] From the early 1960s enthusiastic teachers and youth workers sought to direct young people's idealism into new volunteer programmes.[22] Many believed that social service by young people had an inherent value at a time when adolescence was being connected with social problems. Others wanted to demonstrate that young people's voluntary service was still needed in Britain even when the state had thrown its mantle over so many of the services previously provided by school missions and settlements.[23] Interest and enthusiasm were sustained through conferences organised by the National Council of Social Service (NCSS) and the Headmasters' Conference. The youth service programmes which emerged in the 1960s were mainly aimed at helping specific demographic groups: visiting, gardening, decorating or shopping for old or disabled people.[24] These new schemes developed at a period when older charitable visiting societies, previously staffed by tens of thousands of middle-class women volunteers, were in terminal decline.[25] From 1958 Alec Dickson had been setting up three- to twelve-month placements for young volunteers in the United Kingdom, a scheme formalised as Community Service Volunteers (CSV) in 1962.[26] At the same time IVS developed a similar 'medium-term' volunteer programme.

The late 1950s and early 1960s marked a period of unprecedented attention on young people as concerns about the potentially disruptive nature of British youth were repeatedly raised by political and social commentators.[27] Echoing concerns which had preoccupied club leaders since the late nineteenth century, the so-called 'unattached' youth – a boy or girl who was not in education or a member of any club or organisation – was identified as especially problematic.[28] The period between boys leaving school at fifteen and entering National Service at eighteen was also seen as a challenging 'gap' to be bridged by participation in schemes such as the Duke of Edinburgh's Award. In a period of increasing affluence, concerns centred on young people's use of their increased leisure time and disposable income.[29] Thus the 1959 Conservative Party manifesto recognised the 'challenge to make the growth of leisure more purposeful and constructive, especially for young people'.[30] Paraphrasing President Kennedy, R. A. Butler noted in 1961, 'it will be wise to think of, not only of what this country can do for its young people, but what these young people can be expected to do for their country'.[31] Many in authority began to recognise the potential of volunteering for channelling youthful energies and idealism into constructive outlets, both at home and abroad. Lady Albemarle's review into the Youth Service in England and Wales, which reported in 1960, argued for a reformed and enlarged service able to engage more young people in adventurous opportunities, skills development and service to the community.[32] A number of long-established youth associations, including the Girl Guide Association, Boys' Brigade, Young Women's Christian Association and London Union of Youth Clubs, undertook reviews of their programmes in the early 1960s, and several such reports recommended creating more practical opportunities for service.[33] Overseas service was particularly valued for providing outlets for responsibility and adventure that young Britons had previously found in empire. Such concerns came to the fore as National Service was wound up between 1957 and 1960.[34] Commentators such as the sociologist Michael Young and the NCSS Director George Haynes proposed increasing opportunities for international voluntary service.[35] In 1958 the Colonial Office set up a committee chaired by Sir Gerald Templar to investigate the idea of a 'Commonwealth Youth Trust' which would promote 'inter-racial friendship and service to the community' among young people of the Commonwealth. The committee's report in July 1959 recommended government support for a new scheme for up to 1,000 young volunteers to be called the 'Queen's Commonwealth Volunteers'.[36]

The development of long-term volunteer programmes needs to be seen in the context of an international movement for technical assistance as well as ongoing reforms to the British overseas civil service, topics which were the subject of several White Papers and reports between 1959 and 1964.[37] Enthusiasm for a period of service overseas had strong historical precedent, and British traditions of imperial and missionary service were routinely invoked by organisers of the new programmes in their early days.[38] In fact British missionary societies continued to provide many openings for overseas service: in 1962 there were 4,500 British missionaries serving in developing countries, two thirds of whom were involved in medical, educational, agricultural and secretarial work.[39] In 1963 there were 18,000 government-supported British people working in developing countries, through the Overseas Aid Service Scheme and other initiatives such as the Anglo-American Teachers for East Africa programme.[40] By the early 1960s long-term volunteering had emerged as a key strand in this broader overseas service agenda, in part thanks to President Kennedy's championing of volunteering and his high-profile Peace Corps scheme.[41] The establishment of the Peace Corps stimulated renewed interest in a government-backed British scheme in 1961, although Templar's proposals had been shelved.[42]

In 1961 and 1962 students at several universities began to develop their own programmes in response to a perceived lack of opportunities for graduate-level volunteers.[43] Such plans were superseded by the Macmillan government's announcement in May 1962 that the Department of Technical Co-operation would part-finance a graduate volunteer programme.[44] A unique feature of the British scheme was the co-operation of autonomous volunteer-sending agencies co-ordinated by a committee chaired by Sir John Lockwood, Master of Birkbeck College. NCSS provided a secretariat, and government contributed half the operating costs of the programme, although host countries were expected to cover volunteers' board, lodging and pocket money. The initial sending agencies were VSO, IVS, the United Nations Association for International Service, the NUS and the Scottish Union of Students. The Catholic Institute for International Relations (formerly Sword of the Spirit) joined the scheme in 1965, and the NUS ceased sending volunteers in 1966.[45] These sending organisations welcomed government finance but remained wary of potential political interference.[46]

In the 1960s voluntary service overseas was a subject on which there was considerable cross-party support, although this did not prevent it becoming an arena for political point-scoring.[47] A Conservative Party report in 1963 strongly urged expansion of the scheme:

> We hear much about the corrosive effects of material affluence. Yet amongst our young people there is a widespread and growing desire to give service to others . . . it would be a devastating condemnation of our society if we left a void and did not try to provide them with challenge and opportunity.[48]

In February 1964, towards the end of the Conservative Party's thirteen years in office, the government announced that funding would increase to cover 75 per cent of the scheme's costs and allow a considerable increase in volunteer numbers.[49] However, it was the new Labour government who, in line with a manifesto commitment to increase overseas aid, set up the Overseas Development Ministry which oversaw the expansion of what became known as the 'British Volunteer Programme'.[50] Government remained sceptical about using volunteers as replacements for technical experts but welcomed volunteers as the human face of development assistance. However, Jef Smith, Vice-Chair of IVS, identified the danger of young volunteers damaging the overall aid programme by stealing the limelight.[51] Indeed between 1964 and 1970, despite a falling aid budget, the British Volunteer Programme remained a well-publicised, though largely symbolic, aspect of Labour's overseas aid commitments.[52] Government support for volunteering in a period of rapid social change at home and decolonisation abroad was part of a need to find new roles for British youth. In the 1960s local authorities began to make public money available to support volunteering and community service at home through councils of social service, schools or the Youth Service. Anthony Steen, for example, drew in funding for his projects with older people – later known as Task Force – from Youth Service departments, which saw young people's volunteering as service for youth.[53] By 1970 around forty local councils of social service in England had started what were known as 'youth action schemes' in partnership with schools, colleges and youth clubs.[54]

Funding commitments brought desire for greater knowledge and understanding of the phenomenon of youth volunteering, and this was considered by several government committees in the 1960s. Under the influence of the Newsom Report (1963) state schools came to see the provision of service opportunities as part of their role.[55] In the long-running debate over raising the school-leaving age to sixteen, community service was repeatedly put forward as a potentially constructive activity to fill the timetables of pupils 'of less than average intelligence' or a 'restive' nature who would be expected to stay on longer at school.[56] However, timetabled or compulsory service was felt by some to be a rejection of the 'voluntary' concept, and some educationalists objected to the approach of 'dragooning' young people into service.[57] The Bessey Committee, appointed in 1965 to draw up a possible scheme for co-ordination of service by young people, was positive about the all-round desirability of young people's service to the community.[58] As a result of such confidence in the potential of volunteering, in 1968 £100,000 of government money was allocated to a new Young Volunteer Force Foundation in order to involve even greater numbers of young people.

Challenges facing youth volunteering in the 1960s

Despite widespread public and government support for young people's service in the 1960s, youth volunteering programmes faced numerous challenges. The difficulty of matching suitable volunteers with appropriate tasks was common to all programmes. A lack of survey data makes it difficult to quantify what many reports judged to be a 'spectacular' upsurge in the numbers of young volunteers in the 1960s.[59] Evidence for an increase is provided by the growth in volunteer numbers claimed by both new and established groups.[60] Since those in education formed a large proportion of young volunteers, any increase was in part the result of greatly expanded numbers in secondary, further and higher education. Greater affluence and increased knowledge about domestic social and international problems were potent factors behind increased interest in volunteering and also influenced the growth of campaigning and protest movements.[61] Moreover, television programmes such as *Blue Peter* – first screened in 1958 as the pioneer VSO volunteers were setting off to their postings – provided new outlets for children's and young people's charity through popular annual appeals.[62] Nevertheless, minutes and reports of youth volunteering organisations reveal ongoing anxieties about recruiting appropriately skilled or committed volunteers. New volunteer schemes in the 1950s and 1960s had to compete for young people's attention with a far wider range of leisure-time activities than ever before. For example, the British Volunteer Programme struggled to meet its ambitious targets, which by 1966 required the successful recruitment of around 3 per cent of all British students leaving universities and colleges.[63]

In the 1950s and 1960s voluntary service was presented as an activity open to all young people, rather than a duty incumbent on the educated middle and upper classes, although volunteering programmes achieved only limited success in broadening the appeal of volunteering.[64] In the late 1950s the first overseas volunteers were recruited mainly from elite public schools, but gradually the programme widened to involve state-educated graduates and industrial apprentices. A new stereotype of 'adolescent lady bountifuls' had emerged, which organisations tried to refute by recruiting 'non-traditional volunteers' including young people at work, at secondary modern schools or from disadvantaged backgrounds.[65] Several reports considered that certain groups of young people might need the opportunities provided by volunteer schemes to develop qualities of citizenship. From the outset the Duke of Edinburgh's Award scheme sought to turn 'unattached' youth and boys in approved schools into volunteers, although it also experienced high drop-out rates among these groups.[66] Some new programmes like the Voluntary Service Scheme of the Methodist Association of Youth Clubs, formed in 1966, offered overseas volunteering opportunities to those unlikely to get a chance through other organisations because of the growing danger of 'an "elite" developing in the field of service'.[67] Domestic youth volunteering in the 1960s has thus been described as being in transition 'from middle-class altruism to an "industry" for the unsuccessful working-class young'.[68] There are in fact a number of parallels with earlier attempts to involve working-class members of boys' and girls' clubs in self-governance or charitable activities. Nonetheless, several evaluations at the end of the decade found that the youth volunteer movement retained a broadly middle-class profile.[69] A 1971 survey argued that work-camps were ineffective in reaching 'non-traditional' volunteers and questioned whether participants were in need of the experiences offered, since middle-class youth had other opportunities for travel and broadening horizons.[70] Even programmes that were successful in enlisting 'non-traditional' volunteers, like some Young Volunteer Force projects, were gradually modified as fieldworkers discovered they had to spend greater time and resources supporting these young people.[71]

Another key challenge was finding suitable roles for young volunteers. There was a widespread recognition that the need was for adults to open up avenues of service. Speaking at a conference in Liverpool in 1960, the minister responsible for the Youth Service, L. C. J. Martin, called on voluntary associations to give young people new opportunities of service.[72] The CSV and IVS model of placing young long-term volunteers in hospitals, children's homes and special schools presented difficulties for these institutions and could leave volunteers in poorly defined roles. Young volunteers facing barriers of red tape heckled the Home Office Minister Lord Stonham at a 'teach-in' on community service organised by CSV in 1965.[73] These issues emerged as part of a wider process of redefining the role of volunteers in the welfare state. Difficulties were exacerbated because the training and preparation of young volunteers was often limited.[74] In contrast, some programmes, such as the Duke of Edinburgh's Award, faced criticism for limiting service by young people to first aid or life-saving training courses.[75] Changing ideas about gender also proved challenging for programme organisers in the 1960s. Allocation of activities was initially dictated by traditional gender roles: girls were more likely to be assigned to volunteer as home helps or in children's homes, boys to gardening or decorating. For example, it was a requirement for girls on UNA work-camps in 1964 to be able to 'cook for a group of six'.[76] However, increasingly girls rejected such activities and youth leaders began to deliberately subvert gender stereotypes, for example placing young men in child-care roles.

In 1965 the United Nations Secretary-General, U Thant, commenting on new developments in voluntary service, looked forward to:

> the time when the average youngster – and parent or employer – will consider that one or two years work for the cause of development, either in a far away country or in a depressed area of his own community, is a normal part of one's education.[77]

Such an aspiration contains an inherent contradiction which cut across youth volunteering schemes in the 1960s. Was youth volunteering to be regarded primarily as providing effective services to communities and clients or was it to be part of the social education of the young? Several pioneers of new models of youth volunteering hoped to combine both objectives in a 'compound of altruism and opportunism'.[78] Teachers felt that the principle of service should be a part of students' 'total educational experience' since through service they could better understand the society they lived in.[79] The Technical Co-operation Secretary Dennis Vosper considered character formation to be a valuable 'side-effect' of overseas service.[80] Indeed, early publicity materials for the British Volunteer Programme emphasised that service combined development assistance with character-building challenges for volunteers.[81] This language of character-building suggests further continuities with pre-war traditions of service. Moreover young volunteers themselves desired to avoid any suggestion that they were 'do-gooders' and sought to emphasis the personal rewards of volunteering.[82]

Concern about this divided emphasis on effective service and educative function was apparent in several reports produced from the mid- to late 1960s. Both the Aves Report (1969) and Mary Morris's 1969 survey of voluntary work expressed fears that client welfare might come second to the interests of young volunteers.[83] Respondents to the Bessey Committee concluded that it would be 'disastrous if other people's misfortunes were to be a trial and error training ground for citizenship'.[84] Alongside a widespread lack of volunteer preparation, there is evidence that young volunteers were often poorly supported and that evaluations of the service they performed were rare.[85] There were few opportunities for volunteers to talk about their experiences, although the few good-practice handbooks published in the 1960s did recommend holding volunteer meetings to encourage peer support. Rural schools and communities faced particular problems in this respect.[86] Morris urged better organisation of youth volunteer schemes, suggesting that although a desire to serve was vital, 'efficiency, reliability and adaptability are important too'.[87] Likewise, the voluntary work-camp movement faced a conflict between the aim of organising successful cross-cultural camps and the goal of meeting community needs.[88]

Organisations sending volunteers overseas developed more thorough programmes of selection, pre-service training, in-country orientation and debriefing for returned volunteers. However, worked out through trial and error, such training often failed to meet the diversity of volunteers' needs.[89] The overseas volunteering programmes were deliberately structured to avoid replicating a 'technical expert' model. Volunteers would live in local communities on as equal a basis as possible, receive subsistence wages, offer friendship as much as technical skills, inspire community members to volunteer and be open to learning from the experience.[90] In its early years under Dickson's leadership (1958–62) VSO stressed the value of adaptability and friendship offered by school-leaver and apprentice volunteers.[91] This ideal was out of kilter with the technical assistance paradigm of the UN's 'development decade', and, increasingly, government and volunteer-sending bodies came to value technical skills and graduate-level qualifications while retaining faith in young volunteers of 'high moral purpose and of profound sensitiveness to the plight of their less fortunate fellows'.[92] The records of the British Volunteer Programme (BVP) reveal considerable difficulties of co-ordinating the work of five independent organisations of very different sizes, levels of solvency and philosophies. Issues dominating the agenda in the first five years of the BVP included selection and evaluation of volunteer projects, training and length of service of volunteers, the place of the British Council as the BVP's overseas representative and concerns over the proportion of the costs paid by government.[93] After an eighteen-month tour of long-term volunteer programmes in 1964–65, Glyn Roberts warned, 'the social and economic future of communities cannot be played with to provide a "rewarding experience" for vast numbers of European and American youth'.[94] Roberts identified a need for more careful selection and placement of volunteers, better training, longer service and closer involvement of local people in the programmes. Others such as A. W. D. James, the director of the NUS volunteer programme, and Adrian Moyes at the Overseas Development Institute stressed the need for the United Kingdom programmes to improve training and length of service in order to compete with volunteers from other countries.[95] At IVS, Jef Smith called for volunteers' 'valuable but limited contribution' to be better 'integrated into an overall philosophy of aid'.[96]

A failure to place volunteer activity in a wider context may have limited the impact of volunteering both on volunteers themselves and on the communities they served. By the late 1960s there was a new recognition that if the contribution of young volunteers was to mean anything more than individual satisfaction and immediate relief, volunteers must be educated to the wider implications of their efforts.[97] Voluntary service often had a profound impact on volunteers that could lead to volunteers forging careers in community or international development assistance. Returned overseas volunteers formed an association in 1960 with the goal of raising awareness of development and volunteering.[98] In the late 1960s some volunteers began to question the value and use of the service they undertook, marking a transition from traditional social 'service' to community 'action'.[99] At universities and colleges older models of fundraising and volunteering were challenged by students seeking a discussion on the philosophy of student involvement in the community and the development of radical forms of student service.[100] These shifts to a more politicised understanding of voluntary service were also reflected in the formation of new campaigning organisations in the 1960s.

Conclusions

This chapter has begun to explore a youth volunteer movement beset by 'unrealistic expectations and inherent contradictions'.[101] It has suggested that there are strong parallels between volunteering in the 1950s and 1960s and that which took place in other periods in British history in terms of the high expectations placed on voluntary service. Official support for volunteering in the 1950s and 1960s was underpinned by a belief that volunteering was a constructive leisure-time activity which would distract young people from anti-social behaviour. Organised youth volunteer schemes thus became a form of youth work aiming to reach 'unattached' young people before they became 'delinquents'.[102] However, despite widely acknowledged enthusiasm for home and overseas service, schemes were beset by problems with recruitment, retention, training and placement of volunteers. Moreover, unrealistic expectations surrounded young volunteers' potential contribution to international and community development. While the majority of young people prioritised adventure and challenge, some did begin to question the value of the service they undertook, with implications for the evolution of young people's service in the 1970s. A central characteristic of young people's service in Britain at different periods of history has been the recognition that it can create a learning experience for the volunteer. What was new in the late 1960s was an understanding that participation did not automatically bring the expected benefits, either to the communities served or to volunteers themselves. However, this remains as yet an under-researched subject, with the archives of the BVP and voluntary organisations including the IVS and Returned Volunteer Action still to be explored.

Notes

1 William Beveridge, *Voluntary action: a report on methods of social advance* (London: George Allen & Unwin, 1948), pp. 141–2.

2 Tim Hastie-Smith, interview, BBC Radio 4 *Today programme*, 1 October 2008.

3 C. Rochester, *Making sense of volunteering: a literature review* (London: Volunteering England, 2006), p. 2.

4 For some examples see K. Simpson, '"Doing development"': the gap year, volunteer tourists and popular practice of development', *Journal of International Development*, vol. 16 (2004), pp. 681–92; D. Lewis, 'Globalization and international service: a development perspective', *Voluntary Action*, vol. 7, no. 2 (Summer–Autumn 2005), pp. 13–23; P. Devereux, 'International volunteering for development and sustainability: outdated paternalism or a radical response to globalisation?', *Development in Practice*, vol. 18, no. 3 (June 2008), pp. 357–70.

5 J. Sheard, 'From Lady Bountiful to active citizen', in J. Davis Smith, C. Rochester and R. Hedley (eds) *An introduction to the voluntary sector* (London: Routledge, 1995), pp. 114–27.

6 T. Dartington, *Task force* (London: Mitchell Beazley, 1971), p. 9.

7 C. Allinson, *Young volunteers?* (London: Community Projects Foundation, 1978); J. Sheard, 'Volunteering and society, 1960–1990', in R. Hedley and J. Davis Smith (eds), *Volunteering and society: principles and practices* (London: NCVO, 1992).

8 Frank Judd, quoted in A. Gillette, *One million volunteers: the story of volunteer youth service* (London: Penguin, 1968), p. 99.

9 G. McCulloch, *Philosophers and kings: education for leadership in modern England* (Cambridge: Cambridge University Press, 1991).

10 A. Devine, *A sympathetic boyhood: the public schools and social questions* (London: P. S. King and Son, 1913).

11 W. Beveridge and A. F. Wells (eds), *The evidence for voluntary action* (London: George Allen & Unwin, 1949), p. 125; *UGS Record* (Spring 1951), p. 261; 'Public school missions', *Conference*, vol. 9, no. 2 (June 1972), pp. 18–20; London Metropolitan Archive, NCSS Archive, 'Young people and voluntary service: report of a conference held on the occasion of the 45th AGM of the NCSS', 3 November 1964.

12 Southwark Local History Library, Peckham Settlement Archive, box 3, Union of Girls' Schools for Social Service, 'A report to the trustees of the Sembal Trust', 1968, p. 5; Marie Lewis, 'Developments in settlements', *Social Service Quarterly*, vol. 36, no. 2

(Autumn 1962), pp. 52–5; *The teen canteen of the Dulwich College Mission: a report* (London: Dulwich College Mission, 1960).

13 E. Best and B. Pike, *International voluntary service for peace 1920–1946* (London: IVSP, 1948); Gillette, *One million volunteers*; David Wainwright, *The volunteers: the story of overseas voluntary service* (London: Macdonald, 1965), p. 28.

14 British Library (hereafter BL), London, NUS Pamphlet Collection, WP 7560, 'Introducing NUS', c.1957, p. 23; International Voluntary Service for Peace, *Annual report 1956* (London: IVSP); Sir John Lockwood, 'The call for Volunteer service overseas', *Social Service Quarterly*, vol. 37, no. 2 (Autumn 1963), p. 50.

15 See special issue of *International Voluntary Service* (Summer 1959); *The hidden force: a report of the international conference on middle level manpower* (New York: Harper and Row, 1963).

16 F. Boyd, A. Dickson and N. Swallow, *Technical assistance* (London: United Nations Association, 1959), p. 3; P. Williams and A. Moyes, *Not by governments alone: the role of British non-governmental organisations in the development decade* (London: Overseas Development Institute, 1964), p. 25.

17 A. Rutter, 'Workcamping in new areas', *International Voluntary Service* (Summer 1959).

18 National Archives, Kew, Richmond, Surrey, CAB 144/4, *The establishment of a Commonwealth youth trust* (1959) [Templar Report], pp. 16–17. For early reaction to the schemes, see 'A year in the Commonwealth for young volunteers', *The Times* (1 December 1959), p. 4.

19 D. Bird, *Never the same again: a history of VSO* (London: VSO, 1998); National Archives, OD 10/35.

20 D. Burley, *Issues in community service* (London: National Youth Bureau, 1980), p. 14; J. A. Graham and B. A. Phythian (eds), *The Manchester Grammar School 1515–1965* (Manchester: MUS, 1965), pp. 143–5.

21 D. Wainwright, *Youth in action: the Duke of Edinburgh's Award Scheme 1956–1966* (London: Hutchinson, 1966).

22 N. Paterson, 'The Voluntary Service Unit', in *Experiments in education at Sevenoaks* (London: Constable Books, 1965), pp. 23–40; L. Bailey, *Youth to the rescue* (Evesham: Arthur James, 1967); 'Voluntary service in schools', *Conference*, vol. 1, no. 1 (July 1964), pp. 13–20.

23 Southwark Local History Library, Peckham Settlement Archive, *UGS Record* (Summer 1956).

24 Dartington, *Task force*; G. M. Aves, *The voluntary worker in the social services* (London: Bedford Square Press of the NCSS, 1969), p. 26; 'Young volunteers: a discussion', *Social Service Quarterly*, vol. 38, no. 1 (Summer 1964), pp. 5–8.

25 F. Prochaska, *Christianity and social service in modern Britain: the disinherited spirit* (Oxford: Oxford University Press, 2006), p. 97.

26 A. Dickson, *A chance to serve* (London: Dennis Dobson, 1976), pp. 116–20.

27 Ministry of Education, *The Youth Service in England and Wales* [Albemarle Report], (London: HSMO, 1960); C. Ellis, 'No hammock for the idle: the Conservative Party, "Youth" and the welfare state in the 1960s', *Twentieth Century British History*, vol. 16, no. 4 (2005), pp. 441–70; C. Ellis, 'The younger generation: the Labour

Party and the 1959 Youth Commission', *Journal of British Studies*, vol. 41, no. 2 (April 2002), pp. 199–231.

28 P. Jephcott, *Some young people* (London: George Allen and Unwin, 1954); *The Duke of Edinburgh's Award Scheme report 1956–8* (London: Duke of Edinburgh's Award, 1959), p. 9.

29 *Accent on youth* (London: Conservative Political Centre, 1961); P. Jephcott, *Time of one's own: leisure and young people* (Edinburgh: Oliver and Boyd, 1967), pp. 10–17; M. Abrams, *Teenage consumer spending in 1959* (London: London Press Exchange, 1961).

30 I. Dale (ed.), *Conservative party general election manifestos 1900–1997* (London: Politico's Publishing, 1999), p. 136.

31 *Accent on youth*, p. 8.

32 Albemarle Report, p. 19.

33 *The report of the Haynes Committee on the work and future of the Boys' Brigade* (London: Boys' Brigade, 1964); J. Hanmer, *Girls at leisure* (London: London Union of Youth Clubs, 1964); *Tomorrow's Guide: report of the working party 1964–66* (London: Girl Guide Association, 1966).

34 Albemarle Report, p. 13; *Times Educational Supplement* (21 October 1960), p. 531.

35 *Social Service Quarterly*, vol. 35, no. 1 (June–August 1961), p. 13; *International Voluntary Service* (Spring 1958), p. 1.

36 Templar Report, p. 17; See also J. M. Lee, 'No peace corps for the Commonwealth?', *Round Table*, no. 336 (October 1995), pp. 455–67.

37 *Service overseas: the young idea* (London: Conservative Political Centre, 1963).

38 HRH Prince Philip, 'Introduction', in D. Wainwright, *The young volunteers* (London: Ministry of Overseas Development, 1965), pp. 4–5; Lockwood, 'The call for volunteer service overseas'.

39 Williams and Moyes, *Not by governments alone*, p. 25.

40 House of Commons debates, 5th series, vol. 712, cols. 873–963, 14 May 1965.

41 E. Cobbs Hoffman, *All you need is love: the Peace Corps and the spirit of the 1960s* (Cambridge, MA: Harvard University Press, 1998), p. 55.

42 National Archives, OD 10/34; 'Not enough use is being made of young volunteer workers', *The Guardian* (27 December 1961).

43 T. Stacey, 'The Peace Volunteers', *Sunday Times* (25 February 1962).

44 Lee, 'No peace corps', p. 462; National Archives, OD 10/34/7.

45 London School of Economics (hereafter LSE), Returned Volunteer Association Archive, Lockwood Committee minutes, box 40.

46 Lockwood, 'The call for volunteer service overseas', p. 69; P. Zealey, 'Need and response in overseas service', *Social Service Quarterly*, vol. 36, no. 3 (Winter 1963), pp. 109–11.

47 House of Commons debates, 5th series, vol. 689, cols 377–82, 12 February 1964.

48 *Service overseas: the young idea*, p. 7.

49 House of Commons debates, 5th series, vol. 689, cols 377–8, 12 February 1964.

50 B. Castle, 'Ministry on the move', *Venture*, vol. 17, no. 1 (January 1965), pp. 12–14.

51 J. Smith, 'Volunteers for what?' *Venture*, vol. 17, no. 4 (April 1965), pp. 13–16.

52 *British volunteers: a contribution to overseas development* (London: Ministry of Overseas Development, 1969).

53 Dartington, *Task force*, p. 8.

54 *Youth in action: a study of councils of social service and community service by young people* (London: NCSS, 1971), p. 27.

55 R. Hadley, A. Webb and C. Farrell, *Across the generations: old people and young volunteers* (London: George Allen & Unwin, 1975), p. 56; Central Advisory Council for Education, *Half our future* [Newsom Report] (London: HMSO, 1963).

56 Newsom Report; The school-leaving age was raised from fifteen to sixteen in 1972.

57 *Youth in action*, p. 8; Bailey, *Youth to the rescue*, p. 111.

58 G. S. Bessey, *Service by youth: a report of the committee of the Youth Service Development Council* [Bessey Report] (London: HMSO, 1965), p. 1.

59 *Youth helps age* (London: NCSS, 1964); *Youth in action*, p. 5; Aves, *Voluntary worker*, p. 25; N. Haycocks, 'The chairman's view III', *Social Service Quarterly*, vol. 39, no. 2 (Autumn, 1965), p. 50; M. Thomas, *Work camps and volunteers: the PEP study of international work camps in Britain and British work-camp volunteers* (London: PEP, 1971).

60 R. Hadley and A. Webb, 'Young volunteers in the social services', *Social Work Today*, vol. 2, no. 7 (July 1971), pp. 21–5.

61 M. Braham, 'Volunteers for development: a test of the post-materialist hypothesis in Britain, c.1965–1987', *University of Oxford discussion papers in economic and social history*, 20 (June 1999), www.nuffield.ox.ac.uk/economics/history/paper30/30braham.pdf (accessed 30 May 2010).

62 *Blue Peter: fifth book* (London: BBC, 1968), p. 17.

63 P. Zealey, 'Need and response in overseas service', *Social Service Quarterly*, vol. 36, no. 3 (Winter 1963), pp. 109–11; House of Commons debates, 5th series, vol. 712, cols 906–7, col. 907, 14 May 1965; National Archives, OD 10/81.

64 London Metropolitan Archive, NCSS Archive, 'Young people and voluntary service'; Hadley, Webb and Farrell, *Across the generations*, p. 8.

65 *Youth in action*, p. 16; Dickson, *A chance to serve*, p. 125; M. and A. Dickson, *Count us in: a community service handbook* (London: Dennis Dobson, 1967), p. 60; 'Police cadets help teach immigrant children', *The Times* (19 December, 1966), p. 7.

66 *Duke of Edinburgh's Award Scheme report 1956–8*, p. 8; *Duke of Edinburgh's Award Scheme report 1961*, p. 14.

67 R. Bedford, *They volunteered* (London: Chester House Publications, 1968), p. 21.

68 Allinson, *Young volunteers?*, p. 3.

69 Hadley, Webb and Farrell, *Across the generations*, pp. 61–2; *Youth in action*, p. 9; Burley, *Issues in community service*, p. 14; Bird, *Never the same again*, p. 47.

70 Thomas, *Work camps*, p. 86–7.

71 Allinson, *Young volunteers?*, p. 29; M. Campbell, *Lend a hand! An introduction to social welfare work for young people* (London: Museum Press Limited, 1965), p. 64.

72 *Times Educational Supplement* (15 July 1960), p. 91.

73 'Red tape bar to social work', *The Times* (27 September 1965), p. 7.

74 M. Morris, *Voluntary work in the welfare state* (London: Routledge, 1969); *Youth in action*, p. 12; Bessey Report, p. 12.

75 A. Taylor, *For and against: a discussion on the award scheme* (Oxford: Pergamon Press, 1967), pp. 26–30.

76 'Voluntary service in schools', p. 15; Campbell, *Lend a hand!*, p. 64.

77 Quoted in Gillette, *One million volunteers*, title page.
78 H. F. G. Carey, 'Voluntary Service Overseas', *Conference*, vol. 1, no. 1 (July 1964), p. 21.
79 Graham and Phythian (eds), *Manchester Grammar School*, p. 144; Paterson, 'Voluntary Service Unit', p. 33.
80 *Hidden force*, p. 119.
81 *Service overseas by volunteers* (Lockwood Committee, 1964); *Graduate service overseas* (NUS, c.1965–66).
82 Campbell, *Lend a hand!*, p. 53.
83 Aves, *Voluntary worker*, p. 26; Morris, *Voluntary work*, p. 124.
84 Bessey Report, p. 12.
85 *Youth in action*, p. 12; Dickson, *Count us in*, pp. 86–7; Hadley, Webb and Farrell, *Across the generations*, p. 5.
86 I. Wallace, 'Community service', *Conference*, vol. 7, no. 3 (October 1970), pp. 31–4.
87 Morris, *Voluntary work*, p. 122.
88 Thomas, *Work camps*, p. 84.
89 IVS Archive, Leicester, IVS Long-Term Service Subcommittee minutes, 16 March 1966; IVS returned volunteer reports 1970–73.
90 Boyd, Dickson and Swallow, *Technical assistance*, p. 12; IVS Archive, 'International Voluntary Service report on long term service to AGM 1965', p. 3; Rutter, 'Workcamping in new areas', *International Voluntary Service* (Summer 1959); Smith, 'Volunteers for what?'
91 M. Dickson, 'Second best and under-used', *Venture*, vol. 18, nos 3–4 (April–May 1966), pp. 3–4.
92 Lockwood, 'The call for volunteer service overseas'; Bird, *Never the same again*, pp. 38–7; House of Commons debates, 5th series, vol. 689, cols 377–82, 12 February 1964.
93 National Archives, Lockwood Projects Sub Committee File, OD 10/81; Voluntary Service Policy File 1966–67, OD 10/65; IVS Archive, 'Minutes of a meeting held 1 December 1964', p. 2, IVS Long-Term Service Subcommittee Minutes 1963–6, box A66.
94 G. Roberts, *Volunteers in Africa and Asia: a field study* (London: 1965), p. 54.
95 Adrian Moyes, *Volunteers in development* (London: Overseas Development Institute, 1966), p. 102.
96 Smith, 'Volunteers for what?' p. 16.
97 Dartington, *Task force*, p. 126; *Youth in action*, p. 30; A. Dickson, 'Foreword', in S. Goodlad, (ed.), *Education and social action: community service and the curriculum in higher education* (London: George Allen & Unwin Ltd, 1975), pp. 7–11.
98 SE, Returned Volunteer Association Archive, 'Report of weekend conference held at Farnham Castle, February 1963', Lockwood Committee minutes, box 40.
99 *Youth in action*, p. 23; C. Dyhouse, *Students: a gendered history* (Abingdon: Routledge, 2006); A. Dickson, 'Student community action', *Community Development Journal*, vol. 5, no. 4 (October 1970), pp. 183–9.
100 A. Barr, *Student community action* (London: Bedford Square Press, 1972); Aves, *Voluntary worker*, p. 25.
101 Sheard, 'From Lady Bountiful to active citizen', p. 117.
102 Morris, *Voluntary work*, p. 127.

9

Voluntary action and the rural poor in the age of globalisation

Jill Roe

Two great paradoxes strike the present-day reader of William Beveridge's *Voluntary action* when trying to relate its principles to the rural poor.[1] The first paradox pertains to the fact that Beveridge extolled mutual and philanthropic endeavour 'outside one's home' for social advancement, but apart from his comments on some activities of the Women's Institutes, there is virtually nothing on voluntary action in rural communities or in aid of the rural poor, though in Australia, at least, this kind of action was nowhere more pronounced than in rural communities.[2]

The second paradox resides in the reality, unimaginable in the late 1940s, that although Beveridge rightly noticed great areas of social need and distress untouched by state action at that time and called for co-operation between the individual, voluntary organisations and the state in future to address those needs, we now see that the future would only in part encourage the sort of progressive co-operative endeavour he envisaged, and most recently has actively discouraged it. Thus in Australia we saw initiatives like women's refuges and rape crisis centres established as responses to feminism in the 1970s, and there was more government spending on services needed by countrywomen. In more recent decades, however, in Australia as elsewhere, there has been a reversal of the trends in state support, owing to cost-cutting and ideological objections to state action, with the state devolving basic services back to the private sector, as with the privatisation of the Commonwealth Employment Service, established in 1946. Likewise 'demutualisation' has meant the end of venerable institutions such as the Australian Mutual Provident Society, which first opened its doors in Sydney in 1849. What the consequences of all this will be have yet to be determined, but it seems likely that remaining rural workers will be among those most seriously effected, as local factors come into play.[3]

Other considerations relevant to the rural poor arise from this late twentieth-century distortion of Beveridge's idealistic notion of voluntary action as a lever for creating the good society.[4] Most obviously, unfavourable economic circumstances may stimulate voluntary action, but they seldom strengthen it in the long run. To draw again on Australian perspectives, good intentions and the most dedicated community action are not likely to be enough to offset recurrent rural crises and the apparently inevitable decline of agriculture and the smaller country towns affected by it. The 'age of globalisation' may simply hasten trends already underway.

In a recent collection of essays entitled *Struggle country: the rural ideal in twentieth century Australia*, the editors, the Melbourne historians Graeme Davison and Marc Brodie, call for a new approach to the rural experience and longer perspectives. The title *Struggle country* refers, they tell us, not only to the harsh economic and environmental realities that have governed the fortunes of rural Australians in the 'pioneer postlude' – a nice phrasing – but also to 'the intense intellectual and political struggles among successive generations of Australians to bring rural ideals into line with the circumstances of a modern capitalist society located in a dry continent'. If the approach of the blockbuster *Australia* starring Nicole Kidman and Hugh Jackman is any guide, a difficult task lies ahead for the historians.[5]

Historical perspective is the key to understanding why Beveridge had so little to say about voluntary action in a rural context. His framework was the wider framework, developed in the years after the Second World War, of the dynamics of free versus totalitarian regimes, not the balance of rural versus urban needs within a society, a balance which in any event had been long since struck in Britain. British people had been importing much of their food from the empire for a century or more, and British society had long been largely urbanised. Towards the end of *Voluntary action* Beveridge did touch on some of the economic challenges that lay ahead; but since the British Commonwealth of Nations was regarded by him as one of the great national achievements – as perhaps it was – it seems unlikely that he envisaged the end of empire or its domestic consequences. Modern British social history has shown that concern about rural poverty at home faded away in the early twentieth century – though telling accounts of rural life continued to appear long afterwards. By the 1960s, concern about rural poverty would become a concern about poverty in the wider world, especially in Africa.[6]

In Australia, the rural dream died hard and later; and while many farmers and the farming communities were entering 'struggle country' by the 1960s, and resentfully so too, it was not really until the report of first national enquiry into poverty in Australia, chaired by the British-born welfare economist Professor Ronald Henderson in 1975, that a clearer but far from complete or forward-looking picture of the incidence of rural poverty began to emerge.[7]

From this benchmark, two major points seem most significant here, one positive and one negative. The positive point that the Henderson Report raised straight away was that rural poverty is not the same as urban poverty, and that in measuring the former, wealth is as important as income: that is to say, there could be great fluctuations in annual farm income due to the ups and downs of markets, but farm families would usually be able to carry on, on credit. As well, there were significant regional variations in its incidence, as in the case of an oversupply and consequent impoverishment of dairy farmers on the north coast of New South Wales, a well-known example.[8]

The main finding of the Henderson Report was that it was the older farmers on small and uneconomic blocks of land, and the rural labourers with uncertain employment opportunities, who were most likely to experience poverty at this time. Henderson believed that these (and other) ills could be remedied by the introduction of a society-wide guaranteed minimum income, the provision of annuities for elderly farmers wishing to stay on the land in return for their estates passing to annuity-providing bodies, and local versions of Citizens' Advice Bureaux. This has yet to be studied closely, but the guaranteed minimum income was never a viable proposition in Australia and nothing came of the annuities proposal, though it is likely that some services did improve.[9]

Subsequently, however, many services have gone into decline. This applies to both private and public provision. The banks began rationalising their branches in rural areas in the 1980s, and the protective tariffs and rural subsidies built up since Federation have been gradually withdrawn in the last quarter of the twentieth century. In retrospect it seems obvious that rural communities and the poor within them would experience the full force of a resurgent capitalism as they entered the age of globalisation.

That this may have had good effects has been suggested by some. The political scientist Don Aitkin is one who has drawn attention to the benefits of change and modernisation in rural communities: he notes that the loss of markets for primary products following Britain's entry into the Common Market encouraged new strategies such as wine production, and cleared the way for investment by the urban rich. Be that as it may, the issue here must be with those who did not or for various structural reasons could not benefit from these new initiatives.[10]

The negative point, only just coming into focus in Henderson's day, relates to the true character and significance of Indigenous poverty. Whereas a number of specialist research reports were undertaken by the Henderson Commission of Inquiry, including two on the Aboriginal experience, in the first overall report there is only limited reference to 'this very difficult question', owing to the importance placed on the need to encourage participation in policy-making. The housing situation was however recognised as dire.[11]

Thirty years on from the heady days of the Henderson Report, further paradoxes have emerged. In the July 2008 issue of *The Humanitarian*, the journal of the Australian Red Cross Society, it was reported that Australians discard about three million tonnes of food a year. The world is not short of food. Yet as we know there is a mounting world food shortage, with protests and even food riots reported in diverse countries, even apparently Italy, and better known in Haiti, Ethiopia and the Philippines, not to mention Zimbabwe. Hunger is again on the world's agenda. Similarly, whether the report was exaggerated or not, Australians are said to have overtaken the Americans as the fattest people in the world, a frightening claim. As we know from the study of the incidence of famine in India and elsewhere, scarcity and plenty can go hand in hand, with unequal distribution and social structures constituting the underlying problem.[12]

This is true even for a rich country like Australia, where we used to speak of pockets of poverty, then of levels. Now it seems that maybe we should be talking in terms of area. There has been widespread concern about the 'rural–urban divide', and although some 1990s research suggested that this was sometimes overwrought and self-interested, it may also be that the major locations of permanent need, as distinct from incidental and crisis want, are hidden away in rural and remote regions.[13]

There is a further twist to the tail of the new inequality. One now forgotten and embarrassing argument for the old, race-based, immigration restrictions of the White Australia Policy was that it facilitated a modern and immensely productive use of land, the food bowl effect, both for the cities and for export. Be that as it may, the agricultural sector itself is now too often in crisis, owing to prolonged drought and the impending effects of climate change. In a dry continent where, unlike North America, soils are thin and fragile, drought is recurrent and usually severe, and the possible consequences of climate change are already widely feared.

Moreover it has been suggested that the family farm will soon be a thing of the past as credit dries up and agri-business takes hold. Certainly there has been a steep decline in rural population since the golden age of the 1950s, with a consequent decline in country towns. By now, an amazingly low proportion of the population lives in rural and regional Australia, approximately 12 per cent of the total, whereas in the 1940s it was more like a third; and as the size of rural communities declines, the issue of leadership, which is said to be vital to effective voluntary action in communities, begins to look bleaker than ever.[14]

On the other hand, alongside the previously mentioned loss of services in small towns, that is those with populations of under 5,000, has come the growth of the larger towns, now known to geographers as 'sponge cities', as in the case of Eyre Peninsula, South Australia's largest and westernmost peninsula. Nowadays people from all over the Peninsula think nothing of driving down the bitumen to Port Lincoln, or cross country to the old iron and steel town of Whyalla, for the weekly shop, whereas sixty years ago it was an event, done over uncovered roads, at best monthly. While the influx of retirees in coastal communities has brought some fresh expertise and renewed strength to voluntary action in many places, this is not the case in more remote or inland locations.[15]

Evidently the issues are not as straightforward as they may seem. Nonetheless the question of whether remote and regional communities based on agriculture can survive the 'double whammy' of climate change and demographic decline during a longer more protracted period of economic challenge remains. No doubt some will succeed. But socio-economic decline can be quite rapid. Only a few years ago the sight of totally deserted railway villages up the spine of Eyre Peninsula came as a shock to the present writer. Once they were effective local centres, each with a school and store and church. Now many are no more than a cluster of huge wheat silos. The very latest reports are of a further exodus to the coast and to the capital cities, and an ongoing ambivalence about loss of the young. In terms of survival much will depend on international markets and the price of oil – and the survival of a local football team.[16] And what will happen to those left behind, trapped by plummeting house prices among other things, with their numbers apparently augmented mainly by welfare escapees from the city seeking cheap housing, for example in those old railway towns?

Experience suggests that for all the general provisos entered above, voluntary action still has a vital role to play, as so often in times past. One of the most effective pressure groups in Australian history is the Country Women's Association (CWA), which has always had as its aim the improvement of the lives of rural women and their children. It was founded by leading rural women in New South Wales in 1922 and provides important services and advocacy for countrywomen in all states of the Commonwealth to the present day. Indigenous communities tell a different story, though as will be shown below, over time the sort of leadership that is integral of voluntary action is slowly emerging (which is not to suggest that state action should be cut back). The role of women is a subtext to both settler and Indigenous action and the survival of rural and regional communities.[17]

I take the Indigenous dimension first, not because I have expertise in the area, but because the simple truth is that those Indigenous Australians in remote and peripheral rural communities are, to echo something Brian Abel Smith once said so memorably in a quite different context, the poorest of the poor. To put matters in social policy categories, for a very long time Indigenous Australians were at best the undeserving poor, with ever-diminishing land rights, their welfare left to Christian missions (which, it must be said, at least saved their clients from starvation, taught some skills, and usually ensured clean water supplies on reserves, which, alas, is not always the case in surviving enclaves today). Moreover, for the remote communities now largely dependent on the state, change has come at a barely perceptible pace, and pathologies have emerged, owing to lack of work and isolation.[18]

It is perhaps too soon to assess the Federal government's 'intervention' in the Northern Territory, implemented by the Howard government and continued today with modifications by the Rudd government. But its most striking feature, the compulsory quarantining of half of welfare payments for which all Indigenous people are entitled as citizens so as to ensure adequate food purchases for families, has been controversial. It has been welcomed by many women in much the same way as temperance was once advocated by women because their priority was to feed their families, but by fewer men, who resent the loss of their authority. They all, women and men, now seem to be travelling greater distances to the towns for supplies, for welfare payments and for grog. To some it sounds rather like a state-sponsored version of the Charity Organisation Society. The problems of leadership and self-help now seem quite acute here. The Arnhem Land leader Galalarrwuy Yunupingu has recently stated that by now the 'Intervention' is 'at the cross roads'.[19]

Even harder for the non-Indigenous citizen to see clearly is what is happening to that higher proportion of Indigenous Australians who live on the outskirts of country towns, the 'fringe-dwellers'. However, memoirs and oral history collections are now yielding evidence of an ever-increasing number of remarkable individuals from such sites, and their achievements are important in promoting self-help. A case in point is the now-documented work being done in the north-western New South Wales town of Collarenabri by Isabel Flick, who died in 2002, having struggled seemingly endlessly to unite her damaged community in such causes as the restoration of a local Indigenous cemetery and to campaign for needs such as better housing and equal pay for cotton-workers at nearby Narrabri. To read her posthumously published memoir is to marvel at her patience, and in the end her effectiveness.[20]

Maybe the lesson of Isabel Flick's life, and the lives of other Indigenous women activists of her generation such as the dedicated Sydney welfare worker 'Mum Shirl', is that there are no quick fixes. It is also clear that the times were on their side, with the rise of combined black-white pressure groups in the 1950s, such as the Sydney-based Aboriginal-Australian Fellowship, established in 1956, and the Federal Council for the Advancement of Aborigines and Torres Strait Islanders (FCAATSI), established in Adelaide in 1958 (both disbanded after the successful constitutional rights referendum in 1967), and the student Freedom Riders to the region in the 1960s. They also had important white allies locally – in the case of Isabel Flick, the local doctor Archie Kalokerinos and the student volunteer intern Paul Torzillo, who facilitated access to recently established support systems in Sydney.[21]

The third main Indigenous grouping is the urban community, which in Sydney is focussed on Redfern on the south side of the City of Sydney local government area. Redfern has been a refuge and locale of support systems for incoming Indigenous people since the early years of the twentieth century, with important voluntarist health and legal-aid schemes established there in the 1970s. In her autobiographical narrative *Don't take your love to town*, published in 1988, Ruby Langford (now Langford Ginibi) has recorded how she and her extended family moved between bush camps and overcrowded city housing, surviving on casual work, welfare payments and charitable aid. To read this classic work, with all its picaresque vitality, is to appreciate how greatly Indigenous workers were affected by changes in the rural economy dating back to the 1950s, and to realise that urbanisation, not social policy or voluntarism, became the common lot (and hope) of the labouring poor, both black and white.[22]

In 1987 the British historian John Iliffe published his remarkable *The African poor: a history*. No such grand synthesis has yet been attempted for the experience of the first Australians, which in any event is scarcely comparable in terms of scale and complexity. For example, despite many severe health problems affecting

Indigenous people in remote and rural areas, there is nothing to compare with the outcast status created for Ethiopian women by birth injuries; and the impoverishing effects of Apartheid in South Africa are too well known for more than passing reference to be necessary here. However, the 'great transition' that Iliffe traces has a wider bearing, in that the world of Indigenous people in Australia was also 'turned upside down' in the age of empire, which we may regard as the first phase of globalisation, and insofar as family supports and self-help have remained vital in both contexts. As Melanie Oppenheimer points out in her study *Volunteering*, if culturally appropriate terminology is used, volunteering is part of Indigenous society, as indeed it has had to be.[23]

As noted at the beginning of this chapter, Beveridge was not strongly focussed on rural poverty; but the principles he sought to defend still resonate in that context. We may note, for example, a resonance in his comparison between totalitarian and free societies:

> By contrast [with totalitarian societies] vigour and abundance of Voluntary Action outside one's home, individually and in association with other citizens, for bettering one's own life and that of one's fellows, are the distinguishing marks of free society.[24]

With that most long-term residents of rural communities would instinctively agree. Likewise although rural communities are now supported by the state to a previously unthinkable and often only grudgingly acknowledged extent, the peculiarities of rural life have always meant what is noted in Jose Harris's monumental biography of Beveridge, that he realised that there may be many areas of social need which are not met by blanket or monetary means, such as the special needs of atypical or distressed minorities.[25] An interesting instance of sharply focussed social aid by voluntary action in contemporary Australia is the work of Anglicare, the Anglican welfare arm, in outer suburban Adelaide, where poor and dysfunctional families are very numerous.[26]

Fashionable preoccupations with sea-changing, tree-changing or back-to-nature ideas in general all confuse the idea of rural poverty. It has been pointed out by the Bristol University sociologist Paul Cloke that there are these days many new players in rural communities, including stockbrokers, and that supposed rural values have proved convenient for the neo-conservatives of the 1980s, who sought to replace state with self-help by imagining new versions of the rural idyll. Impervious as many of us may be to such versions of the world, it has a ring of truth, even with the dyed-in-the-wool rural poor in sunny Australia, who, research has suggested, may not be especially miserable, thanks largely to lifestyle factors. On the other hand the rural idyll is of limited value where, for example, distance is an issue, and where voting is compulsory, as in Australia. Even though rural populations are much diminished, small winning margins and preferential voting, not to mention the national ethos and now climate change, mean that at least some attention must be paid to the needs of rural and regional areas.[27]

There is little doubt that the current phase of globalisation has been putting severe strain on the rural sector. A paper from the Australian Catholic Social Justice Commission issued in 1993, dramatically entitled 'The spiral down to poverty', posited 'a tragedy of epic dimensions', fearing that Australian farmers were being downgraded to 'peasant status'. Based on interviews with the farming community, it reported as follows:

> Drought, coupled with spiralling interest rates, bank charges and margins (often in excess of an effective interest rate of 30%), commodity price falls and the rising cost of inputs (seeds, pesticides, fuel, fertilisers, machinery and parts – mostly controlled by overseas interests) meant that many farmers were unable to service their loans and were either forced off their properties or remain in a state of 'suspended animation' – reduced to tenant farmers or 'a form of peasantry to the banks'.[28]

The paper points to particular 'hot spots' such as the western division of New South Wales, where so many Indigenous people are located, and South Australia's 'debt-ridden' Eyre Peninsula, which also has a significant Indigenous population in remote areas and the far west. Whereas in Henderson's report the rural poor were found along the coast, now it is the inland area that is being highlighted.

Given that research into rural poverty today is still thin on the ground, and work on the role of religion-based action in alleviating rural distress is even harder to come by, some observations on the Social Justice Commission paper are in order: first, that Catholic social action has always included advocacy for the small farmer; second, that concern about the social impact of drought and its reflection in rising suicide rates in rural areas was intense at the time of writing (as it has been several times since); and third, that the discussion strengthens the case for more respectful historical perspectives. It sounds like the 1890s all over again, with the paper's stress on the dire combination of extended drought and bank foreclosures in favour of the big players and the corporates. A similar story could be told of the 1920s, when for various reasons a high proportion of returned soldier settlers on small blocks of land failed to make good on the land. One new point seems to be that the churches are now bigger players, especially the Catholic Church. As the largest religious denomination in modern Australia, it has both the resources and the clout to make a difference, though how much activity has been focussed on the rural poor is unclear.[29]

Statistics cast some light on the voluntary principle in rural society today. However, as Oppenheimer has pointed out, they do not extend back very far. According to estimates made by the Australian Bureau of Statistics in the 1990s, some 2.6 million people, or 19 per cent of the population aged over fifteen, undertook some form of voluntary of work at that time. The highest state rate was that of South Australia, where 33 per cent of the population was involved; and higher rates in the country than the city have been noted in several subsequent surveys. As well, a gender difference is apparent. The split of interests in volunteering in

2007 showed that about one third of effort went into welfare and community activities, with similar proportions found in the areas of arts, sport, recreation and hobbies, and in education, training and youth development. That is to say, the situation overall may sound impressive, but the distribution of energies suggests that the relationship between volunteering and welfare may be quite tenuous and that it often depends on women.[30]

That may suggest that the future for rural communities is likely to be bleak. However, many encouraging signs of rural pride and self-helping are apparent today, and material collected for this chapter from regional and rural New South Wales suggests an ongoing responsiveness to need. For example, the medium-sized mid-western New South Wales town of Cowra has a 'no interest loans' service run by Josephite nuns, an Education Foundation offering grants to school leavers to help them continue their education provided by GrainCorp, a Christian umbrella group providing housing assistance for low-income refugee families and a graduate scholarship scheme run by local women graduates. The extent of possible voluntary activity in country towns is highlighted by the astonishing statistic that the small northern community of Gloucester boasts 170 voluntary organisations, including a 'snow-fest' with snow trucked in![31]

Another remarkable instance of effective local initiative in hard times is the Bendigo Bank. Bendigo is an old gold town in north-eastern Victoria with a population of 140,000, and Bendigo Bank is a community bank. It was set up following the town's loss of banking services, and has now spread to other centres. It has become so successful that it has been suggested it could become the subject of a takeover bid by one of the major banks.[32]

In 1975 Professor Henderson pointed out that there was 'no evidence' that voluntary gap-filling organisations would become redundant – he was probably thinking of the religious and migrant welfare services which sprang up in the wake of the mass immigration programme after the Second World War – and that voluntary organisations are not just alternatives to statutory service but essential to any welfare system.[33] So it has proved to be. Oppenheimer has shown that over 30 per cent of today's voluntary organisations have their origins in the 1970s, and most of the Indigenous services, now state-supported, date from that time.[34] Meanwhile new issues are forever arising, such as AIDS, which has been treated as a medical issue in Australia and responded to in association with a gay-based AIDS Council. Aitkin has underlined the point by asserting, no doubt correctly, that hardly a new medical issue arises but that a new group calling for assistance is set up. Certainly there is plenty of evidence of fresh voluntary action in regional and rural communities as new issues arise, some of which relate to men in crisis over sexuality, alcoholism or impoverishment, all worsened by hard or changing times.[35]

There is also a good deal of evidence that the underlying Beveridge–Henderson messages about the need to encourage voluntary action are now being heeded by governments. A considerable amount of public funding has gone to rural and regional Australia in the past decade with the objective of strengthening communities and families, including Indigenous ones. Partly this was due to the policies of the Howard government, which always preferred voluntary to state action, but much was done at state and local levels too. Public documents are often opaque and generalist, but there is no gainsaying the statistics. Issues of *Year Book Australia* over the past decade show that the funding for support services has doubled, with an allocation of $A240 million over four years in 2001, and A$500 million in the next period to 2009.[36]

How this is playing out as a buffer against pressures from within and without only time will tell. At present it may seem like whistling in the wind; and it needs to be said at some point that voluntary action has not always been sufficiently inclusive in times past, when 'my lady bountiful' attitudes were still in place. However, times have changed, and there have always been energetic and resourceful women and men on the ground; and the emergence of effective Indigenous leadership is especially significant. These are the people who will make a difference in rural and regional Australia in the future, as in the past; and it seems clear with the worsening economic outlook that they will be needed. As Australia's first woman Governor-General, Quentin Bryce, reminded us in her first big speech, delivered in Canberra in October 2008, 'the smugness of good times' is over. After visiting the archetypal New South Wales outback town of Bourke and noticing there 'the human response to hardship and suffering . . . and a collective sense of social responsibility', her message was, as the headline had it, that the vulnerable are the responsibility of us all.[37]

Notes

1 I thank the Sydney researcher Kerry Regan for assistance with data collection and other support during the preparation of this chapter.

2 Lord Beveridge, *Voluntary action: a report on methods of social advance* (London: George Allen & Unwin, 1948), pp. 110, 135–6.

3 Beveridge, *Voluntary action*, part III, 'The needs that remain in a social service state'.

4 Beveridge, *Voluntary action*, p. 320.

5 Graeme Davison and Marc Brodie (eds), *Struggle country: the rural ideal in twentieth century Australia* (Melbourne: Monash University ePress, 2005), p. xii.

6 A. Howkins, *The death of rural England: a social history of the countryside since 1900* (London and New York: Routledge, 2003), pp. 183–5, points out that real problems of rural poverty and deprivation have persisted, and may even have worsened, in the late twentieth century, despite rising prosperity in many rural areas.

7 Australian Government Commission of Inquiry into Poverty (Professor R. F. Henderson, Chair), *Poverty in Australia: first main report* (Canberra: Australian Government Publishing Service, 1975), vol. 1.

8 Australian Government Commission of Inquiry into Poverty, *Poverty in Australia*, ch. 11, 'Rural poverty', pp. 178, 181.

9 Australian Government Commission of Inquiry into Poverty, *Poverty in Australia*, pp. 185, 191, 194.

10 D. Aitkin, *What was it all for? The reshaping of Australia* (Crows Nest, NSW: Allen & Unwin, 2005).

11 Kathleen F. Hill, *A Study of Aboriginal poverty in two country towns: research report* (Canberra: Australian Government Publishing Service, 1975); Fay Gale and Joan Binnion, *Poverty in Aboriginal families in Adelaide: research report* (Canberra: Australian Government Publishing Service, 1975); and Australian Government Commission of Inquiry into Poverty, *Poverty in Australia*, pp. 258, 267. A third report by the Department of Sociology at the University of New England, *Rural Poverty in northern New South Wales: research report* (Canberra: Australian Government Publishing Service, 1974), included a study of welfare programmes for Aborigines in the region, and the conclusion expressed concern for poor whites as well (p. 157).

12 A. Sen, *Poverty and famines: an essay in entitlement and deprivation* (Oxford: Clarendon Press, and New York: Oxford University Press, 1981).

13 B. Davidson and J. Lees, *An investigation of poverty in rural and remote regions of Australia* (Armidale, NSW: Rural Development Centre, 1993), pp. 53–4.

14 *Year Book Australia* (Canberra: Australian Bureau of Statistics, 2001), p. 143, table 5.19, 'Rural population percentage of total population'.

15 Jill Roe and Helen Bartley, 'Eyre Peninsula', in W. Prest and K. Round (eds), *Wakefield companion to South Australian history* (Kent Town, SA: Wakefield Press, 2001), pp. 183–5.

16 'Big dry leads to sporting drought', *Sydney Morning Herald* (23 October 2008), p. 3.

17 B. Kingston, *A history of New South Wales* (Port Melbourne, Vic.: Cambridge University Press, 2006), p. 139 (on the CWA); M. Alston (ed.), *Australian rural women: towards 2000* (Wagga Wagga, NSW: Centre for Rural Research, Charles Sturt University, 1998).

18 'Missions battle with poor water, sewage', *Sydney Morning Herald* (13 November 2008), p. 6.

19 *Sydney Morning Herald* (16 October 2008), p. 7.

20 I. Flick and H. Goodall, *Isabel Flick: the many lives of an extraordinary Aboriginal woman* (Sydney: Allen & Unwin, 2004).

21 F. Bandler and L. Fox (eds), *The time was ripe: a history of the Aboriginal-Australian Fellowship* (Chippendale, NSW: Alternative Publishing Cooperative, 1983); Federal Council for the Advancement of Aborigines and Torres Strait Islanders, *Encyclopaedia of Aboriginal Australia* (Canberra: Aboriginal Studies Press, 1994); A. Curthoys, *Freedom ride: a freedom rider remembers* (Crows Nest, NSW: Allen & Unwin, 1988). 'Mum Shirl: Colleen Shirley Smith, AM, MBE, c.1924–1998', National Federation of Australian Women website, http://nfaw.org.women-s-history (accessed 16 May 2010).

22 Kingston, *History of New South Wales*, p. 173; G. Davison, 'The exodists: Miles Franklin, Jill Roe and the "drift to the metropolis"', *History Australia*, vol. 2, no. 2 (June 2005), pp. 35.1–11.

23 John Iliffe, *The African poor: a history* (Cambridge: Cambridge University Press, 1987) p. 277; C. Hamlin with J. Little, *The hospital by the river* (Melbourne: Pan Macmillan Australia, 2001); and M. Oppenheimer, *Volunteering: how we can't survive without it* (Sydney: UNSW Press, 2008), p. 175.

24 Beveridge, *Voluntary action*, p. 10.

25 J. Harris, *William Beveridge: a biography*, 2nd edn (Oxford: Clarendon Press, 1997), pp. 458–9.

26 'Hope for the bruised and broken', *Weekend Australian* (2–3 August 2008), p. 30. I thank Andrew Strickland for alerting me to this work.

27 'Sea-changing' and 'tree-changing' are Australian colloquialisms for population movements from the city to the coast or to the bush, often occurring at retirement. P. Cloke, 'Rural poverty and the welfare state: a discursive transformation in Britain and the USA', *Environment and Planning*, vol. 27, no. 6 (1995), pp. 1001–16; J. Byrnes and G. Harris, *Expenditure patterns of low income households: a pilot study* (University of New England: Rural Development Centre, 1992), pp. 33–4.

28 Australian Catholic Social Justice Commission, Noela Lippert, 'The spiral down to poverty', Occasional Paper, ACSJC, Canberra, March 1993, p. 4.

29 Suicides by geographical area 1988–98, Australian Bureau of Statistics, Publications 3309.0, *Suicides, Australia 1921 to 1998*, Canberra, 2000, www.abs.gov.au/AUSSTATS, p. 31 (accessed 17 May 2010).

30 Australian Bureau of Statistics, Publications 4102.0, *Australian social trends*, 1997, www.abs.gov.au/AUSSTATS, pp. 1–6 (accessed October 2008); *Year Book Australia*, vol. 89 (Canberra: Australian Bureau of Statistics, 2007), chapter 12, p. 367; Volunteering Australia, submission to the Productivity Commission, October 2004, copy in my possession.

31 Cowra data collected by Marianne Payten for this project, copy in my possession; for Community Builders, Gloncester, see www.communitybuilders.nsw.gov.au/rural_regional/programs, 2008 (accessed 17 May 2010).

32 City of Bendigo and Bendigo Bank websites, January 2009.

33 Australian Government Commission of Inquiry into Poverty, *Poverty in Australia*, vol. 1, p. 11.

34 Oppenheimer, *Volunteering*, p. 21.

35 Aitkin, *What was it all for?*, pp. 208–9.

36 'Stronger families and communities strategy funding', *Year Book Australia* (Canberra: Australian Bureau of Statistics), vol. 83 (2001), p. 267, vol. 86 (2004), p. 200, vol. 88 (2006), p. 219.

37 '"Vulnerable are all our responsibility", says Governor-General', *Sydney Morning Herald* (17 October 2008), p. 3.

10

Voluntary action in Britain since Beveridge

Pat Thane

What is 'voluntary action'?

One of the difficulties of discussing voluntary action, which has perhaps become even more acute since Beveridge's day, is the sheer variety of forms of activity that it can encompass. Indeed, in recent decades in Britain, the very language we use to discuss them has become more diverse and contested. Some organisations which were once staffed mainly by volunteers are now highly professionalised with a substantial salaried workforce, and receive significant government funding while pursuing the same aims as before. They are perhaps better described as non-governmental organisations (NGOs). However, a new term – 'the third sector' – has recently emerged as a descriptor of the whole voluntary/NGO sector, and was favoured by the most recent Labour government. For a while 'civil society' was in vogue as a descriptive term, following the end of the Cold War and the forefronting of ideas downplaying the role of the state and promoting the untrammelled market society, minimally regulated by the state. The unhelpful ambiguity of the term in this context has been well discussed by Jose Harris.[1] At present, alongside modernised, professionalised organisations lie a diversity of others which are indeed voluntary, many of them small and community-based, others larger and national or inter-national, pursuing a range of goals, whether charitable, humanitarian (for example helping refugees), government-lobbying, environmental, leisure-oriented or of other kinds. One thing that is clear is the sheer number of organisations still active within this broad sector.[2]

Also in Britain an important area of voluntary action has long been part of government. In particular, the magistracy, the ancient lower tier of the justice system, in which it plays an important role, is voluntary, as is the equally important jury service.[3] So also, until recently, were all elected local councillors, a key tier of government, though one with diminishing significance and independence, especially since the 1980s. Governors of state schools continue to be volunteers.

This sector, then, includes, as it long has done, a great variety of activities and institutional forms, which are in constant flux. There is such variety that there seems to be no satisfactory comprehensive typologies, despite the efforts of some social scientists.[4] But it is clear is that we are talking about a lot of associations and forms of association, a lot of people involved in them, now and in the past, and a very wide range of activities. Accurate measurement of change over time in this field is, in practice, impossible, because the terrain includes, and always has included, many organisations which are short-term and ephemeral and leave few traces or records behind, which does not mean that they were, or are, unimportant or ineffective. They may be single-issue groups that achieve their aims, or fail to do so, then fold because they have no reason to continue, for example campaigners against road or airport developments. We have no accurate measure over time of the number of such organisations or of their size. It is unclear, indeed, how to measure the scope and impact even of large, long-lasting organisations. Should it be done in terms of numbers of donors? Of activists? Of amount of income, or turnover? It has been no one's duty to record such data on a national scale.

We just do not know whether there are more 'voluntary' organisations, or more volunteers, now than when Beveridge wrote in 1948, or whether there were more, or less, in 1948 than before. Whatever the numbers, most people most of the time probably are not involved in any such association, though many may be involved at some point in their lives. But, however we look at it, it seems clear that this terrain of associations, which often have their origins outside the sphere of government, often pursuing aims which in the end require action by local or central government, is and has long been heavily populated, with ephemeral associations continually replaced by others, and other organisations long surviving while pursuing either unchanging or shifting objectives.

The cultural and political pessimism which leads to the argument that voluntary action and associationalism directed towards improving socio-political conditions has in some sense declined in Britain over the past century, or half century, seems to be mistaken. A United Kingdom Home Office survey in 2003 found that 30 per cent of adults in England and Wales had 'formally' volunteered within the previous twelve months; that is, they had participated in some form of institutionalised voluntary activity.[5] Many others are known to volunteer 'informally', for example helping out neighbours with difficulties, but they are difficult to quantify. Whether this is a higher or lower proportion of the population than in previous decades is, again, unknown owing to lack of comparable statistics, but voluntary action is clearly still very strong in early twenty-first-century Britain.

This strength is given a pessimistic spin by some commentators who see it as a substitute for genuine political activity at a time when participation in political parties (another, definitely declining, form of voluntary action) and voter turn-out are both at low levels.[6] On the other hand, it can be seen optimistically as a sign that very many people are committed to working for the community and to helping others. There has always been a complementary relationship in Britain between formal politics and political and social movements outside the formal political structures.[7]

A changing sector

The change in language applied to what was once routinely described as the voluntary sector has been slower than the transformation of some organisations that were once truly voluntary. Until relatively recently, the term 'non-governmental organisation' was applied only to international, mainly humanitarian, organisations. It is now applied increasingly to domestic ones.[8] It seems to signal a rather belated recognition that not all of the organisations that used to be called 'voluntary' are now 'voluntary' in the way they once were. Organisations such as the Child Poverty Action Group (CPAG) or One Parent Families/Gingerbread still make some use of voluntary workers and voluntary funding, but they are also highly professionalised, with paid professional staff, and often gain significant government funding.

The CPAG was founded in the 1960s as a professionalised, media-savvy, lobbying organisation.[9] One Parent Families was founded in 1918 as a wholly voluntary organisation, the National Council for the Unmarried Mother and her Child (NCUMC), dedicated to supporting a stigmatised group of people. It transformed itself from the 1960s into a highly professionalised institution, and in 2008 merged with a smaller voluntary organisation, Gingerbread, which had been formed as a self-help group for single mothers by Tessa Fothergill in 1970 after her own marriage ended.[10] The combined organisation was known as Gingerbread from January 2009.[11] It must be said, however, that even in the nineteenth and early twentieth centuries unpaid voluntary work could be highly 'professional' in the sense that it was dedicated, experienced and, sometimes, trained and many organisations largely staffed by volunteers employed at least some paid workers.[12]

But surely the greatest change in much, though not all, of this sector since 1948 is the reduced dependence on purely voluntary work and donations. The broad objectives of the type of organisation under discussion have remained fairly constant over the past 100 years and more: essentially organising for the achievement of socio-economic, legal and/or cultural equalities within the United Kingdom and/or internationally. Different organisations focus on different aspects of inequality at different times, and different aspects of inequality become prominent on the public agenda at different times, often propelled there by these organisations. They use various techniques, sometimes lobbying government and/or campaigning publicly, sometimes giving practical support to the social group with whom they are concerned, sometimes all of these things.

For example, the League of Coloured Peoples, established in 1931, was the first large organisation formed in Britain to campaign against racial discrimination.[13] Gypsies and Travellers, the minority group who arguably experience most discrimination and disadvantage in Britain still in the twenty-first century, formed no campaigning group until the Gypsy Council was created in 1966.[14] Voluntary associations composed wholly or mainly by another, very large, disadvantaged group, women, campaigned for gender equality through much of the nineteenth century and, particularly actively and effectively, immediately after the extension of the franchise to women aged thirty and above in 1918. It is possible to identify at least twenty changes in family, property, criminal and other aspects of the law in the 1920s, as well as improvements in state welfare provision (such as the granting of widows' and orphans' pensions in 1925) in the direction of greater gender equality and/or improvements in women's lives, which were, to some degree, the outcome of lobbying, demonstrating and drafting legislation and manoeuvring it through parliament (with the assistance of mainly male MPs) by women's associations. Arguably, newly enfranchised women worked to employ their new political legitimacy through associations because of their relative weakness as individuals in the political system. Their chances of being elected to parliament were slight; they could achieve more by working collectively outside parliament. They were generally most effective when associations combined to pursue a goal.[15] This gives some credence to the notion that voluntary action can provide alternatives to formal politics for those who feel excluded from the political system.

Some of the women's organisations founded between the wars continued to be active through at least to the 1960s. Some, such as the Fawcett Society (founded in 1866), are today more active than ever in campaigning for gender equality, after a period of relative obscurity from the late 1960s to the 1990s. Before the Second World War such associations were overwhelmingly genuinely voluntary, their personnel and funding relying upon unpaid work and voluntary donations. Now, the Fawcett Society, for example, is highly professionalised, with a permanent paid, often highly qualified, staff, though still dependent upon voluntary donations and still dedicated to the cause for which it was founded.[16] It changed in the later twentieth century as other organisations changed.

Voluntary action in the welfare state

Why these changes since 1948? The immediate post-war period seems to have been a time of uncertainty for voluntary organisations, though it has been too little researched – a black hole between the work of historians and social scientists.[17] The post-war Labour governments (1945–51), led by Clement Attlee, seemed to be divided between hostility and ambivalence to 'charity', as much voluntary action was seen at the time. This was understandable, given that this was the first ever majority Labour government, dedicated to improving the lives of working people, and many working people had bitter memories of being dependent on charity, in particular during the economic Depression of the inter-war years. But providers of relief to the poor were not the only voluntary organisations.

More surprisingly, as Daniel Weinbren (in Chapter 5) and others have acknowledged, Labour also proved rather unsympathetic to friendly societies, which were non-profit, non-governmental savings institutions, mostly founded in the eighteenth and nineteenth centuries, run by and for working people, mainly on a voluntary basis, and designed to enable them to support themselves in sickness, unemployment and old age. Labour appeared to believe that the twentieth-century state should be able to provide for all basic needs and that voluntary organisations should have a much smaller role in the expanded post-war welfare state. One of the many ways in which the Attlee government ignored the advice in Beveridge's otherwise influential 1942 report, *Social insurance and allied services*,[18] was in rejecting his belief that there were limits to how much 'welfare' the state could or should provide or afford. Beveridge had argued that the state should ensure that everyone in need had access to a sufficient income for subsistence, but that voluntary action, including personal saving through non-profit, voluntarily run friendly societies, should be encouraged in order to supplement state provision for those wanting, and able to afford, an above-subsistence standard of living. However, of course, Beveridge also, throughout his life, supported voluntary action, above all because he believed that its vibrancy signified a good, cohesive, society whose members felt committed to helping one another with their money, their time or both.[19]

Attlee himself had a background in voluntary action, having been (as had Beveridge) a resident in his youth at the Toynbee Hall Settlement in east London, where he had been converted to socialist politics (as the Liberal Beveridge had not). Attlee even became President of Toynbee Hall while he was Prime Minister after 1945. But his government did little to encourage voluntary organisations, though some received small subsidies when they were seen to be complementing the work of the state.

Many established organisations seem to have languished in the late 1940s and early 1950s, uncertain of their role now that the state was taking over much greater welfare responsibilities and often short of funds, perhaps because donors thought them no longer necessary in the new welfare state. Levels of taxation were also high throughout the period of Labour government, taking from the better-off, who might have contributed to voluntary action, to help poorer people both through government investment in economic development and job creation and through the expansion of state welfare services and benefits.[20] As a result, Toynbee Hall itself went through a period of uncertainty about its role and experienced a shortage of funding in the immediate post-war period.[21]

However, new voluntary organisations also emerged during and immediately after the war, as specific needs were identified for which the state was not providing. Indeed they were often formed to campaign for the needs of disadvantaged groups to be included in the government's plans for the promised 'New Jerusalem'. For example, the Old People's Welfare Committee was founded in 1940 in response to revelations of the poverty of older people in a wartime government social survey, and it continued to be active after the war and until the present day. The National Corporation for the Care of Old People was founded in 1947 (with support from the voluntary Nuffield Foundation) for similar reasons. Both still survive, now under the names of Age Concern and the Centre for Policy on Ageing respectively. The latter changed its name in 1980 'in recognition of the organization's transformation from a grant-giving to a policy-oriented agency'.[22]

In 1946, the Association of Parents of Backward Children (renamed the National Association for Mentally Handicapped Children in 1955, then MENCAP in 1969, which it remains) was formed by Judy Fryd and other parents concerned about the lack of support that they received for caring for their disabled children. In the same year, the National Association for Mental Health (later MIND) was formed. Both were responses to the very poor state, at the time, of provision for the mentally disabled and mentally ill, a serious gap which they campaigned for the promised welfare state to fill. They may have influenced the relative improvement in provision of this kind in the newly founded National Health Service from 1948. Certainly they increased public awareness of these issues. In 1953 the Spastics Society was founded to support the still neglected group of sufferers from cerebral palsy. It was renamed SCOPE in the 1990s in view of the negative popular connotations of the word 'spastic'. All five organisations have survived and become highly professional NGOs, still campaigning for improvements in the lives of older or mentally ill or disabled people.

Through the 1950s some older organisations faded away, but others, such as the settlements and the NCUMC, which had also faltered immediately after the war, found their feet and attracted funding again by recognising that they had a complementary role to the welfare state, filling the many gaps which were becoming evident, identifying unmet needs and campaigning for more comprehensive state action.

The 1960s and 1970s

Major changes came in the 1960s and early 1970s. The 1960s saw the foundation of new organisations with new characteristics. In the welfare field, among others, the CPAG was founded in 1965, following revelations by researchers (see below) of the unexpectedly high levels of poverty among larger families. Shelter was founded in 1966 by the Revd Bruce Kenrick to campaign for the homeless and the large numbers of people still living in deplorable housing. Its immediate success was much assisted by the coincidence that a film by Ken Loach about a young homeless couple, *Cathy come home*, was screened on television shortly afterwards and watched by twelve million viewers. Shelter, Scotland was formed in 1968. The Disablement Income Group (DIG) was founded in 1965 by Megan du Boisson. Suffering from the early stages of multiple sclerosis, she discovered that there were no state benefits available to married women, such as herself, who were not in paid employment and hence outside the national insurance system. They could apply for means-tested Supplementary Benefit, but this did not cover the costs of disability or chronic illness. DIG Scotland was formed in 1966 by another disabled woman,

Margaret Blackwood, inspired by du Boisson's work. DIG in both countries began on a voluntary basis but quite rapidly grew and attracted paid, trained support. With the support of sympathetic MPs, the groups played an important role in persuading the Labour government to introduce the Chronically Sick and Disabled Persons Act of 1970, which required all local authorities to register disabled people and publicise the services available to them. A full range of cash benefits for disabled people and their carers was introduced, though all of these measures were under-resourced and under-funded. All of these organisations supported issues which were not new but for which there had not been specific previous campaigning and support groups.

These and others were campaigning and lobbying groups, sometimes also providing services and raising voluntary funds, often with support also from central and local government and, increasingly, from the European Union, after Britain's entry to what was then the European Economic Community in 1973. They were staffed by media-savvy professionals, and had more arresting, memorable, media-friendly names than their antecedents. Often, and increasingly though the 1970s and 1980s, they moved from campaigning for disadvantaged groups to campaigning with them, becoming more inclusive as many disadvantaged people themselves became more assertive.

Alongside these professionalised NGOs, another kind of association developed, especially in the late 1960s and the 1970s, consciously less bureaucratised and professional, often less concerned to lobby and work with government, even rather oppositional to it, and more public, street-wise and inclusive. These included the Gay Liberation Front (GLF), founded in 1970, and the Women's Liberation Movement (WLM), founded in 1969, both of which were linked with wider, international gay, feminist, anti-racist, anti-war movements. These were 'new' social movements, as political scientists call them, in the sense that they took up (or, more accurately, brought more clearly into public view) new causes, rather than having anything new about their forms of organisation.[23] The GLF was outspoken about an old inequality in quite a new way. Previous campaigns for equal rights for homosexuals (the term 'gay' – Good As You – became current only in the 1970s when promoted by GLF), such as the Homosexual Law Reform Association (formed in 1958), had been highly discreet and consciously respectable in view of the illegal status of any expression of their sexuality. The GLF gained confidence from the 1967 Sexual Offences (England and Wales) Act, which decriminalised private homosexual activities between consenting adult men, providing the first legal sanction since the Buggery Act of 1533 had made sodomy punishable by hanging. This suggests how wider cultural attitudes were changing at this time.[24]

The issues particularly taken up by the WLM had all too often been the subject of past failed campaigns: domestic violence, about which women had campaigned unsuccessfully in the late nineteenth century; and rape and sexual violence, which had been pursued by women's organisations in the 1920s, though less openly at a time when sexual matters were not publicly discussed. The WLM succeeded in putting these issues permanently on the public agenda, though not, alas, in eliminating them. These organisations sought to change public attitudes and political actions as the professional NGOs did, not through employment of professionals, lobbying and mastery of the media but often through public, sometimes dramatic, events, such as the sabotaging of the Miss World contest by the WLM in 1970, which took place in the Royal Albert Hall before a large television audience.

These and other groups, who often employed less flamboyant or oppositional tactics and were more willing to work with government, campaigned for equal rights for excluded and disadvantaged people who had previously been marginalised or publicly silent. They were initiated by people who experienced these inequalities, and were overwhelmingly voluntary and poorly resourced and often militantly publicly active. They included the deliberately innocuously titled Minorities Research Group, which was formed in 1963 to provide counselling and contact for isolated lesbians and to inform public opinion and promote research. The Campaign Against Racial Discrimination (CARD) was founded in 1964, a broadly based group of black and white activists focussing on lobbying for legislation to outlaw race discrimination at a time when popular racism was increasingly evident. The Race Relations Act, introduced by Labour in 1965, began to address its concerns by declaring unlawful any discrimination in certain public places on grounds of colour, race, ethnic or national origin, and provided for the establishment of a Race Relations Board.

The Gypsy Council was formed in 1966 to protect the most disadvantaged, often forgotten, minority ethnic group in Britain. It held its first meeting in a Kentish pub displaying an all-too common 'No Gypsies' sign. Its manifesto called for camping sites in every county to be open to Travellers, equal rights to education, work and houses and equal standing through respect between themselves and their settled neighbours.[25] The Committee for Homosexual Equality (CHE) was founded in 1969, two years after the Sexual Offences (England and Wales) Act. The CHE campaigned for extension of the legislation to Scotland (achieved, eventually, in 1980) and Northern Ireland (achieved 1982), and for equal rights and respect for homosexuals in society generally.

Among the drivers of these changes in the 1960s and 1970s was the 'rediscovery of poverty'. This work, in particular that of Richard Titmuss, Peter Townsend and Brian Abel-Smith at the London School of Economics (LSE), revealed the extent of continuing poverty in the welfare state, especially among children (as we have seen, leading directly to the formation of the CPAG) and older people.[26] Secondly, more social service professionals were being trained in universities, for example in Titmuss's Department of Social Science and Administration at the LSE. Many of them believed they should go on to improve social conditions, acquiring a strong commitment to paid public service. The Labour Party's return to government between 1964 and 1970, for the first time since 1951, was also seen as making change possible, as it was thought to be more responsive than their conservative pre-decessors to pressure to redress inequalities. It was also perhaps the subject of excessive disillusionment when it did not deliver big changes immediately, despite the adverse economic climate, a situation which led to the formation of campaign-ing groups aiming to promote further cultural and policy change.[27]

Other reasons for change during this period included a less deferential mass media, willing, indeed eager, to publicise campaigns critical of government. A better-educated, less courteous population began to emerge from the relative prosperity of the post-war years, less willing to allow well-meaning people to act on their behalf and more willing to speak up for themselves if they felt disadvantaged. After the Second World War, middle-class married women were no longer largely debarred from paid work, as they had previously been. This removed an important reservoir of voluntary labour but created a substantial pool of people who were trained and paid to work in social services, both statutory and non-governmental. Older organ-isations at the same time took on similar characteristics to the newcomers such as the CPAG and Shelter, with more trained professional staff, and adopted snappier, more media-friendly names, which were often also responses to social change and to changing sensibilities about language. For example, NCUMC in 1973 became the National Council for One Parent Families in response to the spread of divorce, unmarried partnership and single parenthood, male and female, at that time. The Old People's Welfare Committee in the 1970s became Age Concern.[28] As we have seen, the National Association for Mentally Handicapped Children became MENCAP in 1969.

Alongside these new, revived and remodelled forms of action of the 1960s and 1970s, which mostly continue in some form to the present day, a third strand of voluntary, often community-based, associations on the much older model has continued to emerge, focussing on specific issues, and continues to do so. These have included self-help groups, such as Gingerbread (founded 1970 and described above). Some later evolved into, or, as Gingerbread has done, merged with, relatively well-funded NGOs. For example, the Zito Trust was founded in 1994 in memory of Jonathan Zito, who was killed by a schizophrenic man who had been released from hospital into 'the community', according to the official policy of the time, but given inadequate care in the community. The Zito Trust was set up to help such people who had been let down by the welfare state and to campaign for reform of mental health policy and of the law. It is now a well-established, well-funded organisation, sadly, because the issues have not gone away. Others remain small voluntary organisations or disappear or merge with other organisations as their objectives change.

But not all voluntary organisations of the 1960s and 1970s supported 'progres-sive' or welfare causes. The National Viewers' and Listeners' Association was founded in 1964 by fundamentalist Christians to clean up the 'disbelief, doubt and dirt that the BBC projects into millions of homes through the television screen', as its manifesto put it.[29] It was publicly prominent but there was little sign that it achieved its aims, as was the case with the Society for the Protection of the Unborn Child, formed in 1966 also by some Christians to oppose the projected legalisation of abortion, which was implemented in 1967.

Since the 1970s

These processes of organising and campaigning, initiated by volunteers, have long been a normal feature of British society and of many others. It is important not to take an evolutionary approach to this subject and to see all real voluntary organisations as existing in the past, superseded now by professional NGOs. There is a constant process of emergence of voluntary and community organisations, by no means all of which pursue 'progressive' causes, and some of which change into more formal NGO-style institutions. Some individuals may support, simultaneously or serially, several different types of organisation, governmental (for example political parties) and non-governmental. New issues regularly emerge. For example, environmental campaigns have been increasingly numerous since the 1970s, with Friends of the Earth established in 1971, Greenpeace in 1977, the Pesticides Action Network in 1986, the Rainforest Foundation in 1989 and Earth First! in 1991.[30]

The modernised organisations were more expensive to run than their voluntary predecessors. They had to pay salaries and often also paid for striking advertising, as well as meeting the costs of their regular services. They needed more funding in a world of increasing competition for donations. This may have increased the potential for dependence on funds from government or other sources, such as the private foundations. Institutions such as the Joseph Rowntree Foundation, the Nuffield Trust and the Wellcome Trust are themselves NGOs, and their role in supporting and developing smaller NGOs has been significant. Among many examples, we have seen (above) the Nuffield Foundation setting up what became the Centre for Policy on Ageing in 1947. The Joseph Rowntree Foundation, which had long funded research into social issues, from 1988 played an important role in funding pioneering research (in which disabled people were directly involved) aimed at facilitating independent living for people with physical and mental disabilities, and funding non-governmental training and support for people with learning difficulties, which influenced government measures to improve provision for these people.[31] The need for funds also stimulated the search for new kinds of fund-raising, some NGOs becoming 'social businesses' and selling goods in support of their cause. Not that selling goods to fund non-governmental campaigns was new: it was practised by the Anti-Corn Law League in the early nineteenth century and by countless organisations since, but the scale of sustained business is new.[32]

Some members of the non-bureaucratised, non-hierarchical movements of the late 1960s and early 1970s later created more formal institutions, which they saw as more effective in achieving their goals. This was perhaps most evident among women campaigning for gender equality. The WLM ceased to exist, but women continued to campaign on a variety of issues. Women were active in seeking peace in Northern Ireland from the late 1960s. In Wales and Scotland women once active in the post-1969 women's movement were very effective in influencing the creation of electoral systems for the devolved governments introduced in 1997, which had a proportional representation basis rather than the first-past-the post system used in elections to the Westminster parliament. This enabled unusually large numbers of women to be elected in 2001 – 50 per cent of the Welsh Assembly, and 40 per cent of members of the Scottish parliament compared with less than 20 per cent in the Westminster parliament.[33] Throughout Britain, similar action in the Labour Party led to the introduction of all-women shortlists for the selection of candidates for the 1997 general election and the exceptionally large number of women elected for Labour in consequence (101 compared with 32 in the previous 1992 general election). Some women's experience of the social movements of the 1960s and 1970s led them to believe that the more effective way to influence government was to participate in it.[34] Nevertheless, independent, voluntary, non-governmental and anti-governmental movements continue to emerge, for example anti-road protesters in the 1990s or environmental campaigners against a third runway at Heathrow in 2008–09.

From the late 1970s until the 1980s and 1990s, many organisations were being encouraged, and often funded by government, to take on larger roles that previously had been those of government, especially in the welfare field, such as running residential homes for older or disabled people. Government subsidies to voluntary organisations were not new in post-war Britain, but they increased especially fast under Mrs Thatcher's governments of 1979–90, and continued under Labour from 1997. This was an aspect of the international movement to cut state welfare spending and in the direction of economic liberalisation, following the 'oil shock' and the economic crisis of the mid-1970s. It posed problems for NGOs. Many did not see their role as taking on large-scale responsibilities, or that this was within their capabilities. This, they thought, was the role of the state. Theirs, they believed, was the complementary role of filling in the gaps, identifying new issues and pursuing them. And for all Mrs Thatcher's rhetoric about 'rolling back the state', with government funding came controls and conditions. The Thatcher governments simultaneously sought to close many voluntary and community organisations of which they disapproved. One reason for the dissolution of the Greater London Council in 1986 was its practice of funding gay, lesbian, anti-racist and other groups.

It was not new in the 1980s for voluntary organisations to receive state funding or to be integrated into the administration of state services. They had done so since before the First World War, when they played significant roles in the administration of the first old-age pensions, National Health Insurance and Unemployment Insurance, children's services and much more. The collapse of friendly societies after they were excluded from the administration of national insurance in 1946, which they had provided since 1911, may be a salutary lesson for non-governmental organisations that become too closely integrated with government. What effect does increasing reliance on government funding have on an NGO? When does it cease to be 'non-governmental' and with what effects? We need more case studies of these processes within actual NGOs. What, for example, has been the effect on housing associations, which were once mainly voluntary but some of which are now staffed by highly paid professionals, of becoming effectively arms of government and major providers of 'social housing' since the 1980s?

Conclusion: who are the volunteers now?

In the early twenty-first century, there is still room for volunteers even in highly professionalised organisations, such as the Red Cross. The volunteering population remains substantial, as suggested above, but, like the organisations discussed here, it has changed over time. Before the Second World War it was made up substantially of middle- and upper-class married women. Since 1945, if such women have wished to be active outside the home, they have increasingly been able to take paid work. As discussed by Georgina Brewis in Chapter 8, they were initially replaced by young people, who were encouraged to volunteer in the post-war decades. For example, the large international NGO Voluntary Service Overseas (VSO) was set up in 1958 to find opportunities for young people to work for a year or so after leaving school or university. Now, an important new resource is the growing number of fit and active retired people. In 2008 28 per cent of VSO volunteers were aged fifty or above, compared with 3 per cent twenty years before.[35] Older people are working in poor countries after retirement, as nurses, doctors and teachers, giving training in office skills and how to start businesses, and improving water supplies, with skills and experience to offer that people aged eighteen to twenty-one do not have. About 27 per cent of people over sixty are active in formal voluntary organisations in the United Kingdom.[36] Many younger people work long hours while bringing up children and have little time to spare. Older people have time, energy and very often skills and experience. The shape of the population changes but does not diminish the commitment to voluntary action in Britain and other countries.

Notes

1 J. Harris, 'Introduction', in J. Harris (ed.), *Civil society in British history: ideas, identities, institutions* (Oxford: Oxford University Press, 2003), pp. 1–12.
2 This is well discussed in J. McKay and M. Hilton, 'Introduction', in N. Crowson, M. Hilton and J. McKay (eds), *NGOs in contemporary Britain: non-state actors in society and politics since 1945* (Basingstoke: Palgrave, 2009), pp. 1–20.
3 T. Skyrme, *History of the justices of the peace* (Chichester: Barry Rose, 1994).

4 D. Halpin, 'NGOs and democratisation: assessing variation in the internal democratic practices of NGOs', in Crowson, Hilton and McKay (eds), *NGOs in contemporary Britain*, pp. 261–80. See also the 'new social movements' literature, for example, S. Tarrow, *Power in movement: social movement and contentious politics* (Cambridge: Cambridge University Press, 1998), and A. Lent, *British social movements since 1945: sex, colour, peace and power* (Basingstoke: Palgrave, 2001).

5 2003 Home Office Citizenship Survey, www.homeoffice.gov.uk/rds/pdfs04/acuact-comm03.pdf (accessed 18 May 2010).

6 The parties are not, understandably, always enthusiastic about releasing statistics. However, it is estimated that Conservative Party membership reached a peak in 1953, at 2.8 million. By 1997 it was estimated to have fallen to around 250,000. It is unlikely to have risen since then. D. Butler and G. Butler, *Twentieth century British political facts, 1900–2000* (London: Macmillan, 2000), pp. 141–2. The Labour Party publishes annual statistics which may be reliable. According to these figures Labour reached peak individual membership (that is, not including those who were members by virtue of membership of affiliated trade unions) in 1952, at one million. By 1998 (when trade union membership had ceased to be recorded) it had fallen to around 392,000. It also is unlikely to have risen since then. Butler and Butler, *Political facts*, pp. 158–9.

7 Harris (ed.), *Civil society*.

8 McKay and Hilton, 'Introduction'.

9 'The poor get poorer under Labour: CPAG's campaigns', witness seminar conducted at the Centre for Contemporary British History, Institute of Historical Research, University of London, 2000: www.ccbh.ac.uk/witness_CPAG_index.php (accessed 18 May 2010).

10 www.oneparentfamilies.org.uk (accessed 18 May 2010).

11 P. Thane, 'Unmarried motherhood in twentieth century England', *Women's History Review*, special issue on 'Lone motherhood', ed. Tanya Evans and Pat Thane (forthcoming 2011).

12 F. Prochaska, *Women and philanthropy in nineteenth century England* (Oxford: Oxford University Press, 1980).

13 A. Spry Rush, 'Imperial identity in colonial minds: Harold Moody and the League of Coloured Peoples, 1931–50', *Twentieth Century British History*, vol. 13, no. 4 (2002), pp. 356–83.

14 B. Taylor, *A minority and the state: travellers in Britain in the twentieth century* (Manchester: Manchester University Press, 2008).

15 P. Thane, 'What difference did the vote make?', in A. Vickery (ed.), *Women, privilege and power: British politics, 1950 to the present* (Stanford: Stanford University Press, 2001), pp. 253–88.

16 www.fawcettsociety.org.uk (accessed 18 May 2010).

17 But see Crowson, Hilton and McKay, *NGOs in contemporary Britain*; K. Bradley, *Poverty, philanthropy and the state: charities and the working classes in London, 1918–1979* (Manchester: Manchester University Press, 2009).

18 William Beveridge, *Social insurance and allied services*, Cmd 6404 (London: HMSO, 1942).

19 J. Harris, *William Beveridge: a biography*, 2nd edn (Oxford: Oxford University Press, 1997).

20 P. Thane, 'Labour and welfare', in D. Tanner, P. Thane, N. Tiratsoo (eds), *Labour's first century* (Cambridge: Cambridge University Press, 2000), pp. 80–118.

21 Bradley, *Poverty*.

22 www.cpa.org.uk/cpa/about_cpa.html (accessed 18 May 2010).

23 Tarrow, *Power in movement*; Lent, *British social movements*.

24 P. Thane (ed.), *Unequal Britain: equalities in Britain since 1945* (London: Continuum, 2010).

25 T. Acton, *Gypsy politics and social change: the development of ethnic ideology and pressure politics among British Gypsies from Victorian reformism to Romani nationalism* (London: Routledge and Kegan Paul, 1974), p. 163; Taylor, *A minority*. For a discussion of campaigning on all major equalities issues since 1945 see Thane (ed.), *Unequal Britain*.

26 B. Abel-Smith and P. Townsend, *The poor and the poorest*, Occasional papers on social administration (London: G. Bell and Sons, 1965); P. Townsend and D. Wedderburn, *The aged in the welfare state*, Occasional papers on social administration, no. 14 (London: G. Bell and Sons, 1965).

27 Thane, 'Labour and welfare', pp. 107–10.

28 www.ageconcern.org.uk/AgeConcern/our-story.asp (accessed 18 May 2010).

29 L. Black, 'There's something about Mary: the National Viewers' and Listeners' Association and social movement history' in Crowson, Hilton and McKay (eds), *NGOs*, pp. 182–200.

30 McKay and Hilton, 'Introduction'.

31 C. Barnes, *Disabled people in Britain and discrimination: a case for anti-discrimination legislation* (London: Hurst and Co., 1991); *Outside but not inside – yet! Leaving hospital and living in the community: an evaluation by people with learning difficulties* (London: People First, 1994).

32 See Crowson, Hilton and McKay (eds), *NGOs* for discussion of these issues.

33 S. Childs, J. Lovenduski and R. Campbell, *Women at the top, 2005: changing numbers, changing politics?* (London: Hansard Society, 2005) p. 19.

34 E. Breitenbach and P. Thane (eds), *What difference did the vote make? Women and citizenship in Britain and Ireland in the twentieth century* (London: Continuum, 2010).

35 *The Guardian* (3 January 2009).

36 2003 Home Office Citizenship Survey.

11

Beveridge, the voluntary principle and New Zealand's 'social laboratory'

Margaret Tennant

The announcement in late 1947 of Lord Beveridge's proposed visit to New Zealand generated many a paean to his distinguished career, his impressive intellect and even, in one instance, his superior physiognomy. Quoting an unnamed London journalist, New Zealand's newspaper *Southern Cross* extolled Beveridge's learned appearance:

> His features fit his faculties. The erect, long-backed head tells you of his power of assimilation. The broad, fine forehead explains his ability for impromptu 'dictation' – an art somewhere between literature and oratory, in which it is difficult to believe that even Mr. Churchill is his superior . . . The grey eyes and fighter's chin give you the born leader to whom an opportunity of taking big decisions on his own initiative is the bread of life.
>
> 'Outside the office' he is the softest-hearted, the gayest of men. But work has always been sacred, and those who neglect or whose relative slowness hold up his dynamic power pay a penalty which leaves on many weaker vessels a permanent scar.[1]

Given this somewhat intimidating description, it was as well that when William and Janet Beveridge began their month-long visit to New Zealand on 11 April 1948, they were, indeed, 'outside the office' and well disposed to their New Zealand hosts, as Melanie Oppenheimer has elaborated in Chapter 6. Guests first of the University of Otago in association with the Otago centennial celebrations, they were later hosted by the New Zealand government with 'every conceivable need or desire met in advance': 'a form of being nationalised which cannot too highly be commended', Lord Beveridge commented.[2] The pair visited government departments, met senior public servants and politicians and attended receptions and sherry parties, but also had time 'off the platform' to include drives around Otago and visits to Rotorua and Auckland before departing for Sydney by plane on 10 May.[3] The trip appeared to have been a great success, and Lord Beveridge spoke in formal and informal contexts on issues then dear to his heart: world government and security were at this time to be at the forefront of his concerns, but he also lectured on the need for voluntary action – or, as William and Janet put it in separate interviews, 'Beveridge is not enough'.[4] The eliding of Beveridge's name with the newly expanded British system of social security was a reference well understood by his Antipodean audiences, and the 'Beveridge Plan' was of particular interest to New Zealanders, whose own social security scheme had preceded that of the 'Mother Country' (as it was still called).

Over previous decades, New Zealanders had been immersed in what has been termed 'Better Britonism'; the notion that the former colony was not simply more British than most other parts of the Anglo-settler world, but a superior and more innovative version of Britain, without many of its negative attributes.[5] Beveridge joined a line of visiting luminaries fascinated by the elaboration – and rejection – of 'Old World' institutions and qualities in a small-scale society of predominantly British descent (among them Sidney and Beatrice Webb, who toured New Zealand in 1898, the American journalist Henry Demarest Lloyd in 1899 and George Bernard Shaw in 1934). The Beveridges subsequently commented on the pheno-menon of British people 'striking out in new conditions in new countries [with] new economic and political requirements', while seeing themselves as part of a greater British whole. The contrasting landscape of 'English Woodland and Volcanoes'[6] identified in their published account of the New Zealand visit was a physical manifestation of the familiar but different social forces that they observed there, and Janet Beveridge warned that it would be 'a mistake to imagine that this free and independent British spirit in a new environment . . . would not be critical of the behaviour of other British groups elsewhere or even inimical to it'.[7] While many New Zealanders still spoke of Britain as 'home' and another wave of assisted British migration was already under way in 1948, the Beveridges expressed con-cern that 'the young and the old may drift apart, that the young in haste or in anger may leave the nest, critical of the attitude of the parent country, impatient with her austerity and perhaps her dictatorial ways'.[8] For all that Beveridge was a distinguished visitor, his opinions were delivered in a country which had long prided itself on a reputation for being a 'social laboratory', to audiences with their own views on what they wanted to hear from him.[9]

And, as we have seen in Oppenheimer's general account of the Antipodean tour, it was on social security, not voluntary action, that New Zealanders most pestered him to speak. New Zealand's Social Security Act had been passed by the first Labour government in 1938, prior to the Second World War and well before the promul-gation of the Beveridge report of 1942. It rapidly fed into pre-existing notions of New Zealand as a small nation which was a testing ground for new ideas and policies. Social security, with its emphasis on payments according to means and benefits according to need, and its aims for universal provision in the areas of medical care and superannuation, rejected the social insurance principle which had informed funding of the British system since 1911. Part of Beveridge's address to his Otago audience entitled 'Public action for social advance' compared the two systems of social security, and he was particularly impressed by the fact that 'The two British communities of New Zealand and of Britain, at opposite ends of the earth, each have Social Security now developed further than any other country'. He also gently undermined the image of New Zealand as a social laboratory, pointing out how 'New Zealand took the same path, sometimes ahead of the Old Country and sometimes behind it', and tactfully conceding that since social security 'these two British communities [were] leaders of the world in this field, running neck and neck'.[10] This was the kind of commentary in which New Zealanders were most interested: if they had to share world leadership, it was at least with the 'Mother Country'.

With regard to voluntary action, New Zealand's international standing was less secure and New Zealanders' interest more muted. The social laboratory was mandated by an implicit rejection of charity, and voluntary action in New Zealand was more popularly directed at recreational and other leisure pursuits than at 'other' directed philanthropy.[11] In his address 'Voluntary action for social advance', Beveridge's comments were less directly comparative and drew substantially upon his recently completed report for the National Deposit Friendly Society. Dividing voluntary action into mutual aid and philanthropy, as in the soon-to-be published book, Beveridge noted that mutual aid was far more extensive in Britain than it was in the British communities of the Antipodes. While trade union membership was on a par, trade unions in New Zealand seldom paid benefits, and functioned within a more highly developed system of industrial arbitration than operated in Britain. On the philanthropic side, charitable trusts had a minimal presence in New Zealand. The address noted the continued need for voluntary action even after social security, the ongoing place for friendly societies to supplement social security and the role of voluntary action in pioneering, experimentation and citizen service beyond formal politics, all themes in his report. Beveridge concluded by emphasising the important role of the state in supporting voluntary effort, financially and ideologically, if the alternatives of totalitarianism and revolution were to be avoided.[12]

While most New Zealanders' interest was in public action for social advance, it is likely that 'Voluntary action for social advance' alerted those potentially interested to the forthcoming book, which later made its way into New Zealand libraries and was cited in at least one address to the New Zealand Institute of Public Administration.[13] The Beveridges' account of their tour, *On and off the platform: under the Southern Cross*, was published in New Zealand and Australia in January 1949, and contained polished and expanded versions of William's lectures, along with other chapters where the voice of Janet Beveridge was more prominent. As a condensed and focussed version of the more disjointed report *Voluntary action*, the lecture is significant in its own right, but it also signals differences in the ways in which voluntary action was manifest across the British world. Whatever the mechanism for New Zealanders' engagement with *Voluntary action*, neither Beveridge's visit nor his publications took place in a void. Voluntary action was plentiful in New Zealand, but many of its separate manifestations had developed differently in a colonial context, and it is worth examining the three main areas on which Beveridge himself focussed to get a sense of this.

First is the role of friendly societies, which had a presence in New Zealand within a year of the signing of the Treaty of Waitangi with Maori in 1840. Names such as those of the Manchester Unity Order of Odd Fellows, the United Order of Druids and the Ancient Order of Foresters made an early appearance in the new colony. Many migrants brought rule and ritual books to found affiliated branches of these familiar associations in their new home, and in a fluid and often transient society, the friendly societies provided a ready means of integration into new communities. The role of friendly societies in advancing social cohesion was more important than any insurance role in the first decades of European settlement, their festivals, parades and picnics providing diversion well beyond their actual membership in communities with few other social outlets.[14] Jenny Carlyon has suggested that, as in Australia, in New Zealand friendly societies were defined by class less than in the home country; they were more socially diverse, drawing upon skilled as well as unskilled workers, but also having a significant minority of petty proprietors, semi-professionals and white-collar workers among their members.[15] As the insurance role of the societies became more important than the social role in the twentieth century, the proportion of the latter groups increased.

By the end of the nineteenth century there were 465 friendly societies and lodges in New Zealand, with a membership of around 40,200. In 1938 total membership had peaked at just over nearly 114,000 (in a population of 1.6 million), the Social Security Act signalling their eventual demise as the principal means of insurance against accident or illness.[16] Proportionately, the numbers were less impressive than in Britain and Australia. David Thomson has argued that in the last years of the nineteenth century 'perhaps one in six or seven adult men (at most) belonged to a society' in New Zealand, rising towards one in four during the peak inter-war years. The nineteenth-century proportions, in particular, were lower than in all the Australian states, except for Western Australia, and considerably lower than in Britain, especially if the full panoply of friendly societies, working men's clubs, shop clubs, building societies and co-operatives there are also taken into account.[17] Beveridge himself commented that on a population basis in the 1940s he would have expected New Zealand to have three to four times the number of friendly society members in order for to be comparable with Britain and Australia, and that some forms of mutualism were virtually absent in the dominion.[18] But if this was one part of his pattern of voluntary action which was considerably weaker in New Zealand, it was not simply because of the numbers involved. New Zealand's friendly societies kept their distance from the state, and so were not incorporated into the state apparatus as happened in the United Kingdom under social insurance. As the state extended its reach, the friendly societies were effectively sidelined, quite deliberately so under social security, and by the time of Beveridge's visit their decline was well and truly underway.[19] Beveridge's hope for revitalised forms of friendly society, including service provision as well as insurance, had a far weaker basis for realisation in New Zealand than in the United Kingdom. To a New Zealand reader, the emphasis on mutualism and on friendly societies in *Voluntary action* is surprising.

Charitable trusts were similarly much less evident in the New Zealand that Beveridge visited, and in its past. His particular concern was with trusts which had outlived their founders' intent and their usefulness. While the long-established charitable trusts and endowments of the 'Old World' did not transport to the new, the laws which framed them did inform New Zealand law. But because there were so few significant charitable trusts, there was no need for a Charities Commission until very recent times (and then for a somewhat different purpose). The colonial rich were notoriously disinclined to bequeath substantial legacies to charitable causes, the Inspector-General of Charitable Institutions claiming in 1898 that 'the social sanction (*noblesse oblige*) . . . in spite of its power in an old country, had failed . . . Some of its most potent elements were incapable of transplantation [to New Zealand], while others were slow-growing and took too long to mature'.[20] Philanthropy more generally was an optional extra for those seeking recognition and social power, and it never acquired the functional value it had in overseas contexts for both new and old elites. For this reason, charities looked to the state for support relatively early in New Zealand's history, and voluntary effort was never seriously seen as an alternative to state activism.[21]

There was nonetheless a range of charities and other forms of voluntary effort based upon British models by the time of the Beveridges' visit. Voluntary action was classified under some seventeen heads in Beveridge's 1948 report *Voluntary action*, and virtually all of these, with the exception of the settlement movement, were represented in some way in New Zealand by voluntary effort, in some cases by societies directly linked to their British counterparts. The range of voluntary effort was less rich and less historically grounded than in Britain, but it was nonetheless significant in a small country. It was underwritten by a sense of a 'new' society supposedly free from many of the evils of the 'old' world but nonetheless very open to external influences and movements – and by a tension between rejection and replication of the world that migrants knew; by a settlement pattern in which the British predominated, but with a disproportionate representation among them of migrants from the Celtic fringes of Scotland, Ireland and Cornwall; by the presence of a strong central state and a relatively weak system of local government, in which social service provision was limited; and by the presence of a significant and increasingly articulate indigenous Maori population, who were eventually to bring the assumptions and flavour of their own cultural dynamics to concepts of voluntarism. Recent analysis of voluntary organisations in contemporary New Zealand suggests a distinct bias towards bodies characterised as 'expressive' rather than 'service'-oriented. This reflects historical dynamics, and the importance of recreation and sport, rather than welfare, as outlets for the volunteer impulse – and especially for male voluntary action.[22] Philanthropic endeavour, on the other hand, was regarded with a mix of approval and suspicion; as worthy, but also as a residue of the British class system, largely unnecessary in a 'new' country so well endowed with natural resources and employment opportunities.

Nonetheless, one of Beveridge's most forceful points, about continuing support for voluntary effort in a changing, less religiously motivated society, was clearly relevant to New Zealand. His 'Voluntary action' address emphasised that the needs of all individuals were not the same, and could not be met by the state alone; that the pioneering role of voluntary effort remained vital; and that there were some areas which the state should definitely leave to voluntary effort. These were all points that had been made by New Zealand organisations faced with the introduction of social security in 1938, views generally accepted by politicians, who gave practical as well as rhetorical endorsement to the value of voluntarism even as the role of the state expanded on virtually all fronts – social welfare, employment promotion and economic interventionism. As the Labour cabinet minister (and later Prime Minister) Peter Fraser said in 1936 of the Plunket Society and the Children's Health Camps movement (two prominent welfare organisations concerned with children's health and welfare), government did not want to quash 'all of that goodwill, all of that wonderful voluntary effort and that wonderful spirit'. He could not imagine 'that anything could take the place of that personal touch and cooperation'.[23] And yet both the Plunket Society and the Children's Health Camps involved voluntary activity underwritten by successive New Zealand governments: in the absence of large financial benefactors, government had become New Zealand's most generous and reliable philanthropist. Beveridge emphasised in his New Zealand address the continued scope and need for voluntary action, alongside the need of the state to make direct grants from public funds to approved philanthropic agencies.[24] This development had started in New Zealand during the early colonial period, and it accelerated markedly after the Second World War. Amid a rhetoric of partnership, the challenge was for the state to do this in a way which did not destroy the independence of the voluntary organisations assisted. Beveridge's reference to the dilemma posed by the Scylla of laissez-faire and the Charybdis of totalitarianism pinpointed an ongoing quandary for governments in terms of both their own actions and their relationships with the voluntary sector.[25]

New Zealand, then, had its own, existing trajectory for working out the nature and extent of voluntary action and its relationship with state activity. Beveridge's 1948 report was one of a number of publications reflecting on the role of the state and democracy with which some of the country's politicians and, more particularly, its public servants engaged. The emergence of the New Zealand Institute of Public Administration in the 1930s provided a forum in which such ideas could be discussed in a semi-academic context, and one such occasion was particularly significant for its reference to Beveridge and to *Voluntary action*. In 1955 the Assistant Secretary for Justice, Dr John Robson, gave a paper to the seventh annual convention of the institute, which stood out from the others. As a New Zealander with a doctorate in law from the University of London, Robson was one of the more widely travelled and better-educated members of the bureaucracy, aware of overseas trends and with international contacts. However, he also acknowledged the intellectual stimulus provided by the Christchurch branch of the Workers' Educational Association (WEA) during the 1930s. Via the WEA he had been exposed to addresses by social activists and members of voluntary groups, as well as politicians and social administrators.[26] When he became Secretary for Justice in 1960, he brought to the position not only wide experience but, as his successor noted, 'a strong humanitarian sense, a positive and coherent philosophy, and a zeal for what came to be called responsible experimentation':

> Dr Robson regarded the participation of private citizens and groups in the work of the Department [of Justice] and of the administration generally as an essential element in a democratic society. He did not see the government and the community as divorced from each other. The informed private citizen had a most important part to play and he gave every encouragement to public service outside the ordinary administrative machinery.[27]

These were sentiments which Beveridge would have endorsed, and the implied sense of partnership and interpenetration between state and voluntary effort (with private citizens drawn into the activities of government departments, and public servants being encouraged to join voluntary agencies) may have been more readily achieved in New Zealand's relatively compact society than elsewhere in the British world.

Robson was certainly aware of Beveridge's work, and is likely to have met him during the 1948 tour. While most speakers at the Institute of Public Administration's 1955 convention talked about either monetary benefits or case work, Robson specifically asked the bigger questions about who should be responsible for social services administration, and whether central government was taking too much responsibility away from local government and voluntary associations. In elaborating on his theme, he drew upon Constance Braithwaite's 1938 book *The voluntary citizen*, A. D. Lindsay's *The essentials of democracy* and, most extensively, Beveridge's *Voluntary action*. His affirmations of voluntary action were very similar to Beveridge's: the social environment characterised by voluntary associations was the one which encouraged the fuller development of human beings and enabled them to make a better contribution to society; it was not enough that they merely participate in the political machinery of democracy. At times the state had shown an 'indecent haste' to strip voluntary bodies of their functions, 'when a little more patience, a little more understanding, and a little more assistance would have brought voluntary bodies to the standard demanded without involving the loss of the services of willing, able and public-spirited citizens'. Robson went on to note that voluntary associations were not the recipients of large grants from the wealthy, and that although they could compensate by seeking smaller donations from a wider base, such activity often took a disproportionate amount of time and energy away from the cause itself.[28] There was a case, then, for the receipt of grants from the state, and while Robson acknowledged that many were already in this position, he addressed the issue of accountability. His view was that to encourage voluntary associations, 'carping controls' should be kept to a minimum, with flexibility as the keynote. Quoting Beveridge, he concluded that 'Voluntary action is needed to do things which the State should not do, in the giving of advice, or in organizing the use of leisure. It is needed to do things which the State is most unlikely to do. It is needed to pioneer ahead of the State and make experiments'.[29]

And this is precisely what Robson and his closest associates encouraged, using the 1955 paper as the basis of a policy change within the Department of Justice which would hugely strengthen the role of voluntary groups concerned with prisoners' aid and marriage guidance.[30] In New Zealand the marriage guidance movement, in particular, had close associations with its British counterpart, and the role of New Zealand public servants in rescuing and nurturing it into a national body provides a first example of how intertwined the state and the voluntary sector could become.

The men and women who brought marriage guidance to New Zealand in 1948 drew on British models, including the use of 'trained amateurs' as volunteer counsellors. However, the use of inadequately selected and trained personnel led to various problems, not least of which was the bad press associated with Christchurch's Parker-Hulme murder case in 1954: this involved two young girls convicted of murdering the mother of one of them, and the consequent exposure of the marital affairs of the other mother, who, unfortunately, was counselling secretary of the Christchurch Marriage Guidance Council.[31] Robson, as Undersecretary and then Secretary for Justice, oversaw the revitalisation of marriage guidance in New Zealand, through the appointment within the department of a national adviser on marriage guidance (a clergyman named Les Clements) and a national advisory committee of academics, church social service personnel, senior public servants and medical personnel to oversee counsellor training and advise government. In the 1960s counsellor selection and training was provided by, and at the expense of, the department, while the finances of local marriage guidance councils were assisted by grants from the department and Golden Kiwi grants from the national lottery.

Traditions of dialogue and exchange between New Zealanders and their British counterparts were apparent in this area, as in many others. Visits to Marriage Guidance headquarters in London by Robson and Clements were reciprocated by the British National Marriage Guidance Council secretary A. J. ('Joe') Brayshaw in 1963, for example. Brayshaw wrote of the high standard of training and close supervision of counsellors that had resulted from Department of Justice initiatives in New Zealand, and also commented on the intimacy in public affairs that was possible in a country with a population of only two and a half million, a closeness 'impossible among vast populations'.[32] Privately, Brayshaw expressed hesitation about the New Zealand Department of Justice's role in providing training for marriage guidance counsellors, a responsibility in Britain of the National Marriage Guidance Council, and he implied that, while Robson's interest in the movement was the best guarantee of its success, New Zealand's volunteer Marriage Guidance Council needed to take greater initiative in leading activities.

Robson's response, though good-humoured, shows the sense of distinctiveness with which New Zealanders could respond to such feedback, with shades, perhaps, of the 'free and independent British spirit' in the new environment that Janet Beveridge had detected earlier. Defending the use of a government-appointed advisory committee on marriage guidance, he asserted that 'It seems to me that under the Advisory Committee system we get the best that the voluntary world can offer and yet at the same time the facilities of the Government Department are available'. Furthermore, he saw the scale of New Zealand society as a significant factor in the configuration of relations between government and the voluntary sector, most especially the tendency to rely on state expertise and organisational strength:

> Cities abroad run to the millions – ours to the thousands. We have a population of $2^1/_2$ million scattered over a territory about one thousand miles in length. An idea can be successfully applied in other parts of the world where there is a high density of population but will fail in New Zealand because not only are the problems for which it is trying to cater scattered over the country but so is the talent that is available for dealing with such problems. This explains why there is a disposition in New Zealand to expect the state to help.

If Brayshaw despaired of the New Zealand approach, he concluded, he was in excellent company, for a series of visitors, including André Siegfried and the Webbs, had concluded that New Zealanders were 'crudely empirical' in their approach to social issues, inclined to respond individually to similar problems without striving for any consistency from a set of principles.[33]

In terms of the relationship between voluntary and public action for social advance, both Robson and Brayshaw implicitly acknowledged the exceptional intimacy and interpenetration of the sectors in New Zealand. Robson's efforts in the Department of Justice stand out because they were underwritten by a more coherent philosophy than this exchange suggests, and because Robson was the New Zealand public servant who most overtly acknowledged the influence of Beveridge at the height of New Zealand's welfare state. Under Robson's benign oversight, relations between voluntary agencies and the Department of Justice were positive and constructive. Rather than the relationship between government and voluntary agencies being pushed towards the 'Charbydis of totalitarianism', there was considerable freedom of action, and any accountability for government grants was relatively relaxed. This was not to last, however, for social changes and the expansion of state contracts in New Zealand from the 1980s rupturing cosy relationships.

Other instances of partnership between government and the voluntary sector did result from initiatives which, if not altogether 'crudely empirical' were pragmatic and *ad hoc*, with cost-saving to government an overt consideration. Provision for the elderly provides another example of voluntary action with state support in post-war New Zealand. Where *Voluntary action* turned to the needs remaining in a social service state, Beveridge placed considerable emphasis on the aged, who required improved provision for independent housing, residential care for those unable to care for themselves and greater medical assistance.[34] Over the 1940s and 1950s parallel concern about the welfare of the aged developed in New Zealand, along with a sense that state action directed towards children, families and those of working age (via benefits, health services and investment in housing) was in striking contrast to provision for the elderly.[35] Although around 50 per cent of the total amount spent in cash benefits under the Social Security Act was devoted to old-aged pensions and universal superannuation by the early 1950s,[36] many were quick to identify and to criticise assumptions that the way to deal with all social ills was to hand out money.[37]

One result of this concern was a vast increase in subsidies paid out to religious and voluntary organisations to provide residential care for the elderly. As a Treasury memo noted in 1950, 'By successfully enlisting the support of voluntary organisations, [the problem of accommodation for the elderly] could be solved more economically than by the assumption of direct responsibility by the State'.[38] Capital subsidies to voluntary and religious organisations for buildings were followed by maintenance subsidies, and provision for the elderly was promulgated as a successful partnership between state and the voluntary sector – indeed, in New Zealand, this was the area where the term 'partnership' started to be used in a social policy sense as early as the 1950s. Comparing provision for the elderly in New Zealand and Britain, the head of New Zealand's first university-based social work course (and recent British migrant), Professor David Marsh, concluded in 1952 that 'the encouragement of . . . co-operation between Statutory and Voluntary bodies in providing special services for old people is perhaps the most important change which [had] appeared in Government policy in [New Zealand and Britain]'.[39] But one consequence was a proliferation of residential facilities which distorted the pattern of care for the aged for several decades. In New Zealand a 1976 report claimed that 34 per cent of those in religious and voluntary sector homes were fit elderly people who would be better cared for in the community with other kinds of support.[40] Further, by the 1970s the scale of residential care and the accountabilities required had pushed church social services away from their parish bases and towards more professionalised, and separate, social service associations. Beveridge might not have endorsed either consequence.

Voluntary action was the product of a particular time and place, and whatever the universality of many of its ideas, voluntary action, its presence and absence, and its various forms, raised different questions beyond the United Kingdom. The third area to which we now turn is one which does not feature in *Voluntary action*. While in New Zealand in 1948, Beveridge had enjoyed a Maori welcome and civic reception in Rotorua. 'There is great fellow-feeling between New Zealanders and British,' he is quoted as saying, 'and that extends to New Zealanders who are Maoris'.[41] Not all Maori, even at this time, would have prioritised an identity as 'New Zealanders', some tribes having a conflicted relationship with government which went back to the struggles and land loss of the colonial era. While New Zealand had long been part of the British world, its colonial history and the existence of a strong, indigenous Maori population meant that there was at least one distinctive element to voluntary action in New Zealand. Apart from a couple of Citizens' Advice Bureaux case studies in an appendix to *Voluntary action*, there is little sense there of ethnicity or of differing cultural perceptions around voluntarism. And yet, by the 1940s, with accelerating Maori urbanisation, the voluntary sector in New Zealand was already having to engage with these issues. Mainstream bodies such as the churches did this through Maori missions, which shifted their focus to cities and to service provision, while some bodies, such as the Crippled Children Society, developed separate budget lines for Maori services and fretted over how best to reach their Maori clientele. Others made no such attempt, assuming the eventual assimilation of Maori into the mainstream culture.

Maori were not passive in these processes, having long formed their own associations, drawing on European forms to further Maori ends. In the post-war era, Maori voluntary organisations proliferated, assisting in adaptation to urban contexts and replacing severed tribal links with other forms of social support.[42] Some pan-tribal associations were to emerge, the most important in the post-war era being the nationally organised Maori Women's Welfare League, formed in 1951. The league had close links to the Department of Maori Affairs, and welfare officers from that department (themselves Maori) often took the lead in establishing branches of the league out in the community – another example of the close links between government and voluntary action in the New Zealand setting. It has been argued that the boundaries between the department and Maori communities frequently 'merged and blurred', and that, despite the power and reach of the Department into Maori communities in the post-war decades, its effectiveness was dependent upon Maori communities, tribal structures and leaders.[43]

The emergence of new Maori organisations promoting Maori sovereignty, Maori language and the redress of past and present grievances was especially apparent from the 1970s. This saw a more contested relationship with the Department of Maori Affairs and the eventual devolution of many of its service functions to tribally based organisations. So-called 'mainstream' organisations also had to take greater account of Maori needs, and to pay heed to the obligations implicit in the Treaty of Waitangi, signed with Maori tribes in 1840. Ethnicity as it informed the voluntary sector in New Zealand involved an indigenous people whose status was that of *tangata whenua*, or 'people of the land', and whose standing resulted from forces quite different from those of new immigrants.

In the vast array of Maori associational life, *whanau*, or extended family, remained vital. Doing for 'others' was complicated by responsibility for *whanau* and by tribal linkages, and, it has been argued, concepts of 'sharing' were more important than the notion of 'giving'.[44] Ultimately, where Maori activities also involved the use of taxpayer revenues, conflict could arise between Maori ways of operating, bureaucratic accountabilities, Maori responsibility to kin and European perceptions of nepotism.[45] Maori efforts may have fitted more with Beveridge's concepts of mutualism than with those of philanthropy. By 1948 New Zealand's indigenous people were already giving a distinctive flavour to voluntary action, and they would do so even more forcefully in the last two decades of the century.

Beveridge's *Voluntary action* was one expression of world-wide debates about the relationship between the state and voluntary organisations, debates which accelerated alongside the advance of state welfare. Beveridge visited a New Zealand which had long experience of state activism and a welfare state symbolised by the 1938 Social Security Act. Voluntary action was nonetheless on the agenda, the Act, or more accurately, the prospect of social security having forced many agencies to reflect upon their purpose and value to government. The configuration of voluntary action in New Zealand to some extent replicated that of the 'Mother Country', but also differed in significant ways. Sporting and recreational pursuits appear to have absorbed a fair proportion of volunteer energies, while philanthropy had a lower profile and more fragile existence than in Britain. Maori had their own organisational forms, which would claim ever greater space within the spectrum of associational life as the century ended. Also shaping the balance of forces within the welfare economy were the weakness of territorial local government, especially in relation to social service provision, and the corresponding strength of central government in a numerically small population.

As a distinguished visitor to New Zealand, Beveridge was honoured as the father of Britain's welfare state. In his presentations he nonetheless gave 'voluntary action for public advance' equal weighting with 'public action for social advance', providing an authoritative referent for those already attuned to the value of voluntarism. His ideas were subsequently mediated by at least one prominent public servant, John Robson, who used public resources to revitalise organisations, encouraging them, as Beveridge had advocated more generally, to experiment in areas where the state had to tread warily, if at all. Voluntary action in New Zealand, as elsewhere, was shaped by the interplay of historical forces and by the faith of individuals in its democratic possibilities.

Notes

1 Archives New Zealand, Wellington, EA1 PM 59/3/301, part I, press cutting, *Southern Cross* (24 November 1947).

2 W. and J. Beveridge, *On and off the platform: under the Southern Cross* (Wellington and Melbourne: Hicks, Smith & Wright, 1949), p. 12. See also *Evening Post* (Wellington, 24 April 1948).

3 See J. and W. Beveridge, *Antipodes notebook* (London: Pilot Press, 1949), for a further account of the trip. See also Archives New Zealand, Wellington, IA 1 152/70 for the official Department of Internal Affairs itinerary for the visit, along with other arrangements made.

4 See, for example, *Auckland Weekly News* (21 April 1948); *Auckland Star* (8 May 1948).

5 This is most extensively elaborated by J. Belich in *Paradise reforged: a history of the New Zealanders from the 1880s to the year 2000* (Auckland: Allen Lane and Penguin Press, 2001); see especially pp. 76–86.

6 Beveridge, *Antipodes notebook*, pp. 36–8.

7 Beveridge, *Antipodes notebook*, p. 42.

8 Beveridge, *Antipodes notebook*, p. 43.

9 Beveridge was particularly keen to speak on world security, without which social security was unattainable, but he found his audiences in New Zealand and Australia keenest to hear about conditions in Britain and his views on social security. Beveridge, *Antipodes notebook*, pp. 84–5.

10 Beveridge, 'Public action for social advance', in *On and off the platform*, pp. 40, 41, 43.

11 For further on this, see M. Tennant, M. O'Brien and J. Sanders, *The history of the non-profit sector in New Zealand* (Wellington: Office for the Community and Voluntary Sector, 2008), pp. 3, 8–9.

12 Beveridge, 'Voluntary action for social advance', pp. 62–78.

13 See J. Robson, 'Social services administration: whose responsibility?', in K. J. Scott (ed.), *Welfare in New Zealand* (Wellington: New Zealand Institute of Public Administration, 1955), pp. 19–36.

14 J. Carlyon, 'New Zealand friendly societies, 1842–1941' (PhD thesis, University of Auckland, 2001), pp. 2, 34–4, 61–6.

15 Carlyon, 'New Zealand friendly societies', p. 247.

16 Carlyon, 'New Zealand friendly societies', pp. 31, 245.

17 D. Thomson, *A world without welfare: New Zealand's colonial experiment* (Auckland: Auckland University Press and Bridget Williams Books, 1998), pp. 40–1.

18 Beveridge, *On and off the platform*, p. 69.

19 Carlyon, 'New Zealand friendly societies', p. 249.

20 Annual Report on Hospitals and Charitable Institutions, *Appendices to the journals: House of Representatives*, 1898, H-22, p. 2.

21 On this see M. Tennant, *The fabric of welfare: voluntary organisations and government in New Zealand, 1840–2005* (Wellington: Bridget Williams Books, 2007).

22 J. Sanders, M. O'Brien, M. Tennant, S. Sokolowski and L. Salamon, *The New Zealand non-profit sector in comparative perspective* (Wellington: Office for the Voluntary and Community Sector, 2008).

23 Archives New Zealand, Wellington, H1 35/14/41 (B.9), Minutes, Health Camps Conference, 10 July 1936.

24 Beveridge, *On and off the platform*, p. 77.

25 Beveridge, *On and off the platform*, pp. 77–8.

26 J. Robson, *Sacred cows and rogue elephants: policy development in the New Zealand justice department* (Wellington: Government Printing Office, 1987), p. 6.

27 Robson, *Sacred cows and rogue elephants*, pp. 282–3.

28 Robson, 'Social services administration', pp. 29, 30.

29 Robson, 'Social services administration', p. 31.

30 Robson, *Sacred cows and rogue elephants*, p. 16.

31 On the history of marriage guidance in New Zealand see J. Daly, *MG reflecting: a portrait of marriage guidance in New Zealand 1949–1989* (Wellington: Marriage Guidance New Zealand, 1989); L. Clements, 'Marriage guidance in New Zealand: the story of a "movement"', in H. Stewart Houston (ed.), *Marriage and the family in New Zealand* (Wellington: Hicks, Smith & Son, 1970), pp. 157–73.

32 A. Brayshaw, 'Marriage guidance in New Zealand', *Marriage Guidance* (February 1964), pp. 24–6.

33 Alexander Turnbull Library, Wellington, John Lochiel Robson Collection, 92-162-10/27, A. J. Brayshaw to J. L. Robson, 28 October 1963; Robson to Brayshaw, 25 November 1963.

34 Lord Beveridge, *Voluntary action: a report on methods of social advance* (London: George Allen & Unwin, 1948), pp. 226–34.

35 D. C. Marsh, 'Old people in the modern state', *Political Science* (March 1952), pp. 22–3.

36 Marsh, 'Old people in the modern state', p. 25.

37 Archives New Zealand, Wellington, H1 104 (25619), press cutting, *North Canterbury Gazette* (25 November 1949).

38 Archives New Zealand, Wellington, H1 104/4 (25575), B. C. Ashwin, Secretary of Treasury, to Prime Minister Holland, 24 March 1950.

39 Marsh, 'Old people in the modern state', p. 24. Marsh returned to the United Kingdom to teach at the University of Nottingham in the mid-1950s, after helping to establish the School of Social Science at Victoria University in Wellington.

40 G. Salmond, *Accommodation and service needs of the elderly*, Special Report no. 46 (Wellington: Department of Health, 1976), p. 89.

41 *Dominion* (5 May 1948).

42 R. Walker, 'Māori people since 1950', in G. Rice (ed.), *The Oxford history of New Zealand*, 2nd edn (Auckland: Oxford University Press, 1992), p. 503.

43 A. Harris, 'Maori and "the Maori affairs"', in B. Dalley and M. Tennant (eds), *Past judgement: social policy in New Zealand history* (Dunedin: University of Otago Press, 2004), pp. 191–206.

44 D. Robinson and T. Williams, 'Social capital and voluntary activity: giving and sharing in Māori and non-Māori society', *Social Policy Journal of New Zealand*, vol. 17 (2001), pp. 52–71.

45 For further on this see M. Tennant, 'Welfare interactions: Maori, government and the voluntary sector in New Zealand', *History Australia*, vol. 2, no. 3 (December 2005), pp. 80.1–15.

12

After Beveridge: the state and voluntary action in Australia

Paul Smyth

Introduction

In 2008, the newly elected Labor government of Australia initiated a public consultation process with a view to establishing a national compact with the voluntary
sector. This was presented as integral to the implementation of its new social policy
agenda: social inclusion. This apparent reanimation of the British social policy
influence in Australia – in eclipse since the 1970s – means that the Beveridge period
in British social policy acquires fresh significance for Australian researchers seeking
to clarify the role of the voluntary sector.[1] Of course, the policy transfer between the
two countries has always been complex, and there is no suggestion that Australia
will simply imitate New Labour's reconfiguration of the voluntary sector. Always
very dependent on the state, the sector had a relatively minor role in Australia in
Beveridge's day but was to achieve significant growth with the late development of
the welfare state in the 1960s and 1970s. Role expectations on the sector changed,
and it fragmented in the 1990s when the influence of neo-liberalism undercut the
post-war social policy roles of the state. This chapter will suggest that the future of
the voluntary welfare sector in Australia will depend on how the roles of the state
and the market are reset within Australia's adaptation of the social inclusion
agenda.

As Tennant has noted, there is a bewildering array of terms attached to 'voluntary
action', and here our focus will be on what she calls the 'voluntary welfare sector',
which was known in earlier periods as 'charitable agencies'.[2] This is a narrower field
than the volunteering which was the subject of Oppenheimer's path-breaking
study.[3] The chapter will emphasise the importance of understanding the sector in
its relation to other welfare providers (the state and the market). As Fyfe has argued,
the sector is best 'conceptualised as lying within a triangular tension field, the cornerstones of which are the state, the market and the informal sector', with the role
of the voluntary sector being constantly shaped and reshaped by the influences
emanating from the other sectors.[4] In understanding this relationship others have
stressed the importance of 'social origins' and with that a sense of national 'path

dependencies'.[5] The notion of a pathway is purposefully dynamic and points to the fact that sector roles are not static but continually evolve in response to changes in the wider environment. The point was of course well expressed by Beveridge in terms of the 'moving frontier'.

Oppenheimer's work on volunteering aside, there has been very limited historical writing on the role of the Australian voluntary welfare sector in the post-war period. Most accounts are older and reflect the once fashionable view that it had been the sector's fate to be displaced by the welfare state. In the United Kingdom it would seem that a kind of revisionary historiography has emerged which positions the voluntary sector as something of a casualty of welfare state development and finds in Beveridge's 1948 salute to voluntary action a call to arms to revalorise its roll.[6] Here it will be proposed that in Australia – as Tennant has found in the case of New Zealand – independent voluntary effort was never seriously seen as an alternative to the state.

The voluntary sector before the Second World War

In 1943 an Anglican clergyman involved in the voluntary welfare sector, F. W. Coaldrake, wrote that Australia was 'on the threshold of the "Social Security State" ... in such a way that every man, woman and child will be provided for with that full measure of "security" which is his inalienable right'.[7] Coaldrake thought that the role of the voluntary sector was to help usher in the day when the state would entirely take over social services from the sector. As it happened, the ideal of a welfare state did not take hold in Australia until the 1970s. This significant difference in the chronologies of welfare state development gave the Australian sector several decades in which to adjust to a new partnership in the co-production of the welfare state. To understand this key difference we need an appreciation of certain distinctive features of Australia's welfare regime.

Speaking to an American audience in 1946, Norma Parker – a true pioneer of social work in Australia and later Professor of Social Work at the University of New South Wales – pointed out the relative underdevelopment of the Australian non-government welfare sector in comparison to that of the United States. 'In comparison with some other countries', she said, 'there would appear to be a relative lack of private initiative and local effort'. The saying 'the government ought to do something about it', she continued, 'is heard many times every day in Australia', and this had led to the low profile of voluntary agencies. Whether it was Australia's 'convict ancestry', its historical need for strong government action to lead economic development or the absence of a 'leisured class', Parker surmised, a 'general national attitude' had been created which had had an important effect on the profile of social services.[8]

This effect has been noted by welfare historians. As Kewley observed, from penal settlement to pastoral expansion and the gold rushes, nineteenth-century governments had carried out 'a wide range of functions which elsewhere mostly remained with private individuals and groups . . . The doctrine of laissez-faire had comparatively few adherents'.[9] In fact, between 1860 and 1914, government played a bigger role in the Australian economy than in that of any other country. In social policy terms, the key government role was to furnish its citizens with economic opportunity. Alongside this was a policy of encouraging self-reliant citizens to manage their own affairs and not to rely directly on the state for the relief of poverty. As many commentators have noted, without the wealth of an aristocracy and with no parish-based infrastructure to implement a poor law, charitable agencies had to be funded by governments to provide this relief. With this residual role it is perhaps not surprising to note with Jones that 'the many visitors to Australia [in the nineteenth century] rarely, if ever, mentioned Australian excellence in voluntary organisations'.[10]

The major departure from the charity model was the development of a system of old-age and invalid pensions in the early years of the twentieth century; however, this was not universal but targeted to the poor. The major extension to the nineteenth-century legacy was the policy combination known as the New Protection which followed federation in 1901. Here economic support for manufacturers was joined with regulation of the wage system to create – through the Harvester Judgement of 1907 – a living or family wage. This completed the policy framework for a market-oriented, wage-earners' welfare society. It provides the context for understanding Beveridge's observation that Australians relied more on 'Public Action' than on 'Voluntary Action' and in particular why trade unions were more focussed on 'industrial arbitration' than in the United Kingdom.

The voluntary sector in transition, 1945–1960

While Coaldrake's wartime anticipation of a welfare state was to prove premature, there were some significant social policy developments at the time. Social security policy was grounded in full employment, and a more comprehensive system of income support introduced – albeit still targeted to the needy. Importantly for later developments, income tax powers were transferred to the national government, allowing it a new leadership role in social policy development. While the development of the welfare state was delayed in Australia – it is often said that there was no welfare state until 1972 when the Whitlam government assumed office – it is important not to over-emphasise the novelty of the 1970s legislative developments. The 1940s and 1950s were also years of important transitions in the roles of both government and the voluntary welfare sector, a development to which the later years can be seen as more the climax than a disruption. Thus Mendelsohn notes that Commonwealth and state social welfare expenditures actually rose from A\$471.9 million in 1950–51 to A\$33,037.2 million in 1969–70.[11] Brian Dickey's history also highlights the 'vast extension' of services which occurred across the interim, both in statutory provision and in the increasingly subsidised voluntary sector.[12]

Mendelsohn's *Social security in the British Commonwealth*, published in 1954, evidenced a widespread uncertainty regarding the role of the voluntary sector.[13] The new statutory provisions for basic material need had cut away much of the voluntary sector's traditional territory, Mendelsohn said; 'Will it wither and disappear?, or, has it a job to do?' Observing a new wave of voluntary endeavour in the postwar period, Mendelsohn noted new emphases on more personal and community development work. He pointed in particular to the emergence of case work by professional social workers in the sector as evidence of what he considered its expertise in 'the handling of human needs and problems where a special degree of tact, devotion and understanding is required'. Reviewing the expert opinion – including the views of Beveridge – he concluded that while provision for material needs must reside in the state, voluntary agencies were needed to 'provide the human touch', to pioneer new ways of addressing need and to oppose state paternalism with an approach based on the values of mutual aid.

One of the effects of the federal government's greater role in welfare was to raise service standards and with that to increase subsidies to welfare organisations. This need to negotiate standards and subsidies together with all kinds of policy issues saw the major welfare agencies developing national bodies including, by 1960, the Australian Council of Social Services (ACOSS). In part a pragmatic necessity, the development also reflected the manner in which industrialisation and urbanisation were changing the nature of social organisations in ways that made the meeting of welfare goals a more complex matter requiring both positive government intervention and greater co-operation between the state and the voluntary sector.

Thus the annual report of the Australian Social Welfare Council (ASWC) in 1956–57 spoke of the way in which technological progress had brought 'comforts and amenities', but stated that its demands and 'specialisations' had placed much greater value on the possession of education, skills and intelligence.[14] This left many feeling helpless and sometimes led to 'personal breakdowns' and resulting unemployment. In a more complex society, the report continued, it was harder for individuals to meet their own needs: they had 'to rely more and more on an intricate system of publicly-provided educational and vocational facilities, health services, income security services and other benefits'. Families continued to provide for many of their members' needs, it said, but 'the social and economic structures prevent them from dealing effectively with all the problem'. It was in this situation that 'there has been in recent years the acceptance of responsibility by Governments' and the associated development of large-scale social welfare programmes. The ASWC, it said, had been 'brought to life' because of the need to develop an integrated welfare system comprising both voluntary and statutory sectors. Each needed to retain its autonomy, the report proposed, while becoming a 'rationalised part of a comprehensive and efficient whole'. Positive social planning based on an intelligent anticipation of need was needed – not an *ad hoc* reactive approach – so that 'purposeful effort' might lead society to 'a fullness of life'.

More or less unnoticed by historians, the period from 1940 to 1960 reveals a voluntary sector learning that indeed it 'still had a job to do'. Beyond the area of income support, older charitable practices suited to a smaller pre-industrial society were giving way to new endeavours oriented to the challenges of a rapidly industrialising world with new kinds of labour markets, high immigration, urbanisation and changing patterns of family life. In this context a new imperative was recognised for the voluntary sector to work with governments to plan social interventions in a much more systematic way, using the latest techniques developing in the social sciences.

The voluntary sector and the rise of the welfare state, 1960–80

Roughly 41 per cent of Australian voluntary sector organisations operating in 1990 were formed in the period 1960–79, and a further 43 per cent in the period 1980–90.[15] A transformation on this scale did not take place without major changes in the wider policy context. In the early 1960s, the old policy regime, consisting of full employment, high minimum wages and a residual 'safety net' that concentrated resources where most needed, was considered to be not without its strengths.[16] However, by this time the objective of full employment had given way to continuous economic growth as the primary focus of economic policy. Less and less did good economic policy appear to equate with good social policy.

The post-war rates of economic growth were so discontinuous with previous experience, according to the economic historian N. G. Butlin, that they demanded 'an equally radical social and cultural adaptation' if Australia was to solve the problems 'of an affluent society'.[17] Moreover the scope for spending on social services was considered quite elastic by economists, with its limits to be determined by the political process rather than economic science. Additionally the period saw the decline of the central role of a minimum family-based wage as the keystone of social protection; as the wage structure became far more dispersed, married women entered the workforce and equal pay was achieved. In 1967 the industrial tribunal indicated that it was not to be thought of as a welfare agency. In these circumstances the limitations of the traditional 'safety net' or wage-earner welfare society model became increasingly apparent and a new articulation of an alternative welfare state began to emerge.[18]

It was an indicator of future directions when the 1966 ACOSS conference theme, 'The voluntary principle in community welfare', was dropped as the title for the published proceedings in favour of 'Citizens as organizers and providers'. The new inflection of citizenship signalled a reframing of welfare around 'rights and duties'. This, together with an emphasis on the organisation of societies, was meant to indicate a new approach in which welfare was 'not a subject of peripheral interest' but of 'central importance to our way of life'. It was to mean a stronger role for government, but what of the voluntary agencies?[19]

In his keynote address on the role of voluntarism, G. T. Sambell, an Anglican Bishop of Melbourne, began with the observation that the 'trite aphorisms' of ten years earlier were no longer so persuasive. Then one would have said that the sector's role was to experiment, pioneer, be more 'selective and qualitative' in services; while government agencies essentially applied on a mass scale, services learnt from the voluntary sector. Citing materials from Beveridge's works, Sambell thought it now undeniable that governments could act creatively and on a vast scale. Moreover voluntary agencies were sometimes so far behind best government practice that they could be 'menaces rather than pioneers'. But, also thinking with Beveridge that voluntary action was essential for the health of a democracy, Sambell was concerned at a certain decline in regard for its role:

> I once heard a description given of the Church as like a dear old lady in the middle of the peak traffic at the central railway station, being pushed and shoved about a bit until a voice says: 'Be kind to her. Don't push her about too much. She's lived a useful and long life, she hasn't much longer to go.' I sometimes wonder when I hear appreciation expressed of the place of voluntaryism whether the same sentiments are present – but unexpressed.[20]

While Sambell thought the role of voluntary action was increasingly difficult to distinguish from that of government, some of the areas he considered more important for voluntary agencies in the future were research-based innovation, bringing community needs into government planning and being a critical voice against government when appropriate.

Nevertheless, at that time greater emphasis did attach to articulating the new welfare role of the state, with voluntarism sometimes being associated more with a passing order. A common observation was the failure to develop systematic social planning in the way in which economic policy had been developed from the Second World War onwards. The pioneer social policy academic R. G. Brown wrote of the prevailing view of welfare governance whereby 'social action was equated with charity' and a pork-barrel approach taken to spending whereby 'the tendency ... [is] ... to do as little as possible in a piecemeal fashion in response to political pressure'.[21] With the post-war successes of Keynesian economic planning in mind, writers like Tierney demanded a 'social development' model in which 'the scale and quality of thinking about welfare shifts to something like the scale and quality of thinking at present devoted to economic planning'.[22] Here the theoretical terms for this new social policy management on a large scale were furnished by overseas writers like Wilensky and Lebeaux and Richard Titmuss, especially through the distinction between institutional and residual modes of welfare governance. It was within this new planning framework that the role of the voluntary agencies needed to be recast.

By the 1970s the idea that society itself might be the object of policy and planning had become a consensual view in Australian politics. The former Liberal Party minister and then Governor-General, Paul Hasluck, opened the seventh national conference of the ACOSS in 1972 with the observation that 'social welfare measures are not only a compassionate task of relieving distress or healing the wounds of those who have been hurt, social welfare measures are also part of a great constructive task of building a better society'.[23] Significantly for the voluntary sector, he emphasised that this was not a task that could be simply handed over to governments 'because unless society is, itself, involved in social welfare it is likely that many of the measures will be incomplete or maybe wholly inapplicable'. Social policy was thus facing a similar challenge to that faced by economic policy in the 1940s, that is, how to reconcile the need for state planning to achieve full employment with the freedom of the market.

An early Australian statement of this challenge had been provided by the future South Australian Premier Don Dunstan at the ACOSS conference of 1964.[24] He cast his paper in terms of Galbraith's concept of 'conventional wisdom' whereby sets of ideas can govern the lives of large majorities of people even though these ideas have little relation to changed objective circumstances. Dunstan proposed that low-density cottage housing for traditional male breadwinner households reflected just such outmoded conventions. Policy needed to recognise and encourage a new diversity of family formation and promote high-density forms of urban development to match. For these new developments to succeed, however, planning had to have effective input from community groups and could not just be left to technicians and local power elites. This he proposed as a new field for voluntary agencies in Australia, while expressing concern that existing voluntary agencies were caught up in conventional wisdom and more likely 'centred on repairing the family image to the conventional ideal'.

This early observation on a potential role for voluntary engagement in planning and policy as a way of extending active citizenship was to develop as a key aspect of the new welfare model. The conference opened by Hasluck, for example, heard the British academic David Donnison argue the need for a 'micro-politics' to complement comprehensive state planning.[25] The expanding role of social services and income support designed to meet human needs on the basis of fairness meant that ever 'larger parts of our economy are abstracted . . . from the operations of the price mechanism'. Without the role of the price mechanism, he argued, it was essential to have an effective 'political market place where the clients . . . have their say'. Here he urged the voluntary sector to invest as much energy in the 'whole "micro-political" world of those who speak for small neighbourhoods and particular groups' as in the macro-world of research and policy planning.

The return of a Labor government in 1972 after sixteen years in the political wilderness triggered a belated Australian social reform effort along lines evolved in the post-war period in Britain and Europe, notably the Scandinavian countries. A Social Welfare Commission was appointed which led to initiatives in the micropolitical world such as the Department of Urban and Regional Development and the Australian Assistance Plan, which were of particular importance for the expansion of the role of the voluntary welfare sector. This link to voluntarism was explored by Jayasuria in his address to the 1974 ACOSS conference. His paper sketched the now-familiar new social agenda wrought by post-war economic, social and democratic changes as well as the case for a model based on universal rights on principles set out by Titmuss, whom he considered the 'archdeacon of "Welfare Statism" in Britain'.[26] Without subscribing to all of Daniel Bell's analysis of the end of ideology, Jayasuria also proposed that Australian society had many of the characteristics of a post-industrial world. Old class politics had receded. Expanding social resources were now being allocated according to a 'planning model through technical forecasting' rather than by the marketplace. It was here, he thought, that the voluntary sector had a new and critical role to play.

The welfare state need not imply an impersonal, bureaucratic form of governance. In this regard his re-reading of Beveridge's *Voluntary action* had proved both 'reassuring and enlightening'. Beveridge, he said, followed the Webbs in making it a 'cardinal principle that extensive state action should be joined with the "utmost use" of voluntary effort'. This understanding, he noted, had been recently restated by the Labour MP Richard Crossman, who wrote of the role of voluntary agencies as 'change agents' who were active in seeking benefits not just for their respective communities but for the nation at large. For this purpose voluntary agencies needed to shed a passive and service-oriented concept of their role and adopt a more critical and activist understanding. As Jayasuria concluded, skills and resources for political participation were not distributed equally among the citizens. Here he pointed to the emergence of what he called 'Animateurs Sociales' – or social planners and community workers – as a promising if untested way of enhancing a participatory welfare estate.

Of course the welfare state model was contested in the wider political arena. For the radical left, welfare could be no substitute for socialism; while, for what Jayasuria dubbed the 'recent school of Liberal Economists', welfare services and benefits would be best left to market allocation, with only residual public provision for those unable to compete successfully. However, at this time the choice between what Beveridge had described as the Scylla of laissez-faire and the Charybdis of totalitarianism looked like being resolved in a new middle way or mixed economy of welfare. Just as the Keynesian economic state had been mandated to solve market failures, so the welfare state would address failures in the social system. The state would not abolish voluntary welfare agencies but work with them. The sector was thought to have a range of capacities not found in the bureaucracy, especially those that enabled service users and local communities to be brought into the political processes of policy and service development: a role described by Brown in terms of creating a 'constituency for the poor'.[27] Of course, all of this happened precisely at the time when the economic policy foundation of the welfare state, full employment, was crumbling around the world.

The voluntary sector in the 1980s: quasi public?

If the challenge of the 1960s had been to adapt Australian social policy to unprecedented economic growth rates, the challenge of the 1980s and 1990s was to adapt newly formed social aspirations to an economy characterised by reduced growth, higher unemployment and inflation. In a first phase of the long-lived Labor government of Hawke and Keating (1983–95) a Scandinavian-styled, corporatist accord sought to re-establish full employment, with wage growth restrained in exchange for an expanded social wage. In social policy terms this allowed for a refurbishment of the Australian way: wage regulation continued to play a key role in welfare outcomes while the advance to a welfare state was contained if not reversed. As Lyons writes, this allowed for the consolidation of the newly expanded role of the voluntary welfare sector.[28]

To understand the changes to the voluntary sector in the 1980s we have first to appreciate the dimensions of the expansion which had occurred in the welfare sector. Commonwealth spending on social security, health education and welfare grew from 5.2 per cent of Gross Domestic Product (GDP) in 1965–66 to 13.4 per cent in 1985–86, with the great bulk of the growth occurring in the years between 1973 and 1975. In terms of employment in community services this translated into employment growth from 10.1 per cent of total employment in 1966 to 15.1 per cent in 1986, having peaked at 17.6 per cent in 1984.[29] While it is not possible to disaggregate these figures to quantify changes to the voluntary welfare sector, what is clear is that this major growth had changed the character of the sector, a change that was even reflected in its popular nomenclature: references to 'charities' or 'voluntary organisations' gave way to terms like the 'community services industry'.

This growth in the sector soon led to more systematic attention from researchers and policy-makers alike. A 1992 study by the Victorian state government noted the expansion in social outlays in that state (including local government) from A\$520 million in 1983 to A\$800 million in 1990.[30] The main new developments had been in the areas of neighbourhood houses providing personal support, advocacy, education and recreation; development of home and community care for people with disabilities and the aged; supported accommodation and assistance for the homeless; and children's services. Reflecting the mixed-economy framework articulated in the 1970s, the report described these developments as corresponding to a 'social justice framework . . . promoted through a planned partnership with local and non – government organisations'. Within this planned partnership framework, the sector was presented less as a discrete and autonomous entity and more as a part of the larger ensemble of service providers making up a community services 'industry'. Within this industry, however, a blurring of the sectoral boundaries presented a new set of issues for those concerned about the distinctive contribution of voluntary action.

Thus, at a conference in 1987 examining the state of what were called 'community services', Andrew Jones used the example of the family day care service which had developed in the early 1970s to highlight what he called the 'transformation of private relationships' which had been occurring within the field of community care.[31] What had once been informal and private was being brought across into what he called a 'quasi-public' sphere. Family day care services, he explained, had once been 'low cost, maternal-like and informal' but had become more regulated and its providers given more status, a status which 'increasingly resemble[d] that of public employees'. The more public a voluntary service became, Jones observed, the greater was the pressure to change role 'expectations, obligations and exchanges'.

The most sustained reflections on this transformation of voluntary action from the private to the quasi-public sphere were provided by feminists writing on gender and social policy. Importantly, the proportion of married women employed in community services had increased from 16.4 per cent in 1966 to 30.3 per cent in 1984, while the proportion of women in voluntary welfare activity was especially high – 70 per cent in one study of South Australia. Vellekoop-Baldock's study *Volunteers in welfare* grew from her interest in the conflicting perceptions of volunteering as a valuable activity for opening up opportunities for self-development and social engagement for women, and of volunteering as a source of 'scab labour' pushing down the wages of paid workers, thus allowing a low-cost service option for governments.[32] She found that the preponderance of women especially in the welfare sector of volunteering was a result partly of gender stereotyping but also of women's marginal attachment to the paid labour force. Vellekoop-Baldock placed high value on the role of volunteers and had no fear that voluntary action would disappear. However, she thought the voluntary welfare sector in Australia was over-inflated with what was in effect exploited female labour. Labour market conditions in Scandinavian countries, she noted, led to the existence of virtually no volunteers in the welfare sector. From this perspective it would seem that the voluntary welfare sector in Australia was stuck somewhere between its charitable past and a more universal-style welfare state future.

Other challenges to welfare voluntarism which emerged in the new mixed economy were also revealed in Vellekoop-Baldock's study. It showed that the more funds voluntary organisations received from governments, the more they needed to organise themselves on bureaucratic and hierarchical principles. This trend conflicted with those practices of 'participatory democracy' evolved in the 1970s, which Vellekoop-Baldock found motivated many organisations. Further, it created pressures to enlist what was called a 'better class of volunteers' and also to tensions between professionals and volunteers within organisations. Voluntary welfare agencies, she noted, had been more reliant on government funding and were more susceptible to these trends than either social action or self-help groups.

In fact, Vellekoop-Baldock's solution to the tensions in the voluntary welfare sector – through a shift into a Scandinavian-style regime – ran against a national and international trend to reduce government's role in both economic and social policy. This conservative turn was reflected in a conference in 1989 convened to consider a campaign by unions for an award to cover what was called the 'social and community services industry'. Scoping the conference theme, 'From charity to industry', Lois Bryson thought it reasonable that community service workers would want their work treated like that of workers in other industries.[33] The work of welfare had been stigmatised by its historical links to poverty and charity, she said, and an award would allow for proper regulation of wages and conditions and open up opportunities for training and career development. At the same time she saw a danger that the positive values of voluntary action might be lost. Turning charities into industries she considered a 'modernising move' which had come late to the sphere of charities. Noting the 'disenchantment of the home' and the commercialisation of amateur sports, she thought that some of the more positive elements of the *noblesse oblige* notion might disappear with the 'modernising' of the voluntary welfare sector. 'Capitalist values of competitiveness, self-seeking, lack of concern, rationalisation and so on', she said, 'could be accentuated to create a heartless world indeed. We might be hastening the construction of that 'iron cage'" of which Max Weber had warned. Her fears were heightened by what she saw as the 'scant support' for the Labor government's 'social justice' agenda.

This last concern was echoed by the then Deputy Prime Minister, Brian Howe.[34] Reflecting on the life of Beatrice Webb, he thought that the 'very best elements of social reform have always been driven by a desire to achieve social justice which is after all much more than the provision of services no matter how equitably they are divided'.[35] By implication, the role of the voluntary sector had to be fundamentally about more than delivering services for governments. By talking themselves into an industry model, Howe believed, people would be locking their minds into the ruling ideas of the day and would become unable to 'think about the fundamental causes and threats to social justice'. However, he agreed with Bryson's assessment that the 'concept of welfare had become marginalised. Nowadays rather than talking boldly about welfare, we become extremely apologetic about welfare'. At the same conference Watts and Weeks argued from class, feminist and social movement perspectives that without such a social justice horizon, the sector could be 'lured by the promise of prestige' into an industry that did little more than administer 'refined techniques of control and social order'.[36]

In the 1980s what had been seen as 'charities' now found themselves as a 'quasi-public' segment of an industry set up within the planned partnership framework of a welfare state. Pressures grew to modernise or professionalise its functions – to regulate its workforce and be accountable for significantly increased government funds. A particular challenge was to prevent the sector from being used simply as a cheap alternative for duly recognised and properly remunerated public services. However, as the decade closed the welfare state framework itself was unravelling as universalism rolled back to residualism and with that the very idea of government having a positive social planning role. In this shift towards neo-liberalism, the public sector became contained and the voluntary welfare sector found itself increasingly exchanging the micro-politics of participatory democracy for the discipline of the market and quasi-markets.

The voluntary sector in the 1990s: a quasi-market?

In the 1990s, the growing influence of economic rationalism, or neo-liberalism, saw Australian governments progressively dismantle their former 'strategic leadership' role in the economy in favour of a static, supply-side approach. In the 1980s the economy was opened to global markets through tariff reductions and financial deregulation, while in the 1990s the focus was on micro-economic reform. The latter was associated with a public sector reform agenda which, as Considine observed, was 'devised as a direct challenge to the role of the post-war Keynesian welfare state, and therefore to the role of social work and welfare practice'.[37] The role of the voluntary welfare sector was remade once more, this time as a quasi-market.

In 1993, the role of wage regulation as a social policy instrument was largely reduced to minimum wage setting, with 'safety net' awards for the bottom 20 per cent of workers, while the goal of full employment was effectively abandoned in 1994. The option for smaller government and the return of residual welfare was reflected in the reduction of the Commonwealth revenue base from 27.8 per cent of GDP in 1986–87 to 24.2 per cent of GDP in 1992, while public expenditures reduced from 28.8 per cent of GDP in 1986–87 to 26.7 per cent of GDP in 1991–92. The welfare sector researcher Peter Allen noted in 1993 that 'the social goal of "distributional justice for all" had become "conditional welfare for the few"'.[38]

The task of promoting, explaining and implementing the new model largely fell to the government's own economic agencies. Their template for micro-economic reform, the Hilmer Report, observed that government monopolies in welfare and community services could be opened to competitive tendering processes with potential savings to the public purse in the order of 20 per cent.[39] The key initiatives shaping the future of the sector soon followed: the reform of employment services and the report of the Industry Commission entitled *Charitable organisations in Australia*.[40]

For the first time in Australia, the latter mapped and quantified a voluntary welfare sector which had grown so much over the previous two decades. It was found to have an annual expenditure of A$5 billion, of which over A$3 billion came from direct and indirect government support. The report also furnished the discourse and instruments of what became known as the 'Contract State'.[41] Using these instruments, governments, it suggested, would increasingly move out of direct service delivery, competitively tendering these to for profit-based and community-based providers.

This reform agenda of government was not typically presented as an attack on the welfare state. In the widely adopted language of the American authors Osborne and Gaebler, the task was presented rather as 'reinventing government', in particular through separating policy-making functions (steering) from service delivery (rowing).[42] However, as numerous authors have observed, such approaches to reinvention were laden with assumptions directly antithetical to the welfare state. This was not a model such as Hasluck had foreshadowed, in which citizens came together in the 'great constructive task of building a better society'. Rather, as Alford and O'Neill observed in their study of what they called the 'Contract State', the 'pervasive assumption' of the 'public choice' theories informing the reinvention was that 'people are self-interested utility maximisers'.[43] Competitive tendering by the Contract State became the means to limit the growth of governments by curbing the 'budget-maximising' behaviours of bureaucrats and the 'rent-seeking' activities of interest groups.

The flagship of the quasi-market approach in Australia was the Job Network. This developed out of an enquiry into the Commonwealth Employment Service in 1994. The resulting White Paper abandoned the traditional understanding of sectors with different but complementary roles. Taking its cue from the Hilmer Report, it recommended the introduction of a measure of 'healthy competition'.[44] Competition, it thought, would drive improved customer service and promote service innovation. A separate government agency was to be established to regulate the competition, while all providers including the government service deliverers would compete for the full range of services. Under the Howard government (1996–07) this was scaled up to become a fully fledged competitive employment services model, known as the Job Network. While it was not all-pervasive across the full range of social services, as Brennan notes, the thinking behind the Job Network was to inform Australian social administration well into the twenty-first century.[45]

Today it is an established consensus that the application of 'quasi-market' theory failed to fulfil the promise of greater customer satisfaction and service innovation. Thus the Job Network is recognised as having been more efficient in terms of savings to the public purse, but at the cost of being overly centralised and regulated. While suited to the delivery of certain mass-scale, standardised products, the model hindered responsive professional practice; and it caused the unique circumstances of localities and individuals to be overlooked.[46] McGregor-Lowndes has catalogued the 'discontents' from the community welfare sector in terms of burdensome and ineffective reporting requirements; adversarial relations replacing trust and partnership both within the sector and between the sector and the bureaucracy; transfers of legal and financial risks to the sector; and the use of funding contracts 'to curb and control criticism of government policy or even participation in its formation'.[47]

Indeed, the quasi-market experiment in Australia is now more clearly seen to have been less about 'reinventing government' as Osborne and Gaebler had proposed than about dismantling government. Rather than complementing the welfare state as in Beveridge's vision, here the voluntary sector was being realigned with the market in an attempted displacement of the welfare state. As McGregor-Lowndes writes: the 'broad implication for the provision of community services is that the Beveridgean welfare model of state-provided services in fulfilment of citizens' rights and entitlements' was 'replaced by notions of contracting out services, of a hollowed-out state and the creation of markets or quasi-markets for community services'.[48]

The voluntary sector today: a new compact with the state

The 'tension field' in which the voluntary sector finds itself in Australia today is once again set for a significant realignment. In the manner of the former Blair government in Britain, the Labor government in Australia (elected in 2008) is seeking to re-establish the partnership with the not-for-profit sector through a formalised compact. The accompanying emphases on 'social inclusion', 'community', 'civil society' and volunteering arouse debate in terms already familiar in comparable countries: do they simply repackage the neo-liberal formulas of the 1990s or do they indicate a crossing of the 'frontier' to a new set of relationships between state, market and community welfare sector? How this question will be answered in Australia will be very much influenced by the distinctive contextual characteristics of Australian social policy evidenced in this chapter. Here I emphasise three.

Firstly, Australia, like New Zealand, does have a strong tradition of voluntary community welfare. However, it has never functioned as a serious alternative to state-based welfare. By the Second World War, the Australian approach to welfare was very much centred on state support for full employment, together with well-regulated wages as a substitute for welfare. Direct state provision of welfare was deliberately residual, and while charities were encouraged as an alternative, they remained very much reliant upon government support. By the 1970s, the welfare state looked set to supersede this model. However, in the spirit of Beveridge's understanding of voluntary action as a supplement to state action, a dramatically expanded, largely government-funded community welfare sector emerged as a 'micro' political partner to the 'macro' role of the welfare state. Even in the 1990s in Australia, the conversion of the sector to the quasi-market model was almost entirely a government initiative.

The second key factor to emerge from this analysis is the unresolved contradictions in the way the roles of state, market and voluntary sectors are currently constructed in the Australian welfare regime. The fiscal crisis of the 1980s arrested the development of a Beveridge-style mixed economy of welfare, creating a curious balance of old 'wage-earner welfare society' elements together with emerging features of a welfare state. The two co-existed uncomfortably with the growing free-market orientation of economic policy. The economic rationalism of the 1990s, however, was increasingly hostile to both wage-earner and welfare state forms of social intervention, leaving the voluntary sector to operate on a quasi-market policy landscape. Today it is unlikely that this extreme form of neo-liberalism could be reinvented. The crucial challenge for Australian social policy is rather to clarify the assumptions on which it seeks to remake its social policy system. In this regard a reassertion of wage-earners' welfare is unlikely, leaving the option of reinventing a state-based system of economic and social rights adapted to the twenty-first century.[49]

In such a reinvention what can we surmise of the role of the voluntary welfare sector? Once again with Mendelsohn we are forced to ask: 'Will it wither and disappear?, or, has it a job to do?' A feature of this history has been the pattern whereby the role was made and remade in the image of whoever was dominant partner in the welfare regime. In the 1970s, at the height of the Beveridge period in Australia, there were clearly delineated roles for the social partners: the role of voluntary agencies was considered indispensable for a successful micro-politics of welfare. However, as the profile of the welfare state grew, we had the proposition that voluntary services become the fully public services into which they appeared to be evolving. While in the quasi-market phase, the sector began to conform more and more to the logic of competition, with its assumptions of no material differences between competing market actors. This movement in roles over time underlines the basic proposition informing this chapter that we cannot begin to reinvent the welfare role of the voluntary sector without being equally clear about our expectations of the state and the market.

Notes

1 C. Jones Finer and P. Smyth (eds), *Social policy and the Commonwealth* (Basingstoke: Macmillan, 2004).

2 M. Tennant, *The fabric of welfare: voluntary organisations, government and welfare in New Zealand, 1840–2005* (Wellington: Bridget Williams Books, 2007).

3 M. Oppenheimer, *Volunteering: why we can't survive without it* (Sydney: UNSW Press, 2008).

4 N. Fyfe, 'Making space for "neo-communitarianism"? The third sector, state and civil society in the UK', *Antipode*, vol. 37, no. 3 (2005), pp. 536–57.

5 L. Salamon and H. Anheier, 'Social origins of civil society: explaining the nonprofit sector cross-nationally', *Voluntas*, vol. 9, no. 3 (1998), pp. 213–48.

6 A. Kidd, 'Civil society or the state? Recent approaches to the history of voluntary welfare', *Journal of Historical Sociology*, vol. 15, no. 3 (2002), pp. 328–42.

7 F. Coaldrake, quoted in J. Handfield, *Friends and brothers* (Melbourne: Hyland House, 1980), pp. 156–9.

8 N. Parker, 'Describing Australian attitudes ... to American social work colleagues', in R. J. Lawrence (ed.), *Norma Parker's record of service* (Sydney: School of Social Work, UNSW, 1969), p. 64.

9 T. H. Kewley, *Social security in Australia* (Sydney: Sydney University Press, 1965), p. 5.

10 M. A. Jones, *The Australian welfare state* (Sydney: Allen & Unwin, 1990).

11 R. Mendelsohn, *The condition of the people: social welfare in Australia, 1900–1975* (Sydney: Allen & Unwin, 1979).

12 B. Dickey, *No charity there* (Sydney: Allen & Unwin, 1987).

13 R. Mendelsohn, *Social security in the British Commonwealth* (London: Athlone Press, 1954), pp. 264–81.

14 Australian Social Welfare Council, annual report 1956–57, unpublished, Australian Council of Social Service, Sydney.

15 Victorian Government, *Welfare as an industry* (Melbourne: Department of Community Services, 1992), p. 1.

16 Commenting on a survey showing that only 6 or 7 per cent of people in Melbourne were poor, the economist Downing observed that the comparable figure in the United Kingdom was 14 per cent while in the United States it was 20 per cent. R. Downing, 'Poverty and social welfare in Australia', in *Anatomy of Australia* (Melbourne: Sun Books, 1968), pp. 51–64.

17 N. G. Butlin, 'Long-run trends in Australian per capita consumption', in K. Hancock (ed.), *The national income and social welfare* (Melbourne: F. W. Cheshire, 1965), pp. 1–9.

18 P. Smyth, 'Closing the gap? The role of wage, welfare and industry policy in promoting social inclusion', *Journal of Industrial Relations*, vol. 50, no. 4 (2008), pp. 647–63.

19 R. J. Lawrence (ed.), *Community service citizens and social welfare organizations* (Melbourne: F. W. Cheshire, 1966), p. viii.

20 G. T. Sambell, 'Voluntary agencies in our changing environment', in Lawrence (ed.), *Community service citizens*, pp. 11–12.

21 R. G. Brown, 'Social policy in Australia', *Australian Quarterly* (June 1966), pp. 82–90.

22 L. Tierney, 'Social policy and disrupted primary group life', in H. Weir (ed.), *Social welfare in the 1970s* (Sydney: ACOSS, 1970), p. 187.

23 P. Hasluck, 'Opening address', in R. B. Burnheim (ed.), *Social welfare consequences of change* (Sydney: ACOSS, 1972), pp. 1–4.

24 D. Dunstan, 'The urban family, higher density housing, and voluntary action', in Lawrence (ed.), *Community service citizens*, pp. 128–38.

25 D. Donnison, 'Planning the urban environment', in Burnheim (ed.), *Social welfare consequences of change*, pp. 5–11.

26 D. Jayasuria, 'Reflections on purposes and strategies', in G. Mills (ed.), *Action for change … whose responsibility?* (Sydney: ACOSS, 1974), pp. 111–31.

27 R. G. Brown, 'Poverty in the 1980s', in *Second poverty inquiry conference* (Melbourne: Brotherhood of St Laurence, 1980), p. 15.

28 M. Lyons, *The third sector* (Sydney: Allen & Unwin, 2001).

29 P. Saunders, 'An economic perspective on the finance and provision of community services', in P. Saunders and A. Jamrozik (eds), *Community services in a changing economic and social environment* (Sydney: SWRC Reports and Proceedings, 1987), pp. 9–50.

30 Victorian Government, *Welfare as an industry* (Melbourne: Department of Community Services, 1992).

31 A. Jones, 'Tensions in community care policy', in Saunders and Jamrozik (eds), *Community services*, pp. 87–106.

32 C. Vellekoop-Baldock, *Volunteers in welfare* (Sydney: Allen & Unwin, 1990).

33 J. Wiseman and R. Watts (eds), *From charity to industry* (Melbourne: VCOSS, 1989).

34 Wiseman and Watts (eds), *From charity to industry*.

35 Wiseman and Watts (eds), *From charity to industry*, p. 5.

36 R. Watts and W. Weeks, 'Sorting the sheep from the goats: conceptualising the social and community services industry', in Wiseman and Watts (eds), *From charity to industry*, p. 24.

37 M. Considine, 'Governance and competition: the role of non-profit organisations in the delivery of public services', *Australian Journal of Political Science*, vol. 38, no. 1 (2000), p. 74.

38 P. Allen, 'The BSL's shift of focus to issues such as employment and taxation in the 1970s and 1980s', in C. Magree (ed.), *Looking forward looking back* (Melbourne: Brotherhood of St Laurence, 1993), pp. 30–38.

39 *National competition policy review* [Hilmer Inquiry], (Canberra: AGPS, 1993).

40 Industry Commission, *Charitable organisations in Australia*, Report no. 45 (Canberra: AGPS, 1995).

41 J. Ernst, 'A competitive future: the industry commission and the welfare sector', in P. Smyth and B. Cass (eds), *Contesting the Australian way* (Melbourne: Cambridge University Press, 1998), pp. 215–27.

42 D. Osborne and T. Gaebler, *Reinventing government* (New York: Plume, 1992).

43 J. Alford and D. O'Neill, *The contract state* (Melbourne: Deakin University, 1994).

44 Commonwealth of Australia, *Working nation: white paper on employment and growth* (Canberra: AGPS, 1994).

45 D. Brennan, 'Government and civil society', in Smyth and Cass (eds), *Contesting the Australian way*, pp. 124–37.

46 C. McDonald and G. Marston, 'Workfare as welfare: governing unemployment in the advanced welfare state', *Critical Social Policy*, vol. 25, no. 3 (2005), pp. 374–401; P. Mwaiteleke, 'The influence of national competition policy in reshaping human service delivery' (PhD thesis, Murdoch University, Perth, 2007); H. Dean, 'Re-conceptualising welfare-to-work for people with multiple problems and needs', *Journal of Social Policy*, vol. 32 (2003), pp. 441–59.

47 M. McGregor-Lowndes, 'Is there something better than partnership?', in J. Barraket (ed.), *Strategic issues for the not-for-profit sector* (Sydney: UNSW Press, 2008), pp. 45–73.

48 McGregor-Lowndes, 'Is there something better than partnership?', p. 47.

49 P. Smyth, 'Closing the gap? The role of wage, welfare and industry policy in promoting social inclusion', *Journal of Industrial Relations*, vol. 50, no. 4 (2008), pp. 647–63.

13

The Great White North and voluntary action: Canada's relationship with Beveridge, social welfare and social justice

Peter R. Elson

Introduction

This chapter will explore the impact of Beveridge's *Voluntary action* in Canada in three parts. Firstly, I introduce the nature of voluntary action in a Canadian context. There is a distinctly Canadian perspective to voluntary action in the Great White North, which influenced how Beveridge's reports in general and *Voluntary action* in particular were either ignored or adopted. I say 'reports', rather than focussing only on *Voluntary action* because while *Voluntary action* was largely ignored, Beveridge's *Social insurance and allied services* and its Canadian counterpart, the Marsh Report, became the blueprint for social welfare expansion in Canada. I then demonstrate how voluntary action in a broader context in Canada was tied to and followed, rather than led, the expansion of social welfare. Finally, I critically explore the relationship of voluntary action to Beveridge's view of social justice and its three underlying principles of universality, unity and integration. While citizen engagement in voluntary action is necessary for social action, it is not, I will argue, sufficient for the achievement of social justice.

Sir William Beveridge built his social reform agenda on three principles: first, an acknowledgment of the past with a full view of the whole of society in the future; second, an acknowledgement that social insurance was one part of a much broader and comprehensive policy of social progress; and third, a belief that social security must be achieved by co-operation between the state and the individual.[1] In this regard his reforms were a practical and progressive social justice agenda, providing support for family benefits, illness, education, housing and unemployment. The co-operation between the state and the individual, as Beveridge states in his third principle, is explicitly addressed in his preface to *Voluntary action*. 'Social advance requires action by the state and action by the individual', states Beveridge, and it is the independent action of the individual, rather than the state, which is his focus in *Voluntary action*.[2] He defines 'voluntary action' as private action, that is to say action not under the direction of any authority wielding the power of the state.[3]

The broader re-statement of these three principles, to which I return later, has been summarised by Guy Perrin as universality, unity and integration.[4] While Beveridge's report refers to the principle of universality of protection, uniformity of contributions and benefits, and the technical and social integration of services and society, there are ways in which these same principles of universality, unity and integration address the fundamental role of voluntary action and its contribution to social justice.

Canada – we're different eh?

At the turn of the twentieth century, Canada, just 300 years old, and thirty-three years post-Confederation, has been described as largely rural, conservative, white, Christian and British.[5] In fact, immigration to Canada was exploding at the time, growing from less than 50,000 immigrants per year in the early 1900s to 400,000 per year by 1913.[6] It was this massive immigration to Canada that led to the creation of hundreds of voluntary ethnic-centred mutual support organisations.[7]

Under the British North America Act of 1867, the relatively minor roles of government were assigned to the provinces, among them 'the establishment, maintenance and management of hospitals, asylums, charities and charitable institutions'.[8] This description was what passed, at the time, as a description of social welfare organisations. In general, health and welfare matters were local, and provinces reassigned their responsibilities to municipalities and voluntary charities.[9] This approach was based on the principle that social assistance should be residual to assistance available from other sources, such as private philanthropy, neighbours, voluntary organisations and churches.[10]

While this period between the late 1800s and early 1900s in Canada and elsewhere has been mythically described as the 'golden age' of philanthropy, it was certainly a period of tight moral control and extensive worker exploitation.[11] Until the 1940s, citizens and religious institutions were the primary drivers of voluntary action and organisations. Methodist and Presbyterian churches, with their decentralised structures, were actively involved social reform networks, particularly at the local and provincial level, but these networks also extended nationally to the church-sponsored Social Services Council of Canada.[12] Governments provided funding when they were obliged to under the Poor Law where it existed, or in agreements with churches or voluntary organisations, but otherwise the provision of social services was viewed as a means to control social unrest rather than a way to address social needs progressively.[13]

The Canadian Council on Child and Family Welfare took a leading role in supporting the provision of health and welfare relief across Canada and in turn developed strong political, economic and community connections.[14] As a result, well-connected yet stressed community-based volunteer networks struggled to provide relief to families; mutual aid organisations and co-operatives worked with the poor and marginalised; and federated fund-raising organisations consolidated appeals for donations. This aid to the poor often came with a moral cost to the recipient, and organised philanthropy, as distinct from independent acts of charity, tended to focus on moral hygiene rather than material aid.[15] An analysis of debates in the House of Commons between 1917 and 1929 shows that MPs were well aware of the role of charities during the First World War and their ongoing contribution to the health, education and welfare of communities.[16] That said, some charities and their representatives or umbrella organisations were as reluctant as government officials to realise that the dire economic situation in the 1930s required adjustments which were beyond the control of the individual.[17]

This 'hands off' approach to social welfare by the Federal government was pervasive, and it was only by political or economic necessity that social action was taken. Income security measures resulting from the Winnipeg General Strike of 1919 and financial aid programmes for First World War veterans and their families signalled the first major entry by the Federal government into the area of social security.[18] The reluctance to engage in social policy reform unless pushed to do so for extraneous political or economic reasons is a feature of the Canadian social policy landscape, and one which continues to put social policy in general and voluntary action in particular in a residual policy context.

For example, Federal social welfare policy platforms at the time met just as much, if not more resistance from major corporate political supporters as they did from provincial governments. Social programmes, when they were introduced (for example pensions for the blind in 1939), were subject to strict and often humiliating means tests.[19] Thus collaboration with voluntary organisations to provide services was driven by necessity, but it was not necessarily collaboration in the context of achieving a common public purpose. The subsequent extension of the welfare state introduced new opportunities and presented new challenges for the voluntary action.

Voluntary action and the extension of social security

Beveridge in *Voluntary action*:

> Voluntary agencies have in fact largely ceased to be concerned with meeting basic needs for food, clothing, or fuel and will be concerned with such things even less in the future, through the extension of social security.[20]

The growth of Canada in general and of voluntary action in particular is attributable to a number of events, including general overall economic growth; an expanding population due to rising birth rates and massive immigration; an expansion of social, health and economic services at every level of government; and the engagement of citizens in civil society.

The end of the Second World War may have launched a dramatic increase in industry, the economy and immigration, but the pervasive insecurity which marked the Depression years was never far from people's minds.[21] Canadians carried this legacy of deprivation with them as they were being asked to fight for Canada in the Second World War. In Canada, as was the case in Britain, social security became a focus of the 'security' soldiers were fighting for, and the federal government made plans to create post-war social security programmes as early as 1942, the year in which *Social insurance and allied services* was released.[22]

The report made headlines not only in Britain but across the world and particularly in North America. It captured the imagination of politicians and citizens alike. As Dennis Guest describes it, 'The Beveridge Report tapped into the core of Canadian aspirations for a postwar world, and addressed with unaffected simplicity and directness, the anxieties engendered in urban-industrial employment, the costs associated with illness and disability, and of penury of old age or retirement'.[23] In 1943, Leonard Marsh, who directed the McGill University's social research programme between 1931 and 1941, wrote a 'made in Canada' version of it, known as the Marsh Report on Social Security in Canada, for the federal government's Committee on Post-War Reconstruction.[24]

Marsh, also a member of the League for Social Reconstruction, was a keen observer of the ravages of the depression in Canada and a former student of William Beveridge at the London School of Economics and Political Science.[25] Like his mentor, Marsh believed that governments should construct a new social order in which physical security was replaced by a broader programme of social security.[26] Marsh too wanted to achieve a society in which there was full employment, a thriving nuclear family and cradle-to-grave social support.[27] According to Antonia Maioni, the Marsh Report became a symbol in Canada for its collective desire for social rights of citizenship, to be established and protected along with political and civil rights.

The Marsh Report contained six main proposals: (1) a national employment programme; (2) sickness benefits and access to medical care; (3) occupational disability and care giver support; (4) a comprehensive system of old-age security and retirement benefits; (5) premature death benefits; and (6) children's allowances.[28] Largely thanks to Marsh's previous ten-year tenure at the McGill Social Science Research Project in Montreal, the report was drafted in less than one month. The Marsh Report outlined a detailed and comprehensive plan for social welfare and the eradication of poverty. Marsh believed that individual risks were part of modern industrial society and that these risks should be met by collective benefits.[29] To quote the Hon. Mackenzie King, Prime Minister of Canada between 1935 and 1946, 'What society fails to prevent, society is in some measure under an obligation to meet'.[30] These measures were intended to contribute to post-war economic readjustment and reconstruction by providing protection to individuals and families against loss of income while also maintaining their consumer purchasing power.

The Marsh Report was followed in quick succession by the Haggerty Report on health insurance and the Curtis Report on housing and community planning. While these reports, particularly the Marsh Report, received the most attention, it should be noted that similar reports which would now be considered enlightened were commissioned around the same time on the ecological approach to managing natural resources and the role of working women. Many of these reforms were implemented, albeit in a piecemeal fashion, and over substantial periods of strained federal–provincial negotiations.[31] This was due to a combination of an immature and reluctant federal administration, lack of public familiarity with universal programmes, federal–provincial jurisdictional issues and a prevailing neo-liberal political ideology.[32]

The leading political advocates of these social welfare reforms in Canada were not charities, but the Co-operative Commonwealth Federation (CCF), Canada's version of the Labour Party, which actually saw charity as a poor and inefficient substitute for economic justice and rights-based income redistribution.[33] Planned social reforms were also overshadowed by a sense of unbounded consumerism, driven by generous tax provisions for businesses and equally generous re-establishment benefits for veterans.[34] The Marsh Report captured the imagination of Canadians, but it was too radical for the federal government, which proceeded to bury it. When social security programmes such as family allowance were later introduced, there was no direct reference to Beveridge or to the Marsh Report.[35] The Liberal government was not charitable enough to acknowledge the work of someone who was aligned with the League for Social Reconstruction and the CCF political party.

The Marsh Report was more comprehensive than Beveridge's *Social insurance and allied services*, primarily owing to the immature state of social service provision in Canada, yet it made no mention of voluntary action or the role of voluntary organisations in the provision of social services. Marsh made the assumption, as did the League for Social Reconstruction, that social services would be delivered by government. By circumstance and design voluntary organisations were often better positioned than the state to provide direct social services such as health and child welfare. First, social services were a provincial responsibility, and therefore any direct intervention by the federal government would require provincial agreement and a constitutional amendment. Second, charities and mutual support organisations had a long-standing presence in communities which provincial governments were unable to duplicate. Third, provincial governments were as politically reluctant as their federal counterparts to make substantive investments in public social welfare services. Provincial politics was dominated by rural representation where social services were often provided by church groups.[36] In some provinces, such as Quebec, the Roman Catholic Church had been providing health, education and welfare services since the early 1600s and operated under provincial authority to do so.[37]

In this context it made political and financial sense for the state to supplement and support services which were already being provided by the voluntary sector, rather than duplicating or nationalising existing services. These included health care, children's aid, settlement services and post-secondary education. During this post-war period voluntary organisations became beneficiaries of new and increased government spending programmes and continued to proliferate and to provide new services. Examples include the Canadian Red Cross Society, which, supported by the St John Ambulance Brigade, started a programme of volunteer blood donor clinics in 1947. The Arthritis Society was established in 1948, the Canadian Diabetes Association in 1953 and the Canadian Heart Foundation in 1957.[38] Federated appeals, once targeted to the well-off, started to appeal to the working class. Donations to community chests increased eight-fold between 1931 and 1959. There is no evidence from this time that increases in taxation which were used to fund welfare services dampened people's interest in making donations to charity.[39] Shirley Tillotson has shown that throughout the 1930s, 1940s and 1950s, as Canadians were paying more taxes to fund the expanding welfare state, they were also increasing their donations to federated charities such as the United Way.[40]

Over time, Canadians benefited from a number of universal income and social support programmes, including unemployment insurance (1940), family allowances (1944), old-age pensions (1952), unemployment assistance (1956) and cost-shared hospital insurance (1958). Cost-shared hospital insurance, introduced in 1958, evolved, after much turmoil, into the Medical Care Act or Medicare in 1966.[41] The 1940 unemployment insurance bill was the precedent which established the contractually oriented 'insurance principle' in social welfare in Canada, as distinct from poor relief or government aid.[42]

The greatest period of growth in health, education and social services took place from the 1960s to the 1980s as social policies were implemented across a growing population and an expanding economy. The direct delivery of many services, such as hospital and home care services, was and continues to be provided by registered charities. The relationship between charities and government social policy was synchronous in many ways and fostered the development of an interdependent partnership. Governments needed specific types of programmes and services to be provided and regulated while also maintaining a 'window' on community needs and trends.[43] Compatible voluntary sector charities had similar programme objectives, needed a reliable source of funds and felt they were in a position to influence government policy.[44] Even today this partnership is not without tension as governments shift funding priorities and demand greater levels of accountability. At the same time voluntary organisations demand greater flexibility to meet community needs, advocate for policy changes and diversify their own programmes to reduce their dependency on government funding.[45]

The type and growth of registered charities has reflected direct federal government funding priorities as well as the priorities inherent in the social welfare

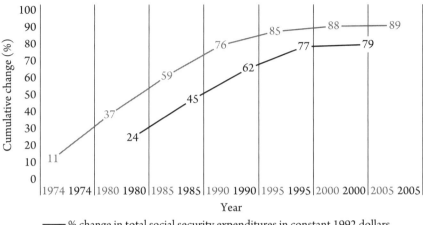

Figure 13.1 Comparison of cumulative change in registration of charities and
total social security expenditures, 1974–2005

Sources: D. Guest, *The emergence of social security in Canada*, 3rd edn (Vancouver: UBC Press,
1997); Peter R. Elson, 'A short history of voluntary sector–government relations in Canada',
The Philanthropist, vol. 20, no. 1 (2007), pp. 36–74.

transfers by the federal government to the provinces and territories. For example,
between 1974 and 1990 the number of registered charities with a welfare focus
increased by 175 per cent; those a health focus by 105 per cent; those an education
focus by 221 per cent; and those with a focus on general benefits to community
by 170 per cent (see Figure 13.1).[46]

As government funding became more widely available, the number of registered
charities and non-profit organisations also grew. The 1960s was a particular period
of rapid growth. The decade saw a proliferation of citizens' movements, many supported by government grant programmes. Social advocates worked to gain support
services and social justice for disadvantaged and disabled Canadians; women's groups
mobilised across Canada to gain women's legal rights and a push for a redefinition
of women in Canadian society; and environmental advocate organisations such
as Greenpeace were launched.[47] Rather than crowding out voluntary action, the
sector grew with and alongside government welfare services, fostering a complex
and often interdependent relationship.

As a result, 74 per cent of all Canadian non-profit organisations, including registered charities, are engaged in service activities. This is significantly higher than
the overall international average of 64 per cent and the similar average for developed
countries. Of these service sectors, 15 per cent are in education; 18 per cent are in
social services; 31 per cent are in health; and 11 per cent are involved in community
development or housing.[48] The voluntary sector in Canada dominates the provision
of health services and post-secondary education. Because these large institutions

dominate the allocation of both paid staff and volunteers, hospitals, universities and colleges are routinely separated out when a statistical analysis of the sector is conducted so that a more balanced picture of the voluntary sector can be seen. For example, government, as a source of revenue, accounts for 51 per cent when hospitals, universities and colleges are included, and only 39 per cent when they are excluded.[49] The voluntary sector in Canada grew with the emergence of the welfare state in Canada; and a significant proportion of charities were and continue to be established to operate as agents for the delivery of public services.

Encouragement of voluntary action

Beveridge in *Voluntary action*:

> Encouragement of Voluntary Action for the improvement of society and use of voluntary agencies by public authorities for public purposes is no less desirable for the future than it has been in the past.[50]

As the number of voluntary organisations increased after the Second World War, so did their reliance on government funding. Some charities, such as children's aid societies and hospitals, received substantial government funding and were subject to accompanying directives and regulations regarding service provision. Many voluntary organisations actively pursue a 'funding mix' and combine fund-raising, charging fees and government contracts to provide services while other voluntary organisations eschew government funding entirely. Overall though, the voluntary sector receives half of its total funding from one level of government or another.[51] The introduction of indirect and direct government funding, combined with federal–provincial cost-sharing programmes and the sheer increase in the number of voluntary organisations over the 1960s, and 1970s, brought the voluntary sector as a whole to the attention of the federal government. It was at this point that the idea of voluntary action made a formal appearance in Canada.

In 1974, twenty-six years after the release of *Voluntary action*, the Secretary of State Hugh Faulkner took steps to try and boost the capacity of the voluntary sector in Canada. Firstly, the Secretary of State created the National Advisory Council on Voluntary Action; and secondly it supported the foundation of the Coalition of National Voluntary Organizations. In November 1974, at the inaugural meeting of the Coalition of National Voluntary Organizations, Faulkner announced the formation of a National Advisory Council on Voluntary Action that would take two years to study the issues and problems affecting Federal relations with the voluntary sector.[52] The Council on Voluntary Action was supported by a departmental secretariat and was asked to address a number of voluntary sector-government relations issues. These issues included developing a workable definition of the sector; problems associated with the recruitment of volunteers and members; the financing of voluntary associations; government use of voluntary resources; and government support to advocacy groups.[53]

According to the council's own report, the council was prevented from exercising the full extent of its mandate. The work of the council was hampered by bureaucratic procedures imposed by the government, instances of outright bureaucratic resistance and a lack of access to information about government programmes that involved the voluntary sector.[54] Nevertheless, the council's report, *People in action*, identified a number of key sectoral issues and made numerous recommendations aimed at increasing the capacity of the voluntary sector at the time. These key sectoral issues, which sound eerily familiar today, included the narrow definition of charity in the context of the scope of voluntary sector in the 1970s; sectoral funding mechanisms, including tax policies and non-financial support by government; and access by voluntary organisations to government information and policy consultation opportunities. Recommendations by the National Advisory Council on Voluntary Action were made to audiences that extended well beyond the Federal government. Recommendations were directed to the relationship of the voluntary sector to the media, local businesses and employers, organised labour and educational institutions. Other recommendations were directed at the voluntary sector itself and addressed operational, governance and financing issues.[55]

The lion's share of recommendations were for the Federal government and included recommended policies and procedures for policy advocacy; direct and indirect financial aid; support services; governance; legal and tax policies; charity registration policy and procedures; research and clearing-house resources; and sectoral representation. Specific recommendations that have still gone unheeded included a re-examination of the definition of charity; simplified, objective and broader registration guidelines; and a transfer of responsibility for charitable registration from Revenue Canada to the Secretary of State.[56]

The council made over eighty recommendations, almost fifty of which were directed at the federal government. Some of its recommendations were implemented, but many more fell by the wayside. The absence of a well-organised representative apex voluntary sector organisation, which could have distilled and prioritised the council's recommendations and then carried them forward, was certainly a mitigating factor in the lack of implementation. The legitimacy of the council's observations and the chronic lack of progress is reflected in the fact that many of the issues identified by the Advisory Council on Voluntary Action were mirrored in the Broadbent Report, released twenty years later by the Voluntary Sector Roundtable, and still remain unresolved.[57]

Voluntary action and social justice

Beveridge in *Voluntary action*:

> Social conscience . . . is to be unwilling to make a separate peace with the giant social evils of Want, Disease, Squalor, Ignorance, [and] Idleness, escaping into personal prosperity oneself while leaving one's fellows in their clutches.[58]

Voluntary action was a deliberate extension of Beveridge's concept of an expanded network of social security services. Beveridge felt that the expansion of state services still left a lot of space for independent and innovative voluntary action, as well as voluntary activities conducted in collaboration with public services. He was clear about what he saw as the relationship between voluntary action and government:

> It is clear that the State must in future do more things than it has attempted in the past. But it is equally clear, or should be equally clear, that room, opportunity, and encouragement must be kept for Voluntary Action in seeking new ways of social advance. There is need for political invention to find new ways of fruitful co-operation between public authorities and voluntary agencies.[59]

As previously demonstrated, the entire environment of voluntary action was changed by the growth of social services. In Britain, health and social services became a mainstream publicly funded, publicly delivered system. Friendly societies provided mutual-aid services, complementing services not provided by the state, with other voluntary organisations providing a venue for a wide range of expressive activities.[60] In Canada, however, this put voluntary action at the forefront of a mixed social economy where health and social services were both publically and privately funded and delivered.[61]

Rather than focus on the mechanics of health and social service delivery, I have chosen to address collective social justice outcomes, and I return to the three principles underlying both Beveridge's *Social insurance and allied services* in general and *Voluntary action* in particular: universality, unity and integration. For if voluntary organisations benefit as a primary delivery agent for public services, as they have done in Canada, do they not too share the responsibility for the intended societal policy outcomes? This is the basis on which I argue that while voluntary organisations have been net fiscal beneficiaries of government policies, there has been an absence of what Beveridge refers to in *Voluntary action* as 'political intervention to achieve fruitful co-operation', particularly in relation to universality, unity and integration.

Three following social justice issues highlight a range of adherence to these three principles in Canada, or, as William Beveridge put it in *Voluntary action*, social conscience 'escaping into personal prosperity oneself while leaving one's fellows in their clutches'.[62] The first case is 'universality', as in access to universal health care for Canadians, reflecting the emergence of health coverage for all Canadian citizens as a matter of right. The second case is an overview of poverty in Canada as seen in the context of income inequality, and is thus a reflection of the principle of 'unity' and therefore of protection, which is egalitarian. The third case is the relationship between the federal government and the Aboriginal peoples in Canada. As such, it reflects Beveridge's principle of social 'integration'. Indigenous peoples are among the most marginalised and vulnerable all over the world, and unfortunately, the same can be said of the Aboriginal peoples in Canada. It is in the treatment of the systematically marginalised citizens, such as Aboriginal peoples, that the relationship of the voluntary sector to social justice finds its true measure.[63]

Universality and access to medical care

The Canadian health care system evolved into its present form over five decades. The primary instigator for a national health system in Canada was not the voluntary sector, or most political parties, but the CCF and its leader Tommy Douglas, now seen as the father of Medicare. The CCF party gathered tremendous momentum, largely due to its social reform agenda in provinces ravished by the depression, winning a majority in 1944 in both British Columbia and Saskatchewan and forcing a reluctant federal government to take action.[64] In 1947 Saskatchewan was the first province to establish public, universal hospital insurance, and ten years later political pressure forced the federal government to pass legislation to share in the cost of these services.[65] By 1961, all ten provinces and two territories had public insurance plans that provided universal access to hospital services.[66] Stephen Kunitz argues that this widespread support for medical insurance reflects a stronger collectivist view of society than exists in the United States.[67]

Fundamentally, as Eugene Vayda and Raisa Deber argue, Canada's health care system is a publicly funded, privately delivered insurance plan which is well respected internationally, administratively efficient and politically immune from major changes which would seriously weaken the five principles of Medicare.[68] While private sector interests periodically promote ready-made solutions to systemic weaknesses, Medicare in Canada continues to receive substantive and continued public support, and any changes are likely to be incremental rather than dramatic.[69] The Canadian health care system is the crown jewel of Canada's social welfare programme, born of a universal view of society where the government, not the individual, had the greatest capacity to meet societal health needs for the greater good of all.

Unity and freedom from want

While Canada's health care system is a genuine source of pride, it would be naive to conclude that health inequities do not exist. They do. While traditionally the sources of health inequities have been factors associated with personal wellbeing, in a study conducted in 2002 by Jim Dunn and in another in 2007 by Armine Yalnizyan, a different relationship between inequalities and health was revealed.[70] In these studies the following conclusions were reached. Cities with an unequal distribution of income have higher mortality rates, and the gap between the rich and the poor has grown over the 1980s and 1990s. For example, in 1973 the top 10 per cent of income earners brought in twenty-one times more than the bottom 10 per cent of income earners.[71] In 1976, the income spread for families had increased to thirty-one times more, and in 2004 it was eight-three times greater.[72]

The poor are getting poorer, and there are more poor people in Canada.[73] The recent economic growth that Canada has experienced has disproportionably benefited families who are well off. While Canada's unemployment figures are low, poor families are earning less now than they did in the 1970s even though they are working even more. According to Yalnizyan the overall trend in Canada is that the rich are getting richer, the poor are not going anywhere, and the mitigating middle class is shrinking. This, Yalnizyan warns, we ignore at our collective peril.[74]

Governments do make a difference, but not the difference they once did. According to separate studies by Jim Dunn and Andrew Heisz, Canada's welfare regime does have an income redistribution effect, but changes in programme benefits since the mid-1990s have reduced its mitigating impact on market income inequalities.[75] Yalnizyan similarly argues that the capacity of federal transfers to mitigate income inequalities has been weakened by cuts to transfers, which would have primarily benefited the poor, and cuts to taxes, which primarily benefit the rich.[76] This conclusion is confirmed in a 2007 study on income inequality by Heisz from Statistics Canada. Heinz's analysis uses the Gini coefficient, another common indicator, to analyse income inequality. The Gini coefficient can have a value between 0 and 1, with 0 indicating that every individual has the same income and 1 indicating that all the income is held by one person. A higher Gini coefficient therefore implies a more unequal distribution of income.

According to Heisz, the Gini coefficient for family market-income inequality rose from 0.361 in 1979 to 0.381 in 1989 (up 0.020) and then rose faster across the 1990s, reaching 0.428 by 2004 (up 0.047) (see Figure 13.2). In 1989, redistribution reduced it by 0.026 more than it did in 1979, more than offsetting the rise in market-income inequality in that decade. Hence, family after-tax-income inequality fell across the 1980s. By 2004, redistribution reduced the Gini coefficient by only 0.009 more than in 1989, so the lion's share of the increase in market-income inequality from 1989 to 2004 was converted to an increase in after-tax-income inequality.[77]

The mid-1990s were a turning-point in the capacity of redistribution policies to mitigate market income inequalities in Canada. It was in the mid-1990s that massive cuts to health and social transfer payments to provinces took place to bring federal debt payments under control. These federal government budget cuts, combined with New Public Management principles, income tax cuts and provincial budget cuts, resulted in a new high in the income gap between rich and poor.[78] Yalnizyan reports that:

> The poorest 20% of Canadian families saw their share of the earnings pie drop from 4.5% from the late 1970s, to 2.6% in the early 2000s. In sharp contrast, the top half of Canadian families saw their share of total earnings grow, from 73% to 79.5% during that same time period.[79]

The poor in Canada have not recovered in any meaningful way. Low unemployment figures belie the underlying plight of the working poor, who need two jobs

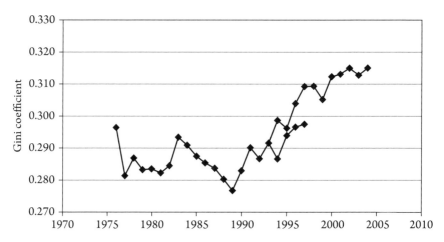

Figure 13.2 Family and after-tax-income inequality indices –
Gini coefficient, 1976–2004
Source: Statistics Canada, Survey of consumer finances and survey of
labour and income dynamics.

to make ends meet. Except for the top 10 per cent of income earners, Canadians are working more and earning less.[80] Single mothers are particularly vulnerable and continue to be so. According to Yalnizyan these data reveal a trend which is bigger than individual luck, lack of training or motivation. She concludes that Canadian families are participating in an economic system that is failing the majority while disproportionately benefiting a select few. Except for the top 10 per cent of income earners, working harder is not resulting in more after-tax income, and even less so than for those same families two decades ago.[81]

The impact of this income disparity is not targeted to one group but has a profound impact on the very nature of Canadian society. Where, we need to ask, is the voluntary sector with its apparent comparative advantage in meeting the needs of disadvantaged people, communities and societies when it comes to addressing income inequity?[82] In all, 74 per cent of voluntary organisations provide services in the areas of education, health, social services and community development or housing.[83] There are now numerous service contracts which explicitly prohibit engagement in advocacy activities. At the same time only a fraction of the permissible allowance for policy advocacy is expended by registered charities, organisations which dominate the provision of social services.[84] Voluntary sector organisations have argued that compatible engagement with government provides an opportunity to influence policy 'from the inside'.[85] Yet the majority of voluntary organisations negotiate their service contract with lower-level bureaucrats who have no policy influence, or are invited to participate in policy discussions only when the agenda has been predetermined.

The service-focussed particularism which dominates the voluntary sector makes it difficult for agencies to see their role in the broad accumulative impact of government policies on the collective lives of Canadians. The dominance of service provision over social justice advocacy by voluntary organisations has become an accessory to growing income inequality.

Integration and the assimilation of Aboriginal peoples in Canada

According to the 2006 census, there are more than one million people of Aboriginal ancestry in Canada, or 3.6 per cent of the Canadian population. The term 'Aboriginal' in Canada refers to First Nation, Métis and Inuit peoples. They comprised of fifty-two nations, including 614 First Nation communities.[86] In many ways the legacy of the treatment and status of Aboriginal peoples in Canada is a reflection of policies which were collectively intended to assimilate rather than integrate Aboriginal people into the broader Canadian society.

Since colonial times, Canada's Aboriginal peoples have been progressively dispossessed of their lands, resources and culture, a process that has led them into destitution, deprivation and dependency. In general, Aboriginal peoples experience worse social, economic and environmental conditions than those of non-Aboriginal people. This burden is associated with unfavourable economic and social conditions that are directly linked to their history of oppression.[87] For example, native spiritual practices were considered illegal under the Indian Act, and any commerce had to be conducted through Indian affairs agents, who returned prices below well below the market rates for their goods.

The life expectancy for Aboriginal peoples has recently improved, but their health status is still much worse than that of Canadians as a whole. On average, First Nations and Inuit peoples live five to ten years less than non-native Canadians.[88] Infant mortality rates among First Nation people on reserves and Inuit are two to three times the overall Canadian rate.[89] Some 20 per cent of Aboriginal people have inadequate water and sewer systems. While Aboriginals make up 3.6 per cent of Canada's population, they account for 17 per cent of the people in prison.[90] The average educational attainment is lower for Aboriginal peoples, fewer Aboriginal peoples are employed, and their average incomes are lower. At least 33 per cent of First Nation and Inuit people, compared with 18 per cent of non-Aboriginal people, live in inadequate, unsuitable or unaffordable housing, according to data from the Canada Mortgage and Housing Corporation. The tuberculosis rate among First Nation people in the 1990s was at least seven times higher than the overall Canadian rate, and over 50 per cent of Inuit in one Baffin Island community had excessive dietary exposure levels of mercury and other chemicals.[91]

Aboriginal people identify the legacy of residential schools as a determinant of their health. This system, which began in 1892, removed children from their homes and placed them in isolated institutions where they were often forbidden to speak their own language and practise their traditions and beliefs. This is in stark contrast to Canada's multiculturalist policy, where new immigrants were not only allowed to continue their spiritual and cultural practices, but also openly encouraged by the federal government to celebrate their culture.[92] In two recent surveys, six out of ten First Nation and Métis respondents identified residential schools as a significant contributor to their poorer health status.[93]

In the early years of residential schools, there was a mortality rate of up to 50 per cent among Aboriginal children due to untreated tuberculosis.[94] Beyond the statistics is a legacy of unmarked graves, family annihilation and cultural dislocation. When residential schools were closed, the child welfare system took over, creating conditions which put more pressure on Aboriginal children to assimilate, as they were even more isolated from their peers in white foster homes than they were in residential schools.[95] Only in the 1980s did negotiations give First Nation people the opportunity to develop their own child welfare service models which would reflect their community, culture and history.

In 2007 a class action lawsuit against the federal government on behalf of residential school survivors was settled. Even now, the structure designed to process these residential school survivor claims can only be described as 'fragile'. The fact that the residential schools were operated under contract to the Federal government by charities, namely churches, is a feature of voluntary sector history which rarely receives attention and calls Canadians as well as the voluntary sector to account. In the nineteenth and twentieth centuries in Canada, cultural (white) and linguistic assimilation and economic isolation dominated the relationship of the federal government with Aboriginal peoples. The *noblesse oblige* orientation of the voluntary sector, combined with its explicit participation in this injustice through residential schools, is an ugly chapter in the history of the voluntary sector in Canada, a history which has yet to be fully addressed. In a broader context, voluntary action has a fundamental role to play in the structural and social integration of society.

Conclusion

In *Voluntary action* Beveridge outlined his recommendations for co-operation with local authorities, statutory provisions, tax policy, ministerial oversight, training and government funding, each of which were insightful and eerily prophetic. Voluntary action was primarily intended to complement the emerging welfare state and government action. Beveridge gave particular attention to mutual aid organisations and friendly societies, but in Canada, the co-operative movement also took hold and continues to make significant contributions in a wide variety of areas, including housing and financial services and producer co-operatives.[96] More important, in my view, is the broader social policy context in which *Voluntary action* was written, namely as a supplementary report to Beveridge's earlier report on social welfare and the role of the state, including his treatise on the importance of social justice.

Universal access to medical care in Canada is one facet of collective social justice about which there is justifiable pride. The leaders of this movement towards universal access to medical care were political, not social, in spite of the fact that the voluntary sector is now a significant beneficiary of this success. Economic inequities in Canada, while mitigated to some degree by government transfer payments to provinces and individuals, continue to grow and have a disproportional impact on women and children. The pervasive particularisation of voluntary sector organisations and the general fragmentation of the voluntary sector as a whole have isolated and marginalised economic inequality as a unifying policy issue.

Important contributions are made by the voluntary sector, but this contribution is not a substitute for greater economic equality, technical and social integration and enforceable guarantees of human rights.[97] Particularism has become the Achilles heel of the voluntary sector's relationship with finding its unifying strength and embarking on the quest for social justice. The voluntary sector has made significant contributions to the delivery of health and social services in Canada, and in this regard the sector has every reason to be proud of its contribution to the principle of universality. However, voluntary sector organisations in Canada have followed, rather than led, attempts to bring the principle of unity and integration to reality.

Since the release of *Voluntary action* in 1948, the voluntary sector in Canada has played a primary role in the delivery of social services, but a tertiary role in the achievement of social justice. If there is one message from *Voluntary action* to be carried beyond its sixtieth anniversary, it is that the voluntary sector as a whole should seek to re-awaken its relationship to social justice and the core principles of universality, unity and integration.

Notes

1 William Beveridge, *Social insurance and allied services*, Cmd 6404 (London: HMSO, 1942).
2 Lord Beveridge, *Voluntary action: a report on methods of social advance* (London: George Allen & Unwin, 1948), p. 7.
3 Beveridge, *Voluntary action*, p. 8.
4 G. Perrin, 'The Beveridge Plan: the main principles', *International Social Security Review*, vol. 45, nos 1–2 (1992), pp. 39–52.
5 A. Cohan, *Lester B. Pearson* (Toronto: Penguin, 2008).
6 J. Bitar, *The emergence of Centraide in the Greater Montreal Area: a case of radical social innovation* (Montreal: HEC, 2003).
7 J. Lautenschlager, *Volunteering: a traditional Canadian value* (Ottawa: Voluntary Canadian Heritage, 1992).
8 United Kingdom Constitution Act 1867, subsection 92 (7), 3.
9 D. Guest, *The history of social security in Canada*, 3rd edn (Vancover: UBC Press, 1997). See www.thecanadianencyclopedia.com/index.cfm?PgNm=TCE&Params=A1SEC828298 (accessed 21 October 2008).

10 J. J. Rice and M. J. Prince, *Changing politics of Canadian social policy* (Toronto: University of Toronto Press, 2000).

11 S. A. Martin, *An essential grace: funding Canada's health care, education, welfare, religion and culture* (Toronto: McClelland and Stewart, 1985), and A. Armitage, 'Canadian social welfare (1900–1988): chronology', in *Social welfare in Canada: ideals, realities and future paths*, 2nd edn (Toronto: McClelland and Stewart, 1988), pp. 270–81.

12 N. Christie and M. Gauvreau, *A full-orbed Christianity: the Protestant churches and social welfare in Canada, 1900–1940* (Montreal and Kingston: McGill-Queen's University Press, 1996).

13 A. Armitage, *Social welfare in Canada revisited* (Toronto: Oxford University Press, 1996).

14 Canadian Council on Child and Family Welfare, 'Proceedings of the eleventh annual meeting: Canadian Council on Child and Family Welfare', *Child and Family Welfare*, vol. 7, no. 1 (1930), pp. 11–45; Library and Archives Canada, Ottawa, MG26-K, M-3179, Canadian Council on Child and Family Welfare, 'Correspondence to R. B. Bennett, Prime Minister, 1933', Microfilm, pp. 604959–61, reproduction copy; R. B. Splane, *75 years of community service to Canada: Canadian Council on Social Development, 1920–1995* (Ottawa: Canadian Council on Social Development, 1996); P. Maurutto, 'Charity and public welfare in history: a look at Ontario, 1830–1950', *The Philanthropist*, vol. 19, no. 3 (2005), pp. 159–67.

15 M. Valverde, 'Introduction to the age of light, soap, and water', in A. Glasbeek (ed.), *Moral regulation and the governance in Canada: history, context, and critical issues* (Toronto: Canadian Scholars' Press, 2006).

16 P. R. Elson, 'A historical institutional analysis of voluntary sector/government relations in Canada' (PhD thesis, University of Toronto, 2008).

17 S. Tillotson, *Contributing citizens: modern charitable fundraising and the making of the welfare state* (Vancouver: UBC Press, 2008).

18 Lautenschlager, *Volunteering*.

19 Guest, *The history of social security in Canada*.

20 Beveridge, *Voluntary action*, p. 308.

21 D. Guest, 'World War II and the welfare state in Canada', in A. Moscovitch and J. Albert (eds), *The 'benevolent' state: the growth of welfare in Canada* (Toronto: Garamond Press, 1987), pp. 205–21, and Lautenschlager, *Volunteering*.

22 Guest, 'World War II', and E. H. Carr, editorial, *The Times* (1 July 1940).

23 Guest, 'World War II', pp. 206–7.

24 L. C. Marsh, *Report on social security for Canada for the Advisory Committee on Reconstruction* (Ottawa: Special Committee on Social Security, 1943).

25 The League for Social Reconstruction was a brain thrust for the socialist Co-operative Commonwealth Federation (CCF) party. The manifesto of the league included 'working for the establishment in Canada of a social order in which the basic principle regulating the production, distribution, and service will be the common good rather than private profit'. See R. B. Blake and J. Keshen, *Social welfare policy in Canada: historical readings* (Toronto: Copp Clark, 1995), p. 205.

26 A. Maioni, 'New century, new risks: The Marsh Report and the post-war welfare state in Canada', *Policy Options* (August 2004), pp. 20–3.

27 Guest, 'World War II'.

28 Marsh, *Report on Social Security*.

29 Maioni, 'New century, new risks'.

30 K. Herman, 'The emerging welfare state: changing perspectives in Canadian welfare policies and programs, 1867–1960', in D. I. Davies and K. Herman (eds), *Social space: Canadian perspectives* (Toronto: New Toronto Press, 1971), pp. 131–41.

31 Guest, 'World War II'.

32 Quebec in particular was leery of any Federal encroachment on provincial jurisdiction. Guest, 'World War II', and A. Moscovitch and G. Drover, 'Social expenditures and the welfare state: the Canadian experience in historical perspective', in A. Moscovitch and J. Albert (eds), *The benevolent state: the growth of welfare in Canada* (Toronto: Garamond Press, 1987), pp. 13–43.

33 S. Tillotson, *Contributing citizens: modern charitable fundraising and the making of the welfare state* (Vancouver: UBC Press, 2008).

34 Guest, 'World War II'.

35 Guest, *The history of social security in Canada*.

36 Christie and Gauvreau, *A full-orbed Christianity*.

37 Martin, *An essential grace*.

38 Lautenschlager, *Volunteering*.

39 Maurutto, 'Charity and public welfare in history'.

40 N. Brooks, 'The role of the voluntary sector in a modern welfare state' in J. Phillips, B. Chapman and D. Stevens (eds), *Between state and market: essays on charities law and policy in Canada* (Montreal and Kingston: McGill-Queen's University Press, 2001), pp. 166–216.

41 M. H. Hall, C. W. Barr et al., *The Canadian nonprofit and voluntary sector in comparative perspective* (Toronto: Imagine Canada, 2005), and Guest, *The history of social security in Canada*.

42 Herman, 'The emerging Welfare State'.

43 Hall, Barr et al., *The Canadian nonprofit and voluntary sector in comparative perspective*.

44 K. L. Brock, 'Sustaining a relationship: insights from Canada on linking the government and the third sector', paper presented at the Fourth International Conference of the International Society for Third Sector Research (ISTR), Dublin, Ireland, 5–8 July 2000.

45 L. Eakin, *An overview of the funding of Canada's voluntary sector* (Ottawa: Voluntary Sector Initiative Working Group on Financing, 2001), and K. Brock, R. Reid et al., *Policy Capacity literature review: report prepared for the Canadian Centre for Philanthropy* (Kingston: School of Policy Studies, Queens' University, 2002).

46 A welfare focus includes housing, food security and legal assistance for those in need; disability, children's and youth services; family crisis services, immigrant aid, disaster relief, rehabilitation of offenders and services for Aboriginal people. See J. D. McCamus, *Report on the law of charities*, vol. 1 (Toronto: Ontario Law Reform Commission, 1996).

47 Lautenschlager, *Volunteering*.

48 Hall, Barr et al., *The Canadian nonprofit and voluntary sector in comparative perspective*.

49 Hall, Barr et al., *The Canadian nonprofit and voluntary sector in comparative perspective*.

50 Beveridge, *Voluntary action*, p. 306.
51 M. H. Hall, M. L. de Witt et al., *Cornerstones of community: highlights of the national survey of nonprofit and voluntary organisations* (Ottawa: Statistics Canada, 2004).
52 National Advisory Council on Voluntary Action, *People in action: report of the national advisory council on voluntary action to the government of Canada* (Ottawa: Secretary of State, 1977), and Joint Tables, *Working together: a government of Canada/voluntary sector joint initiative – report of the Joint Tables* (Ottawa: Voluntary Sector Task Force, Privy Council Office, 1999).
53 National Advisory Council on Voluntary Action, *People in action*.
54 National Advisory Council on Voluntary Action, *People in action*.
55 National Advisory Council on Voluntary Action, *People in action*.
56 National Advisory Council on Voluntary Action, *People in action*.
57 E. Broadbent, *Building on strength: improving governance and accountability in Canada's voluntary sector* (Ottawa: Panel on Accountability and Governance in the Voluntary Sector, 1999), and Hall, Barr et al., *The Canadian nonprofit and voluntary sector in comparative perspective*.
58 Beveridge, *Voluntary action*, p. 9.
59 Beveridge, *Voluntary action*, p. 10.
60 One of the main theories for the emergence of voluntary organisations is 'public failure' – the inability of the state to meet the needs of citizens beyond the majority of voters. G. D. H. Cole, '*Voluntary action*: a report on methods of social advance (book review)', *Economic Journal*, vol. 59, no. 235 (1949), pp. 399–401. Expressive voluntary activities are ones in which an individual has an opportunity to express herself or himself, such as environmental, sports and recreation and arts and cultural activities.
61 M. Valverde, 'The mixed social economy as a Canadian tradition', *Studies in Political Economy*, vol. 47 (Summer 1995), pp. 33–60.
62 Beveridge, *Voluntary action*, p. 9.
63 Social integration in Beveridge's context would be what is now referred to as social inclusion.
64 A. Maioni, 'Parting at the crossroads: the development of health insurance in Canada and the United States, 1940–1995', *Comparative Politics*, vol. 29, no. 4 (1997), pp. 411–31.
65 S. J. Kunitz, 'Socialism and social insurance in the United States and Canada', in C. D. Naylor (ed.), *Canadian health care and the state: a century of evolution* (Montreal and Kingston: McGill-Queen's University Press, 1992), pp. 104–24.
66 Health Canada, 'Canada Health Act overview', 2002, www.hc-sc.gc.ca/ahc-asc/media/nr-cp/2002/2002_care-soinsbk4_e.html (accessed 22 August 2007).
67 Kunitz, 'Socialism and social insurance'.
68 E. Vayda and R. A. Deber, 'The Canadian health-care system: a developmental overview', in Naylor (ed.), *Canadian health care and the state*, pp. 125–40.
69 C. N. Tuohy, *Accidental logistics: the dynamics of change in the health care arena in the United States, Britain and Canada* (Oxford: Oxford University Press, 1999).
70 J. R. Dunn, *Are widening income inequalities making Canada less healthy?* (Toronto: Health Determinants Partnership: Making Connections Project, 2002), and A. Yalnizyan, *The rich and the rest of us* (Ottawa: Canadian Centre for Policy Alternatives, 2007).

71 Dunn, *Are widening income inequalities making Canada less healthy?*

72 Yalnizyan, *The rich and the rest of us.*

73 Dunn, *Are widening income inequalities making Canada less healthy?*

74 Yalnizyan, *The rich and the rest of us.*

75 Dunn, *Are widening income inequalities making Canada less healthy?*, and A. Heisz, *Income inequality and redistribution in Canada: 1976 to 2006* (Ottawa: Statistics Canada, 2007).

76 Yalnizyan, *The rich and the rest of us.*

77 Heisz, *Income inequality and redistribution in Canada.*

78 B. M. Evans and J. Shields, 'The third sector: neo-liberal restructuring, governance and the remaking of state–civil society relationships', *CERIS*, no. 18 (Centre of Excellence for Research on Immigration and Settlement, May 2008), pp. 1–9.

79 Yalnizyan, *The rich and the rest of us*, p. 4.

80 Armine Yalnizyan, 'Income inequality and the pursuit of prosperity', paper presented at the Walter Gordon Massey Symposium, March 2009.

81 Yalnizyan, *The rich and the rest of us.*

82 D. Billis and H. Glennerster, 'Human services and the voluntary sector: towards a theory of comparative advantage', *Journal of Social Policy*, vol. 27, no. 1 (1998), pp. 79–98.

83 Hall, Barr et al., *The Canadian nonprofit and voluntary sector in comparative perspective.*

84 P. Elson, 'Where is the voice of Canada's voluntary sector?', *Canadian Review of Social Policy*, nos 60–1 (Fall 2007–Winter 2008), pp. 1–20.

85 S. D. Phillips, 'Fuzzy boundaries: rethinking relationships between governments and NGOs', *Policy Options*, vol. 15, no. 3 (1994), pp. 13–17.

86 R. Stavenhagen, *Report of the Special Rapporteur on the situation of human rights and fundamental freedoms of indigenous peoples: Mission to Canada* (New York: Economic and Social Council, United Nations, 2004).

87 H. L. MacMillan, A. B. MacMillan et al., 'Aboriginal health', *Canadian Medical Association Journal*, vol. 155, no. 11 (1996), pp. 1569–78.

88 Canadian Institute for Health Information, *Improving health of Canadians: Aboriginal people's health.* See www.cihi.ca/cihiweb/disPage.jsp?cw_page=media_25feb2004_b3_e (accessed 24 August 2007).

89 MacMillan, MacMillan et al., 'Aboriginal health'.

90 R. Stavenhagen, *The situation of human rights and fundamental freedoms of indigenous people* (New York: United Nations, 2005).

91 Canadian Institute for Health Information, 'Improving health of Canadians'.

92 L. A. Pal, *Interests of state: the politics of language, multiculturalism and feminism in Canada* (Montreal and Kingston: McGill-Queen's University Press, 1993).

93 Canadian Institute for Health Information, *Improving health of Canadians.*

94 B. Curry and K. Howlett, 'Natives died in droves as Ottawa ignored warnings', *Toronto Globe and Mail* (Toronto, 2007).

95 A. Armitage, *Comparing the policy of Aboriginal assimilation: Australia, Canada and New Zealand* (Vancouver: UBC Press, 1995).

96 Based on 2004 'Cooperatives in Canada survey' results received from 5,753 non-financial co-operatives representing 5.6 million members, C$27.5 billion in total revenues and

C$17.5 billion in assets. These co-operatives employed 85,073 people, of whom over 76 per cent were full-time employees, in businesses including wholesale co-operatives and federations. Of these co-operatives, 926 were agricultural, representing over 363,000 active memberships and employing over 33,000 individuals with total revenues of C$14 billion and assets of C$5.6 billion.

97 L. Arbour, LaFontaine-Baldwin Lecture 2005, Dominion Institute, Quebec City.

Index